AF441426

MathFlare

Name: ____________________

Class: __________

Teacher: ____________________

Introduction

As parents and educators, we recognize the pivotal role mathematics plays in shaping a child's academic journey and future success. Yet, the path to mathematical proficiency can often seem daunting, fraught with challenges and complexities. That's where the transformative power of MathFlare Workbooks shine through, illuminating the way forward with clarity, precision, and purpose.

Introducing MathFlare Workbooks – a beacon of guidance, a testament to excellence, and a catalyst for achievement. Crafted with meticulous care and expertise, MathFlare Workbooks stand as paragons of educational excellence, designed to nurture young minds, ignite a passion for learning, and develop a deep-rooted understanding of mathematical concepts.

Picture this: your child eagerly delves into the pages of Mathflare Workbook, greeted by a step-by-step guide illuminated with vivid examples that demystify complex mathematical concepts. With each turn of the page, they embark on a journey of discovery, encountering thoughtfully curated practice questions that reinforce learning and hone problem-solving skills. And when they unveil the answers to those very questions, a sense of accomplishment blossoms within them – a tangible reward for their hard work and dedication.

But MathFlare Workbooks are more than just tools for learning; they are pathways to comprehension, fostering a deep-seated understanding of mathematical concepts through a sequential, logical flow. From fundamental principles to advanced problem-solving strategies, every chapter builds upon the last, ensuring a robust foundation upon which future knowledge can be constructed.

As parents, we yearn for nothing more than to see our children thrive, to witness the spark of inspiration ignited within them as they conquer academic challenges with confidence and poise. MathFlare Workbooks serve as partners in this noble endeavor, offering not just practice questions, but the keys to unlocking a world of opportunity.

And for teachers, MathFlare Workbooks stand as invaluable allies in the quest to cultivate mathematical proficiency in the classroom. With answers readily available, instructors can focus on guiding and nurturing their students, confident in the knowledge that MathFlare Workbooks provide a solid framework upon which to build.

In the pages of MathFlare Workbooks, we find not just the promise of academic excellence, but the seeds of a brighter tomorrow. So let us embrace the power of mathematics, let us champion the journey of learning, and let us pave the way for a generation of young minds poised to shape the world. With MathFlare Workbooks as our guide, the possibilities are infinite, and the future, bright.

Table of Contents

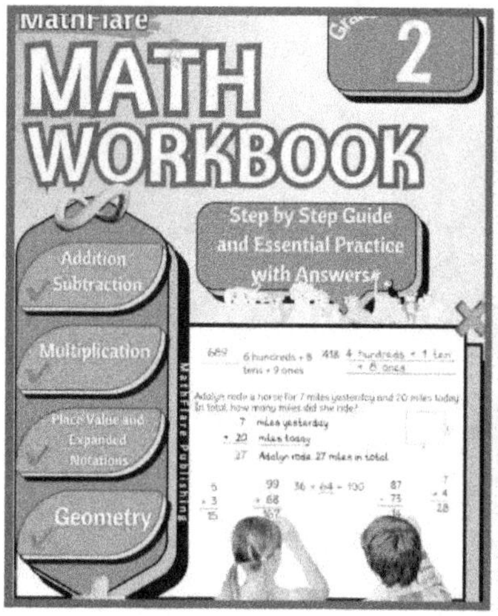
MathFlare
2
MATH
WORKBOOK
Step by Step Guide and Essential Practice with Answers
Addition Subtraction
Multiplication
Place Value and Expanded Notations
Geometry
MathFlare Publishing

MathFlare
2-3
MATH
WORKBOOK
Step by Step Guide and Essential Practice with Answers
Addition Subtraction
Multiplication and Division
Place Value and Expanded Notations
Geometry
MathFlare Publishing

MathFlare
3
MATH
WORKBOOK
Step by Step Guide and Essential Practice with Answers
Multiplication and Division
Decimals
Place Value and Expanded Notations
Fractions and Geometry
MathFlare Publishing

MathFlare
1
MATH
WORKBOOK
Step by Step Guide and Essential Practice with Answers
Counting and Numbers
Addition and Subtraction
Place Value and Expanded Notations
Understanding Time
MathFlare Publishing

MathFlare
1-2
MATH
WORKBOOK
Step by Step Guide and Essential Practice with Answers
Counting and Numbers
Addition and Subtraction
Place Value and Expanded Notations
Understanding Time
MathFlare Publishing

MathFlare
3-4
MATH
WORKBOOK
Step by Step Guide and Essential Practice with Answers
Addition Subtraction
Multiplication Division
Place Value and Expanded Notations
Fractions and Geometry
MathFlare Publishing

MathFlare
4
MATH
WORKBOOK
Step by Step Guide and Essential Practice with Answers
Addition Subtraction
Multiplication Division
Place Value and Expanded Notations
Fractions and Geometry
MathFlare Publishing

MathFlare
4-5
MATH
WORKBOOK
Step by Step Guide and Essential Practice with Answers
Multiplication Division
Place Value and Expanded Notations
Fractions and Geometry
Unit Conversion
MathFlare Publishing

5
MATH
WORKBOOK
Step by Step Guide
and Essential Practice
with Answers
Multiplication
Division
Place Value and
Expanded
Notations
Fractions
and Geometry
Unit
Conversion
MathFlare Publishing

5-6
MATH
WORKBOOK
Step by Step Guide
and Essential Practice
with Answers
Multiplication
Division
Place Value and
Expanded
Notations
Fractions
and Geometry
Units and
Statistics
MathFlare Publishing

6
MATH
WORKBOOK
Step by Step Guide
and Essential Practice
with Answers
Integers and
Statistics
Arithmetic and
Pre-Algebra
Fractions
and Geometry
Ratio and
Percentage
MathFlare Publishing

6-7
MATH
WORKBOOK
Step by Step Guide
and Essential Practice
with Answers
Arithmetic and
Pre-Algebra
Ratio, Percent
Proportion
Geometry
Statistics
MathFlare Publishing

7
MATH
WORKBOOK
Step by Step Guide
and Essential Practice
with Answers
Pre-Algebra
Ratio, Percent
Proportion
Geometry
Statistics
MathFlare Publishing

7-8
MATH
WORKBOOK
Step by Step Guide
and Essential Practice
with Answers
Pre-Algebra
Ratio, Percent
Proportion
Geometry and
Cartesian
Plane
Statistics
MathFlare Publishing

8-9
MATH
WORKBOOK
Step by Step Guide
and Essential Practice
with Answers
Pre-Algebra
Ratio, Proportion
and Percentage
Linear
Equations
Geometry and
Cartesian Plane
MathFlare Publishing

8
MATH
WORKBOOK
Step by Step Guide
and Essential Practice
with Answers
Pre-Algebra
Percentage
Linear
Equations
Geometry
MathFlare Publishing

Chapter. 01

Addition and Subtraction

Addition with Regrouping

When we do addition, we combine numbers. But sometimes, when we're adding numbers, we might need to regroup. Regrouping means we have to move a number from one place to another, usually to the next column, to get the right answer.

For Example: Let's take an example of adding 6533 and 7579 together:

$$\begin{array}{r} 6533 \\ +\underline{7579} \end{array}$$

First, we start by adding the digits in the ones place: 3 + 9 = 12. We write down the 2 in the ones place and carry over the 1 to the tens place.

$$\begin{array}{r} 1 \\ 6533 \\ +\underline{7579} \\ 2 \end{array}$$

Now, we add the digits in the tens place, along with the carry-over: 3 + 7 + 1 = 11. We write down the 1 in the tens place and carry over the 1 to the hundreds place.

$$\begin{array}{r} 11 \\ 6533 \\ +\underline{7579} \\ 12 \end{array}$$

Now, we add the digits in the hundreds place, along with the carry-over: 5 + 5 + 1 = 11. We write down the 1 in the tens place and carry over the 1 to the hundreds place.

```
1  1 1
 6 5 3 3
+7 5 7 9
   1 1 2
```

Now, we add the digits in the thousandth place, along with the carry-over: 6 + 7 + 1 = 14.

```
 1 1 1
 6 5 3 3
+7 5 7 9
1 4 1 1 2
```

This process of carrying over helps us accurately add numbers, especially when they're larger.

Subtraction with Regrouping

Subtraction is a key math operation where we find the difference between two numbers. Sometimes, when we subtract, we might need to regroup, which means borrowing from the next column.

Let's take an example of subtracting 8436 from 6563:

First, we start by subtracting the digits in the ones place: 3 - 6.

Since 3 is less than 6, we need to regroup. We borrow 1 from the tens place, making it 5 tens instead of 6, and add it to the ones place.

So, 3 becomes 13, and then we subtract 6.

8 5 6 13

-6 4 3 6

7

Now, we subtract the tens place digits: 5 - 3 = 2

5

8 5 ~~6~~ 13

-6 4 3 6

2 7

Now, we subtract the hundreds place digits: 5 - 4 = 1

5

8 5 ~~6~~ 13

-6 4 3 6

1 2 7

Now, we subtract the hundreds place digits: 8 - 6 = 2

5

8 5 ~~6~~ 13

-6 4 3 6

2 1 2 7

This process of regrouping or borrowing helps us accurately subtract numbers, especially when the top digit is smaller than the bottom one.

Let's solve problems from exercises:

6,133	6,650
+ 9,978	- 5,798
16,111	852

Word Problems

Word problems are like little puzzles that help us use addition in real-life situations.

For instance:

1. **Jake has 6 carrots. He gets 2 more carrots. How many carrots does he have now?**

To find out how many carrots he has now, we add the number of carrots he started with (6) to the number of carrots he got (2).

So, we add 6 + 2, which equals 8. Jake now has 8 carrots in total!

2. **Jake saved up 4 dollars to buy pencils. He spent 2 dollars on it. How much money does he have left?**

To solve this problem, we need to start with the number of dollars Jake started with and subtract the number of dollars he spent on the pencils.

So, we subtract 2 from 4, which equals 2: Jake has 2 dollars left after buying the pencils.

We need to understand what the problem is asking and what information it provides. Then, we can use addition or subtraction, depending on whether we're combining or taking away objects, to find the answer.

Let's solve problems from exercises:

Ayden bought a pair of shoes for 32 dollars. Later, Ayden bought another pair of shoes for 60 dollars. How much money did Ayden spend in total??

$32	spent on 1st pair of shoes
+ $60	spent on another pair of shoes
$92	Ayden spent in total

Sandra has 38 bananas. She ate 29 of them. How many bananas does Sandra have left?

38	Sandra had 38 bananas
- 29	She ate 29 of them
9	she has 9 bananas left

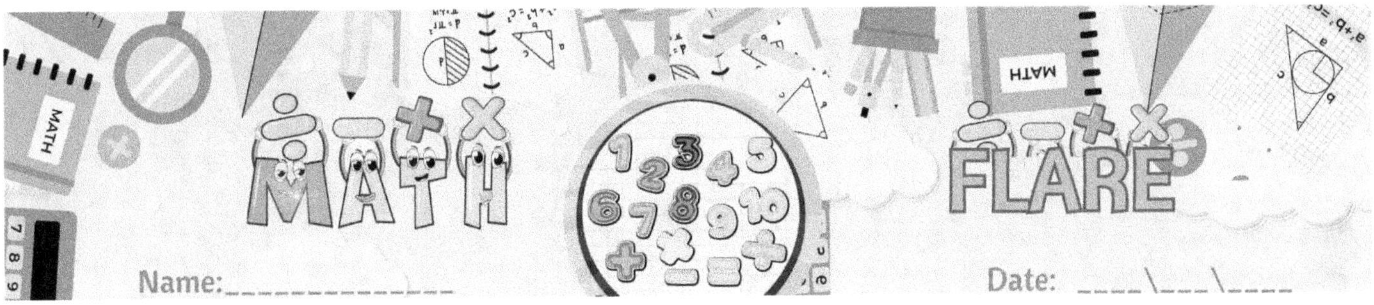

Addition with Regrouping

Find the sum.

1) 6,133 + 9,978 = 16,111

2) 3,131 + 9,989 = 13,120

3) 5,685 + 8,957 = ______

4) 7,835 + 9,478 = ______

5) 3,711 + 9,599 = ______

6) 1,186 + 9,979 = ______

7) 3,591 + 9,739 = ______

8) 3,125 + 8,995 = ______

9) 4,287 + 9,837 = ______

10) 6,177 + 5,944 = ______

11) 2,798 + 9,588 = ______

12) 1,763 + 9,979 = ______

13) 8,179 + 3,963 = ______

14) 9,912 + 9,499 = ______

15) 3,681 + 7,659 = ______

16) 1,172 + 9,979 = ______

17) 3,487 + 8,685 = ______

18) 6,355 + 5,898 = ______

19) 2,268 + 9,854 = ______

20) 6,295 + 9,857 = ______

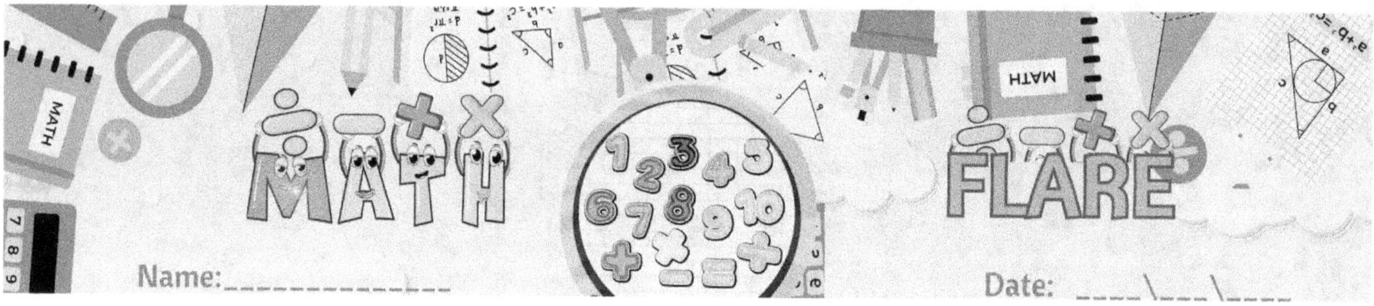

21) 2,818 + 9,592 = ____	22) 1,188 + 9,982 = ____	23) 4,761 + 7,379 = ____	24) 5,922 + 9,599 = ____
25) 9,533 + 2,888 = ____	26) 9,831 + 4,779 = ____	27) 3,353 + 7,957 = ____	28) 2,684 + 9,949 = ____
29) 9,115 + 3,998 = ____	30) 1,968 + 9,972 = ____	31) 9,141 + 8,979 = ____	32) 6,798 + 6,355 = ____
33) 9,368 + 2,856 = ____	34) 3,392 + 9,869 = ____	35) 4,376 + 7,886 = ____	36) 7,238 + 3,972 = ____
37) 4,516 + 6,795 = ____	38) 4,137 + 9,975 = ____	39) 9,111 + 9,999 = ____	40) 6,168 + 9,972 = ____

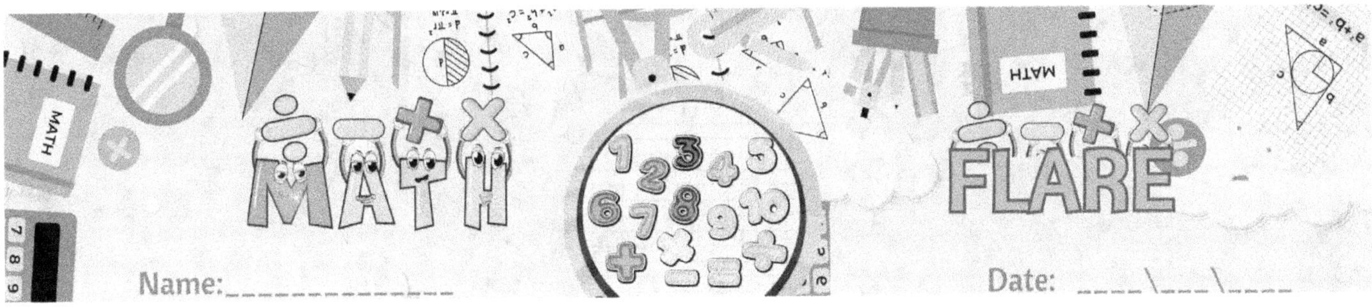

41) 7,839 + 9,494	42) 9,959 + 1,871	43) 7,521 + 6,589	44) 6,575 + 7,539
45) 1,611 + 9,499	46) 6,482 + 9,769	47) 1,166 + 9,974	48) 1,311 + 9,799
49) 6,783 + 4,739	50) 2,843 + 8,669	51) 4,985 + 6,657	52) 7,125 + 3,987
53) 5,611 + 7,699	54) 1,242 + 9,899	55) 2,821 + 8,499	56) 7,843 + 9,569
57) 6,931 + 8,199	58) 5,182 + 9,938	59) 8,382 + 5,958	60) 8,833 + 3,997

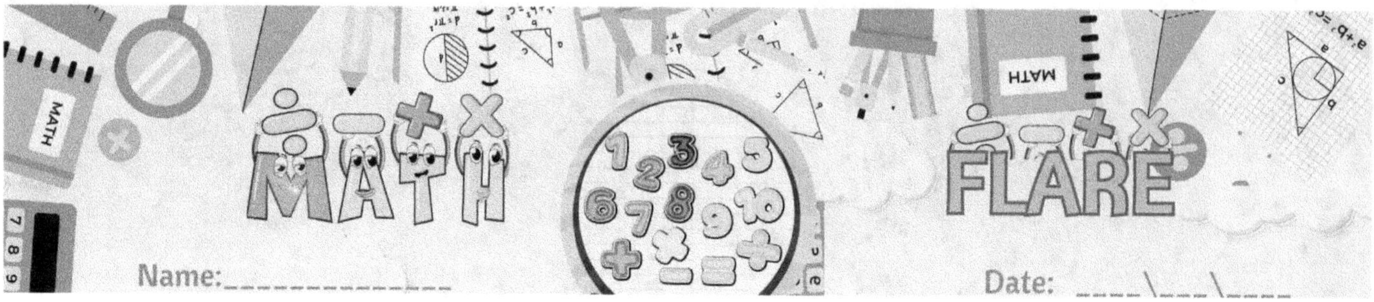

61) 5,581 + 5,869 = ______

62) 9,714 + 4,999 = ______

63) 2,144 + 8,977 = ______

64) 2,986 + 8,148 = ______

65) 6,416 + 9,695 = ______

66) 3,433 + 9,989 = ______

67) 7,717 + 3,594 = ______

68) 6,816 + 8,296 = ______

69) 3,285 + 7,959 = ______

70) 6,241 + 9,879 = ______

71) 6,171 + 9,949 = ______

72) 5,718 + 8,493 = ______

73) 2,568 + 8,997 = ______

74) 3,236 + 9,999 = ______

75) 9,291 + 1,979 = ______

76) 6,181 + 7,929 = ______

77) 5,897 + 8,888 = ______

78) 8,124 + 9,988 = ______

79) 5,912 + 9,199 = ______

80) 1,964 + 9,559 = ______

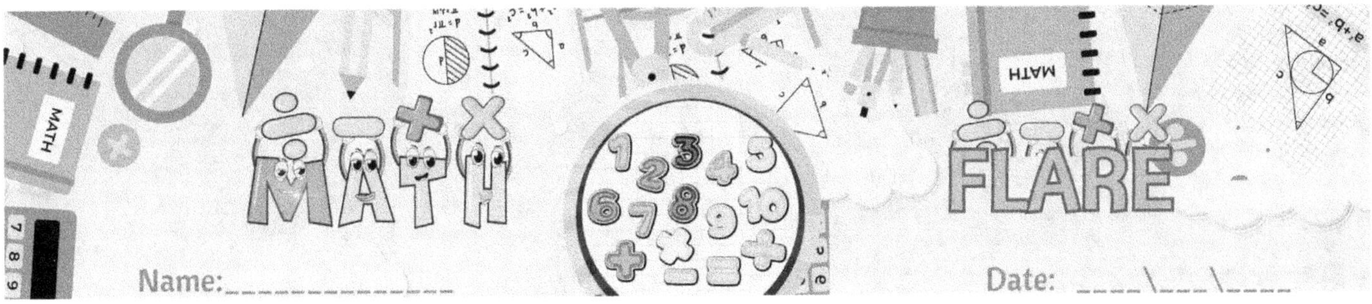

Name:______________ Date: ___________

81) 5,692 + 8,999 = ______

82) 1,211 + 9,999 = ______

83) 1,135 + 9,979 = ______

84) 2,857 + 9,367 = ______

85) 4,349 + 8,869 = ______

86) 7,346 + 3,879 = ______

87) 9,716 + 8,996 = ______

88) 7,782 + 5,638 = ______

89) 1,155 + 9,976 = ______

90) 3,396 + 8,726 = ______

91) 5,834 + 8,986 = ______

92) 1,853 + 9,778 = ______

93) 4,591 + 7,629 = ______

94) 9,471 + 8,859 = ______

95) 5,539 + 7,694 = ______

96) 7,311 + 9,799 = ______

97) 6,988 + 8,765 = ______

98) 5,149 + 6,973 = ______

99) 9,737 + 3,573 = ______

100) 8,198 + 9,993 = ______

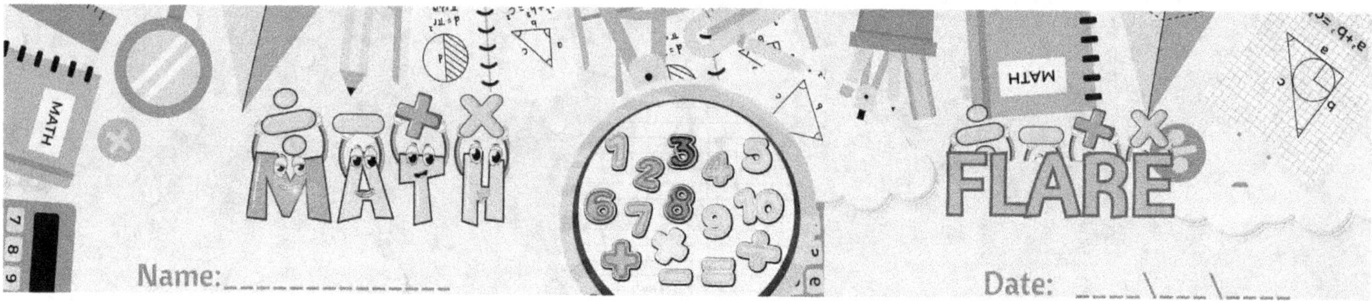

Subtraction with Regrouping

Find the difference.

1) 5,050 − 4,571 = 479	2) 6,650 − 5,798 = 852	3) 4,330 − 2,741 = ____	4) 2,100 − 1,722 = ____
5) 2,100 − 1,293 = ____	6) 8,860 − 3,975 = ____	7) 9,760 − 6,981 = ____	8) 2,680 − 1,998 = ____
9) 9,240 − 5,695 = ____	10) 8,550 − 7,671 = ____	11) 4,000 − 2,513 = ____	12) 8,820 − 5,933 = ____
13) 5,540 − 4,969 = ____	14) 4,440 − 1,584 = ____	15) 4,840 − 1,969 = ____	16) 5,880 − 4,993 = ____
17) 4,470 − 2,893 = ____	18) 2,060 − 1,675 = ____	19) 6,330 − 3,876 = ____	20) 3,400 − 2,735 = ____

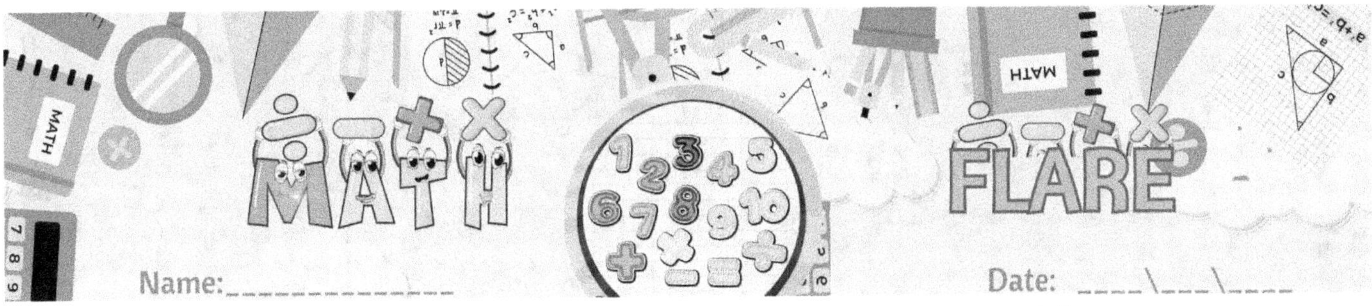

21) 2,480 - 1,692	22) 7,710 - 2,821	23) 8,720 - 3,847	24) 2,360 - 1,576
25) 7,010 - 1,964	26) 6,820 - 3,958	27) 5,000 - 4,854	28) 6,080 - 1,598
29) 2,040 - 1,382	30) 3,880 - 2,996	31) 2,200 - 1,414	32) 3,060 - 2,972
33) 7,480 - 1,999	34) 9,860 - 6,976	35) 6,770 - 4,882	36) 7,360 - 4,479
37) 4,060 - 3,991	38) 7,820 - 1,937	39) 6,320 - 4,558	40) 7,820 - 2,945

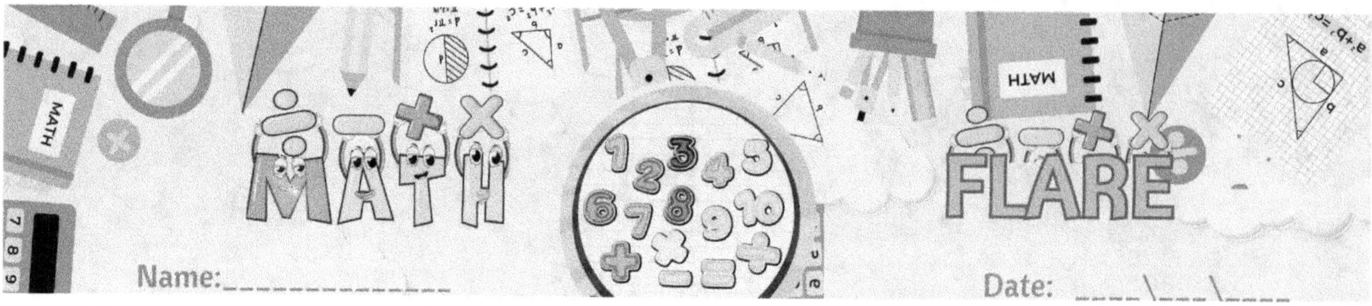

Name:______________ Date: ____________

41) 6,860 − 3,982 = ____	42) 4,880 − 2,991 = ____	43) 5,880 − 1,998 = ____	44) 3,580 − 2,994 = ____
45) 8,210 − 7,445 = ____	46) 6,820 − 4,933 = ____	47) 2,530 − 1,794 = ____	48) 7,720 − 1,895 = ____
49) 2,500 − 1,956 = ____	50) 5,640 − 4,977 = ____	51) 4,080 − 2,399 = ____	52) 4,380 − 1,494 = ____
53) 5,070 − 1,483 = ____	54) 2,180 − 1,599 = ____	55) 2,740 − 1,958 = ____	56) 5,680 − 2,791 = ____
57) 3,070 − 1,795 = ____	58) 2,240 − 1,585 = ____	59) 6,110 − 5,999 = ____	60) 4,510 − 3,893 = ____

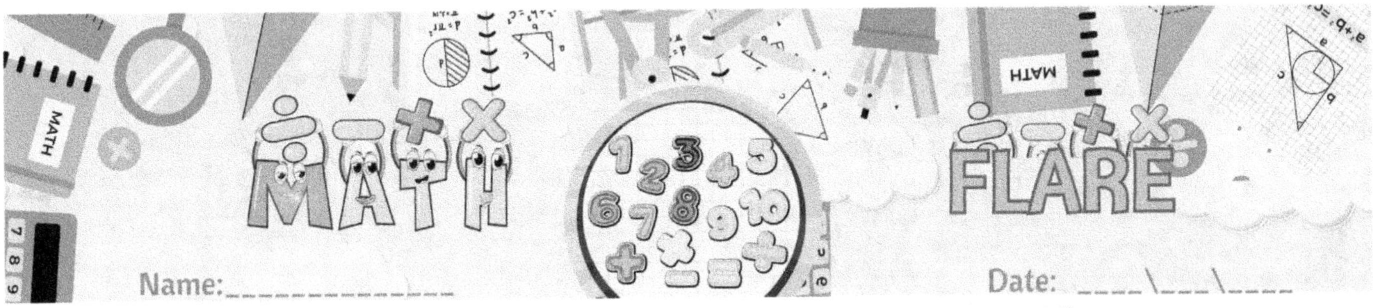

61) 8,770 − 5,985 = ____	62) 8,240 − 6,479 = ____	63) 8,800 − 1,992 = ____	64) 4,280 − 3,892 = ____
65) 3,880 − 2,992 = ____	66) 9,830 − 7,954 = ____	67) 2,030 − 1,365 = ____	68) 8,480 − 2,691 = ____
69) 9,800 − 3,971 = ____	70) 8,320 − 4,955 = ____	71) 9,420 − 7,746 = ____	72) 3,050 − 1,583 = ____
73) 4,340 − 1,952 = ____	74) 4,270 − 1,489 = ____	75) 5,040 − 4,955 = ____	76) 5,280 − 1,399 = ____
77) 5,800 − 4,983 = ____	78) 8,570 − 6,994 = ____	79) 6,640 − 4,995 = ____	80) 3,480 − 1,899 = ____

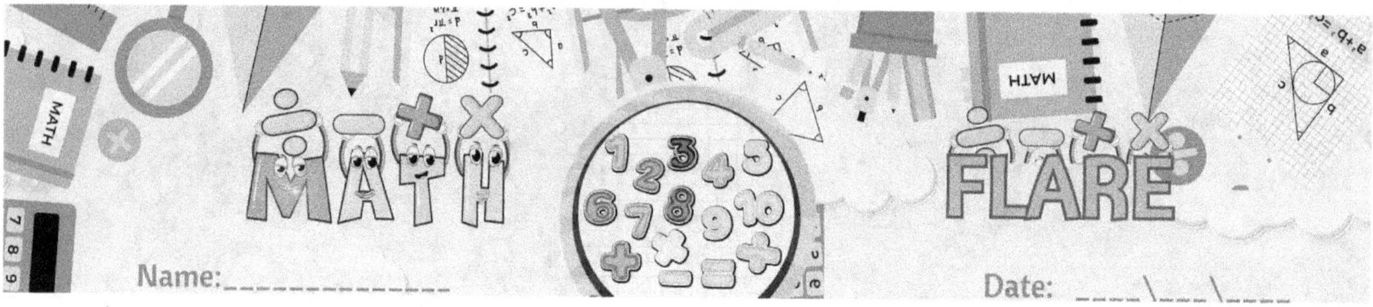

Name:________________ Date: ____________

81) 7,710 - 2,853	82) 3,480 - 2,994	83) 5,710 - 4,981	84) 3,320 - 1,687
85) 3,820 - 2,974	86) 8,000 - 2,877	87) 3,330 - 2,976	88) 7,440 - 1,557
89) 4,000 - 2,564	90) 4,370 - 2,982	91) 7,750 - 2,997	92) 4,720 - 1,866
93) 4,250 - 3,794	94) 4,200 - 1,813	95) 2,880 - 1,999	96) 6,310 - 2,979
97) 2,210 - 1,668	98) 7,160 - 5,488	99) 5,710 - 4,986	100) 7,840 - 5,952

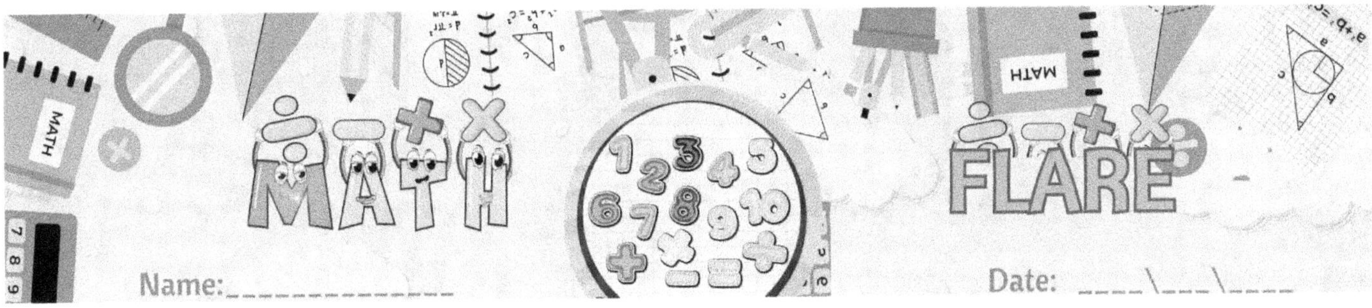

Addition Word Problems

1) Ayden bought a bag of shoes for 32 dollars. Later, Ayden bought another bag of shoes for 60 dollars. How much money did Ayden spend in total?

$32	spent on 1st pair of shoes
+ $60	spent on another pair of shoes
$92	Ayden spent in total

2) Evan spent 41 hours studying for the history exam on Monday and 31 hours studying for the science exam on Tuesday. How many hours did Evan spend studying in total?

3) Levi had 28 dollars in the morning and earned 12 more dollars in the afternoon. How many dollars Levi have in total?

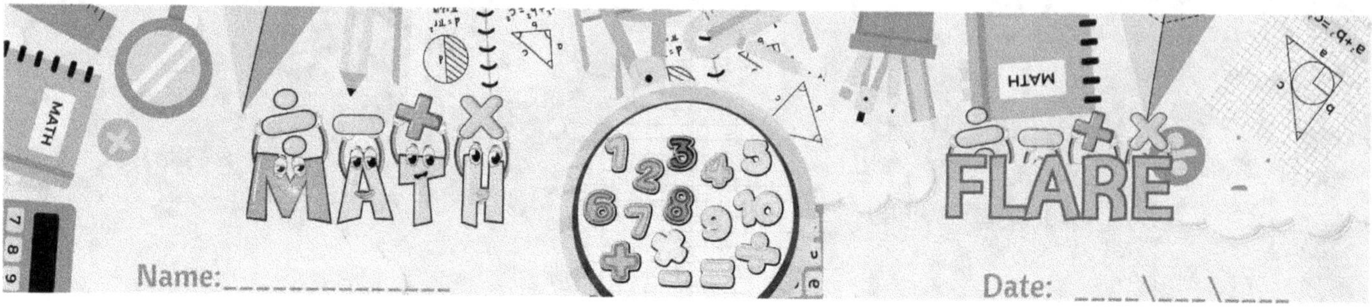

4) Joseph has 56 bandages. He gets 15 more bandages as a gift. How many bandages does Joseph have now?

5) Emma wrote 32 pages of her book yesterday and 24 pages today. How many pages did she write in total?

6) The weight of an empty container is 44 pounds. If the container is filled with 94 pounds of bananas, what is the total weight of the container and its contents?

7) Miles has 100 fish in an aquarium. If Miles adds 14 more fish to the aquarium, how many fish will be in the aquarium in total?

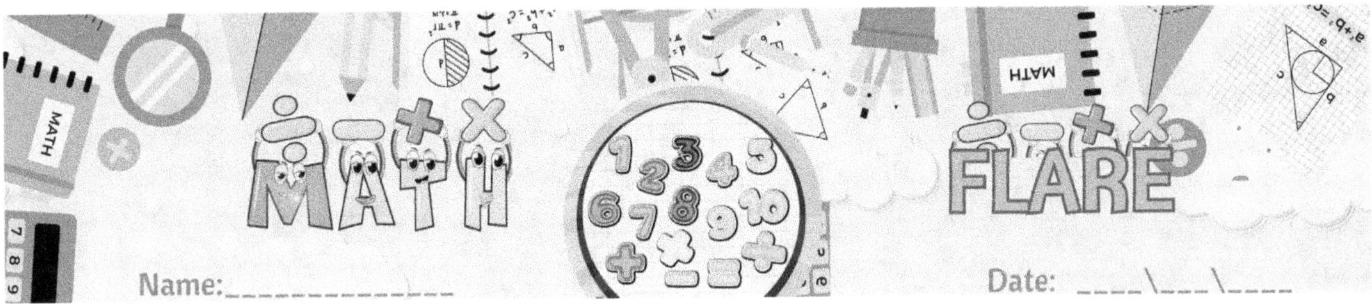

8) Sebastian bought 43 pencils and 5 pens. How many writing instruments did Sebastian buy in total?

9) Claire walked 91 miles yesterday and 67 miles today. How many miles did Claire walk in total?

10) Carter spent 41 dollars on Monday and 40 dollars on Tuesday. How much money did Carter spend in total?

11) Julian has 85 red marbles and 77 blue marbles in a jar. How many marbles does Julian have in total?

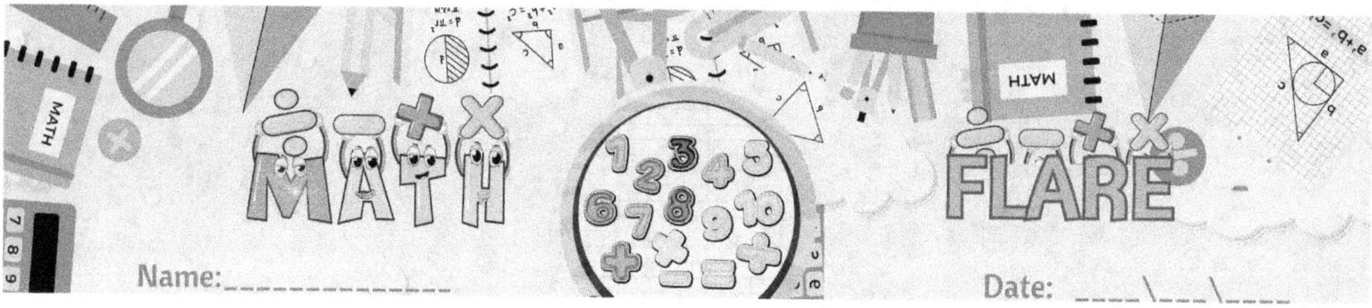

12) Sadie has 19 surgical masks. She buys 91 more surgical masks at the store. How many surgical masks does Sadie have now?

13) There are 93 spoons on the shelf. Isabelle puts 13 more spoons on the shelf. How many spoons are there on the shelf now?

14) Elizabeth has 84 flosses in a bag. If Elizabeth adds 87 more flosses to the bag, how many flosses does Elizabeth have in total?

15) A machine has 96 parts. If 16 more parts are added, how many parts does the machine have now?

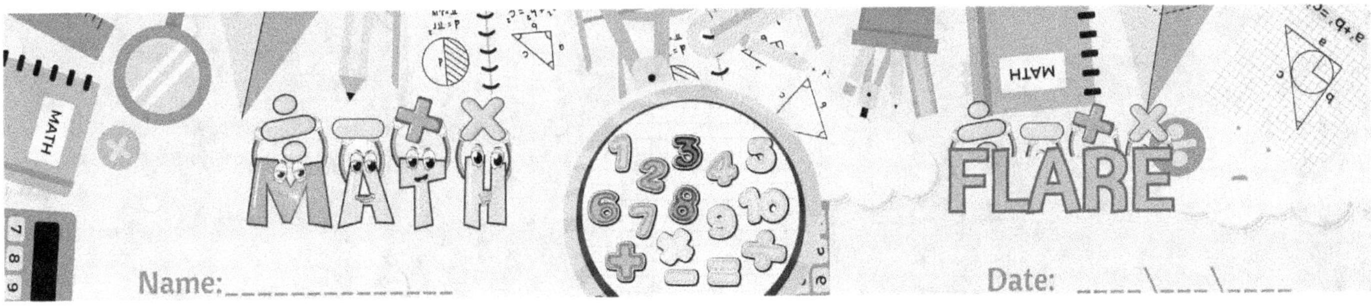

16) Aubrey sold 56 tissues on Monday and 58 tissues on Tuesday. How many tissues did the she sell in total?

17) Tristan has 88 apples and 97 oranges in a basket. How many fruits does Tristan have in total?

18) Gemma has 86 stethoscopes. Her friend gives her 20 more stethoscopes. How many stethoscopes does Gemma have now?

19) At the beginning of the day, there were 96 trees on the shelf. By the end of the day, 62 more trees were added to the shelf. How many trees are on the shelf now?

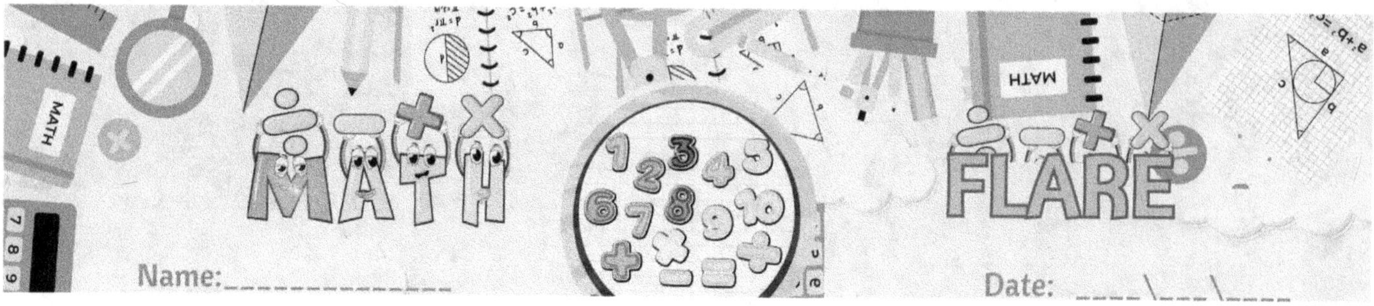

Name:______________ Date: ____________

20) Zara has 78 liters of water in a container. She pours in 77 more liters of water. How much water is in the container now?

21) There are 65 fishes in the pond. 55 more fishes join them. How many fishes are in the pond now?

22) Anthony has 79 headphones. His sister gives him 83 more headphones . How many headphones does Anthony have now?

23) Thomas has 64 cups. He gets 25 more cups. How many cups does he have now?

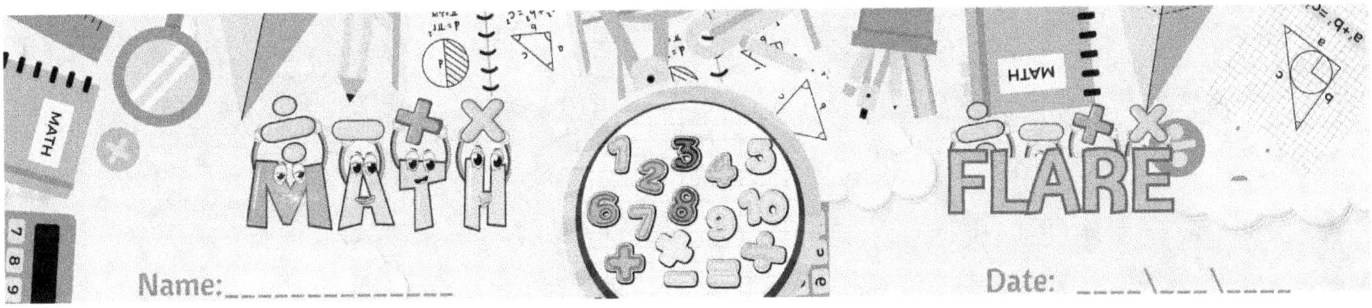

24) A pack of gum contains 69 pieces of gum. If 33 more pieces of gum are added to the pack, how many pieces of gum will the pack contain?

25) Aiden has a basket with 25 chocolates in it. After buying 59 more chocolates, how many chocolates does Aiden have in total?

26) On Monday, Brooklyn read 48 pages, and on Tuesday, 48 pages. How many pages did Brooklyn read altogether?

27) Miles has 77 balls. He finds 55 more balls. How many balls does he have now?

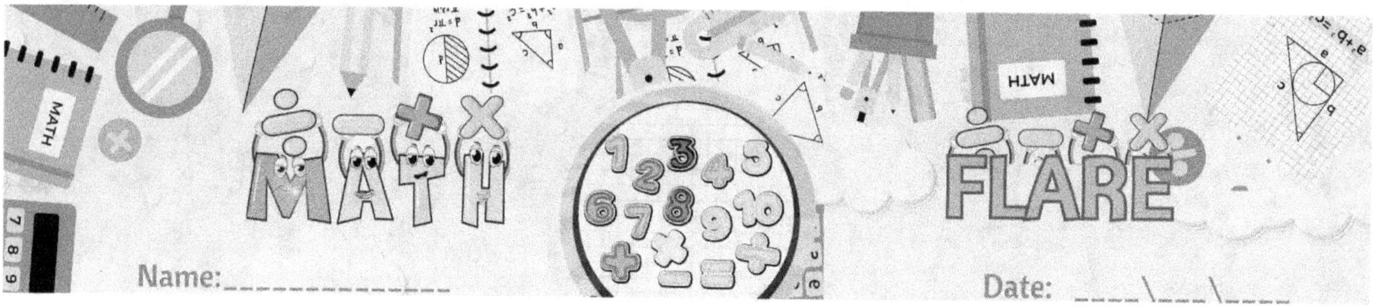

28) Grayson has 21 needles and buys 55 more needles. How many needles does Grayson have in total?

29) Maria baked 41 cakes yesterday and 51 cakes today. How many cakes did Maria bake in total?

30) There are 38 crows on a tree. 15 more crows land on the tree. How many crows are on the tree now?

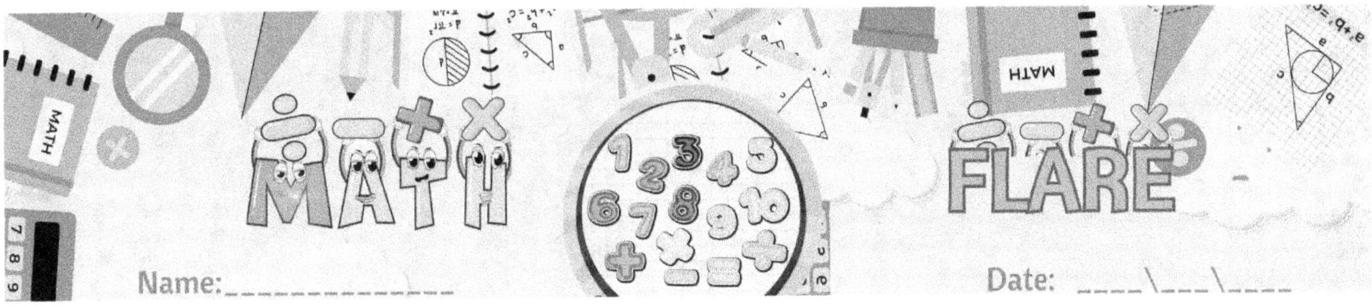

Subtraction Word Problems

1) Sandra has 38 bananas. She lost 29 of them. How many bananas does Sandra have left?

38	Sandra had 38 bananas
- 29	She ate 29 of them
9	she has 9 bananas left

2) Ellen baked a 35 cookies. 27 of them were chocolate chip cookies and the rest were oatmeal raisin cookies. How many oatmeal raisin cookies did Ellen bake?

3) If you have 72 pears and you give away 28, how many pears do you have left?

Name:______________ Date: ____________

4) Adam has 81 dollars. He needs to buy plums that costs 99 dollars. How much money will he have left after buying the plums?

5) Marcie wants to buy oranges, which costs 3 dollars. She has 1 dollars and plans to save the rest. How much more money does she need to save to buy oranges?

6) A pizza has 62 slices. Marin ate 2 slices. How many slices of pizza are left?

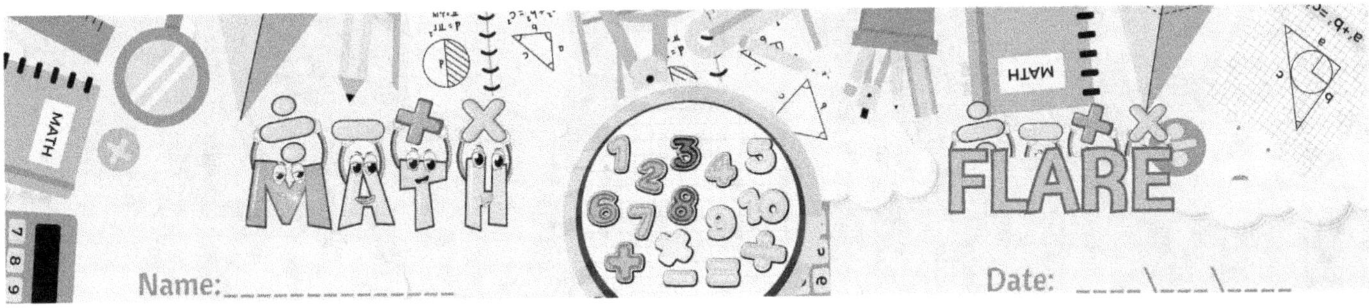

7) There are 20 fish in a pond. Janet caught 3 fish. How many fish are left in the pond?

8) A plums costs $42 and a pen costs $16. How much more expensive is the plums than the pen?

9) A cake recipe calls for 4 cups of flour. 4 cups of flour have already been added. How many more cups of flour are needed?

10) A cake recipe requires 90 cups of sugar. Jennifer only has 47 cups of sugar. How many more cups of sugar does Jennifer need?

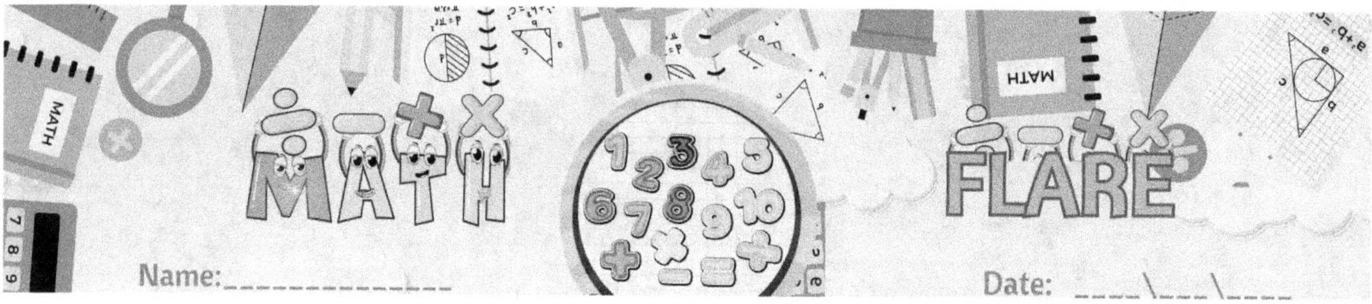

11) Paul has 26 dollars. He wants to buy mangoes that costs 11 dollars. How much more money does he need to buy the mangoes?

12) A pack of gum had 12 pieces. Marcie took 5 pieces of gum. How many pieces of gum are left in the pack?

13) Michele bought peaches for 96 dollars. She received 8 dollars in change. How much did peaches cost?

14) A box of pears weighs 40 pounds. If you remove 40 pounds from it, how much does it weigh now?

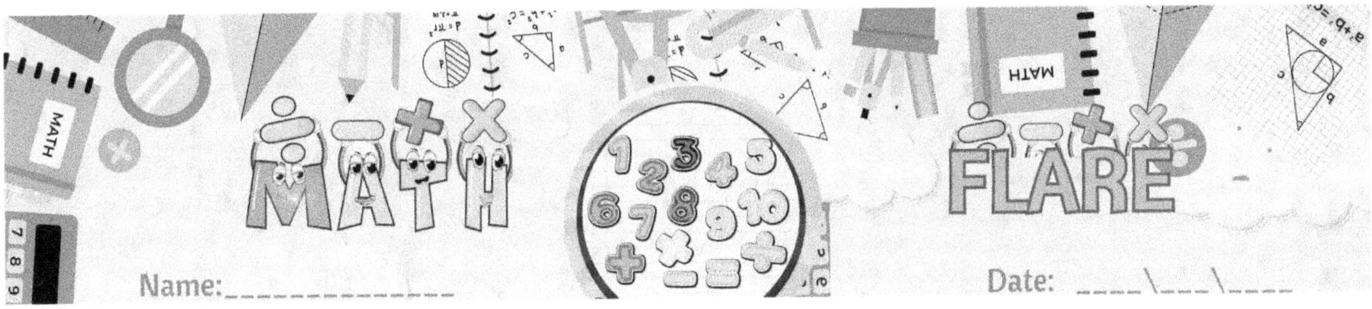

15) Mangoes originally cost 87 dollars, but it is now on sale for 48 dollars. How much money can you save by buying it on sale?

16) Allan saved up 8 dollars to buy pears. He spent 4 dollars on it. How much money does he have left?

17) Amy has 64 plums in her collection. She gave 39 of them to her friend. How many plums does Amy have now?

18) Audrey has 22 peaches. She gave 3 peaches to Sharon. How many peaches does Audrey have now?

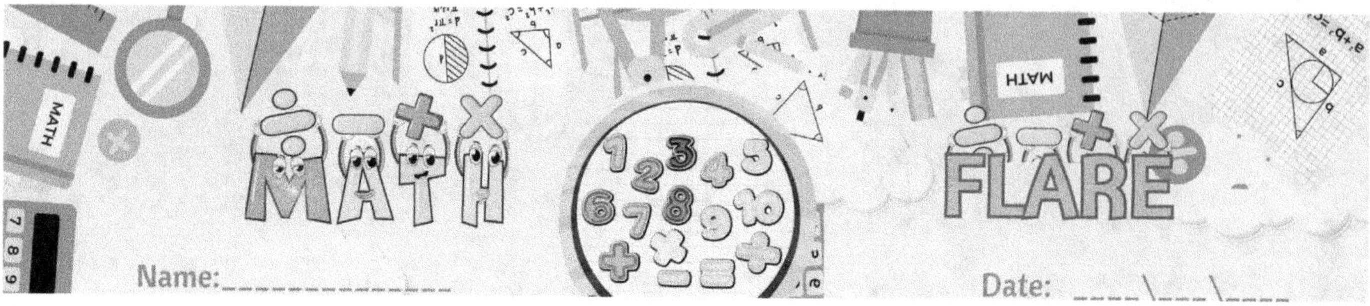

19) A small bag of chips has 21 chips in it. Donald ate 2 chips. How many chips are left in the bag?

20) There are 38 oranges. 33 oranges are blue and the rest are red. How many red oranges are in the box?

21) Steven had 81 apples. He gave 20 apples to Jackie. How many apples does Steven have left?

22) Janet and Michele went on a shopping spree and bought 88 pears. After returning home, they realized that they didn't need 78 of them. How many pears did they end up keeping?

23) There are 51 cars in a parking lot. Jake took 6 cars out of the lot. How many cars are still in the lot?

24) Amy bought peaches for 83 dollars but later found out it was on sale for 60 dollars less. How much did she overpay for peaches?

25) Sandra and Marcie had 95 apples altogether. Marcie gave 21 apples to Paul. How many apples do they have left?

26) Ellen bought plums for 16 dollars. She later returned some plums and received a refund of 14 dollars. How much money did she end up spending on plums?

Name:_______________ Date: ____________

27) Brian has 83 mangoes. He traded 34 of them with his friend. How many mangoes does Brian have now?

28) Sharon and Marcie went shopping for bananas. They had 56 dollars to spend but 23 dollars ended up being spent. How much money do they have left?

29) Oranges costs 92 dollars. If you paid $29. How much change will you get back?

30) Steven has 27 plums in his collection. He sold 26 of them at a sale. How many plums does he have left in his collection?

Chapter. 02

Multiplication and Division

Multiplication

Multiplication is an easy way of adding numbers together quickly. Instead of adding the same number repeatedly, we use multiplication to find the total much faster.

For instance, rather than adding 2 + 2 + 2 + 2 + 2, we can multiply 2 by 5 to get the same result: 2 x 5 = 10.

Here, the first number (2) is called the multiplicand, second number (5) is the multiplier. The answer we get, in this case, 10, is called the product.

Let's think of multiplication as repeated addition.

Take 2 x 5, for example. It means adding 2 together five times, which we can illustrate as: 2 + 2 + 2 + 2 + 2 = 10

Multiplication can also be visualized as groups of objects. Imagine we have 2 groups, each containing 5 oranges.

To find the total number of oranges, we multiply the number of groups (2) by the number of oranges in each group (5):

2 groups of 5 oranges = 10 oranges

Expressed as multiplication: 2 x 5 = 10

In summary, multiplication offers various ways to approach it: through repeated addition or by envisioning groups of objects. It's a powerful tool that makes solving math problems much quicker and more efficient!

We can also use the following table to quickly remember multiplication facts. The intersection of two points shows the product of two numbers.

For instance, the product of 5 x 6 = 30, or 6 x 5 = 30.

	1	2	3	4	5	6	7	8	9	10
1	1	2	3	4	5	6	7	8	9	10
2	2	4	6	8	10	12	14	16	18	20
3	3	6	9	12	15	18	21	24	27	30
4	4	8	12	16	20	24	28	32	36	40
5	5	10	15	20	25	**30**	35	40	45	50
6	6	12	18	24	30	36	42	48	54	60
7	7	14	21	28	35	42	49	56	63	70
8	8	16	24	32	40	48	56	64	72	80
9	9	18	27	36	45	54	63	72	81	90
10	10	20	30	40	50	60	70	80	90	100

Let's solve problems from exercises:

$$\begin{array}{r} 1{,}202 \\ \times \quad 4 \\ \hline 4{,}808 \end{array} \qquad \begin{array}{r} 83 \\ \times\ 86 \\ \hline 498 \\ +664 \\ \hline 7138 \end{array} \qquad \begin{array}{r} 552 \\ \times\ 908 \\ \hline 4416 \\ 0000 \\ 4968 \\ \hline 501216 \end{array}$$

Commutative Property of Multiplication

The commutative property of multiplication is a special rule in math that tells us the order of the numbers being multiplied doesn't affect the result.

For instance, let's take 2 x 5. If we switch the order of the numbers, multiplying 5 by 2 instead, we'll still end up with the same answer: $2 \times 5 = 10$, or $5 \times 2 = 10$.

So, whether we multiply 2 by 5 or 5 by 2, we get 10. That's the commutative property of multiplication in action!

Division

Division is like the opposite of multiplication. It's all about sharing or distributing items equally among a certain number of groups or people.

When we divide one number by another, we're essentially splitting a number into equal parts. We're figuring out how many groups of a certain size can be made from that number.

For instance, let's divide 20 by 4.

When we divide 20 by 4, we're essentially asking, "How many groups of size 4 can we make from 20?"

Now, there are several parts or terms involved in the division process:

- **Dividend:** This is the number being divided, which in this case, is 20.
- **Divisor:** This is the number we're dividing by, which is 4.
- **Quotient:** This is the answer we get after dividing. It tells us how many groups of divisors can be made from the dividend. In this case, the answer is 5.

So, when we divide 20 by 4, we found out that 5 groups of 4 can be made from 20.

Let's solve problems from exercises:

```
   4
4)16
 -16
   0
```

```
     42
12)504
   -48
    24
   -24
     0
```

```
   477
6)2,862
  -24
   46
  -42
   42
  -42
    0
```

Multiplication and Division Word Problem:

Anthony can run four laps in 1 hour. How many laps can Anthony run in 18 hours?

```
   4     1 hour 4 laps
 ×18     how many laps can he run in 18 hours?
 +32
 + 4
 =72     Anthony can run 72 laps in 18 hours
```

How many 12 cm pieces of rope can you cut from a rope that is 420 cm long?

```
    35
12)520
  -36        35 pieces can be cut
    60
   -60
     0
```

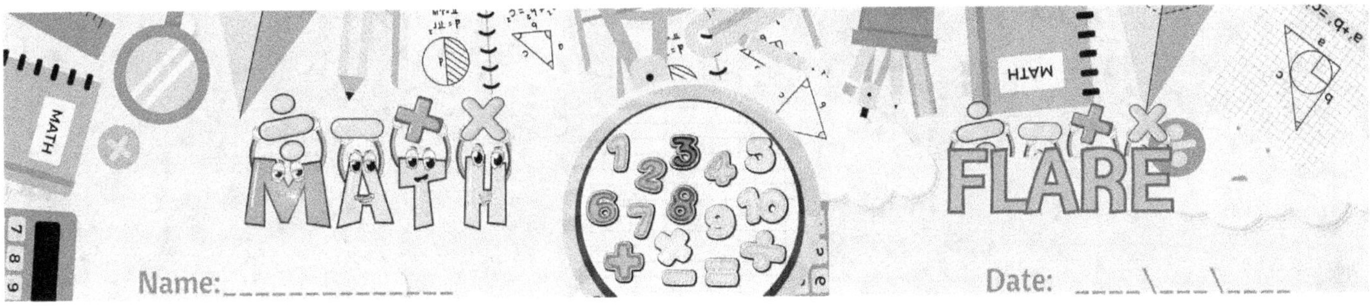

Multiplication: 2 x 1

Find the product.

1) 10×3 = 30	2) 11×3 = 33	3) 10×4	4) 22×3
5) 23×2	6) 21×2	7) 32×2	8) 44×2
9) 23×3	10) 30×3	11) 10×5	12) 40×2
13) 22×4	14) 20×3	15) 43×2	16) 41×2
17) 21×4	18) 21×3	19) 11×4	20) 24×2

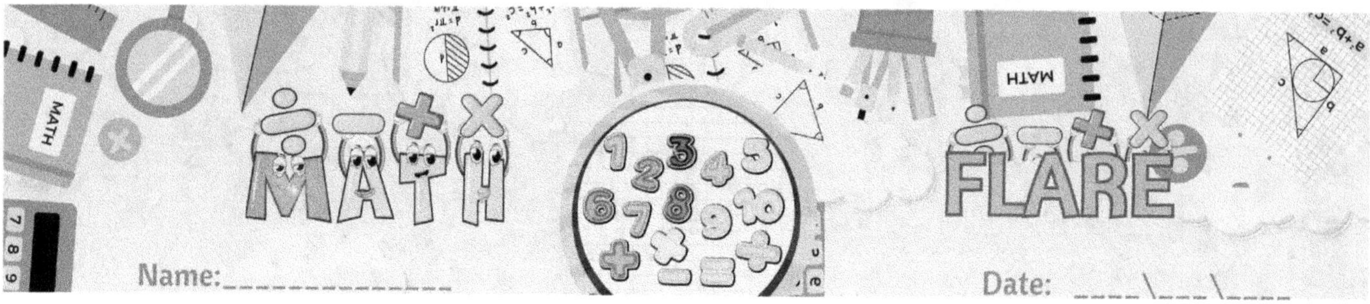

21) 10×2	22) 54×1	23) 33×3	24) 12×4
25) 20×4	26) 41×1	27) 31×3	28) 75×1
29) 32×3	30) 14×2	31) 57×1	32) 49×1
33) 61×1	34) 14×1	35) 20×2	36) 12×3
37) 42×2	38) 12×2	39) 11×2	40) 11×5

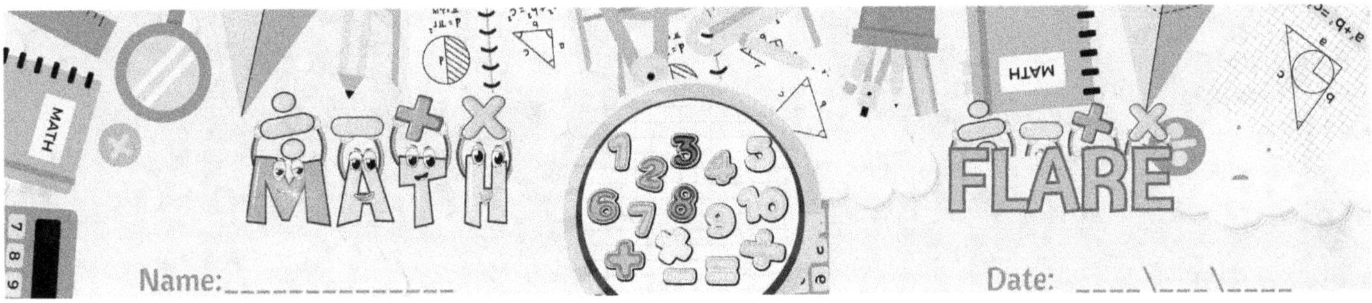

Multiplication: 3 x 1

Find the product.

1) $202 \times 4 = 808$

2) $211 \times 4 = 844$

3) 103×3

4) 120×3

5) 441×2

6) 213×2

7) 403×2

8) 121×3

9) 711×1

10) 123×2

11) 110×5

12) 340×2

13) 341×2

14) 658×1

15) 120×4

16) 113×2

17) 843×1

18) 532×1

19) 100×5

20) 222×3

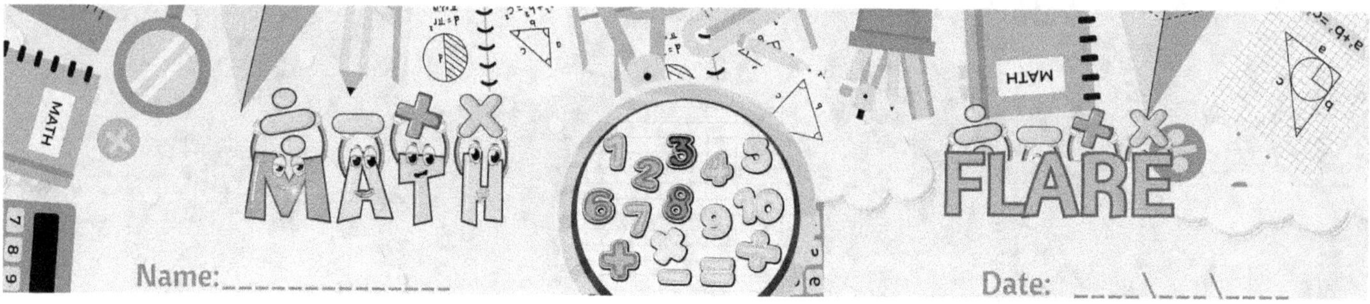

Name:______________ Date: ____________

21) 595 × 1	22) 111 × 5	23) 213 × 3	24) 331 × 2
25) 112 × 4	26) 300 × 2	27) 210 × 3	28) 101 × 4
29) 211 × 3	30) 102 × 2	31) 242 × 2	32) 231 × 3
33) 101 × 5	34) 212 × 4	35) 222 × 4	36) 301 × 3
37) 412 × 2	38) 333 × 2	39) 321 × 3	40) 233 × 3

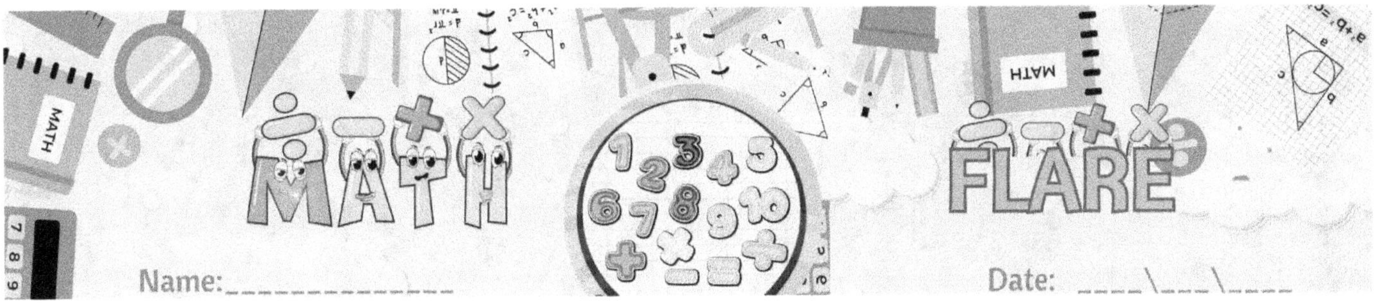

Multiplication: 4 x 1

Find the product.

1) $1{,}202 \times 4$ = 4,808

2) $1{,}110 \times 3$ = 3,330

3) $1{,}222 \times 4$

4) $1{,}223 \times 2$

5) $1{,}110 \times 4$

6) $3{,}224 \times 2$

7) $1{,}011 \times 4$

8) $2{,}210 \times 4$

9) $1{,}133 \times 2$

10) $1{,}101 \times 4$

11) $2{,}111 \times 3$

12) $2{,}222 \times 4$

13) $1{,}111 \times 4$

14) $1{,}300 \times 3$

15) $1{,}032 \times 3$

16) $1{,}101 \times 5$

17) $2{,}000 \times 4$

18) $8{,}620 \times 1$

19) $2{,}130 \times 2$

20) $2{,}031 \times 3$

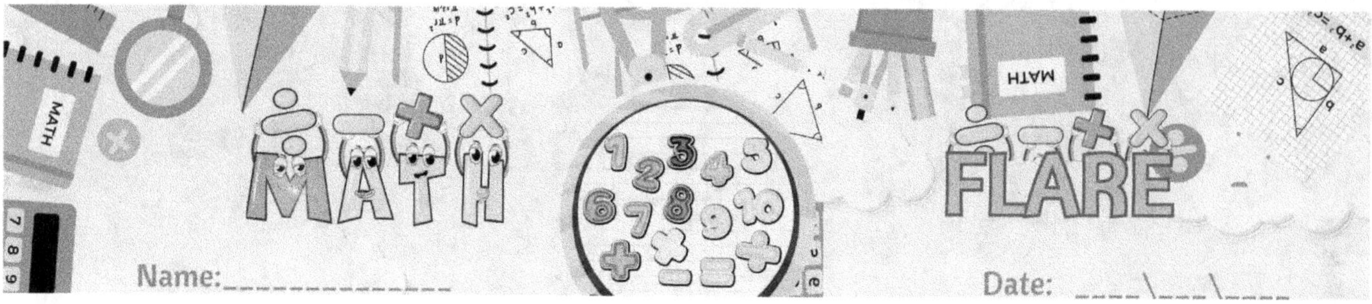

21) $4{,}132 \times 2$

22) $6{,}210 \times 1$

23) $2{,}231 \times 3$

24) $2{,}032 \times 3$

25) $3{,}103 \times 2$

26) $1{,}022 \times 4$

27) $2{,}113 \times 3$

28) $1{,}430 \times 2$

29) $3{,}313 \times 3$

30) $9{,}216 \times 1$

31) $2{,}320 \times 2$

32) $2{,}302 \times 3$

33) $2{,}013 \times 1$

34) $3{,}344 \times 2$

35) $1{,}012 \times 4$

36) $1{,}143 \times 2$

37) $2{,}201 \times 2$

38) $2{,}023 \times 2$

39) $3{,}130 \times 3$

40) $2{,}001 \times 3$

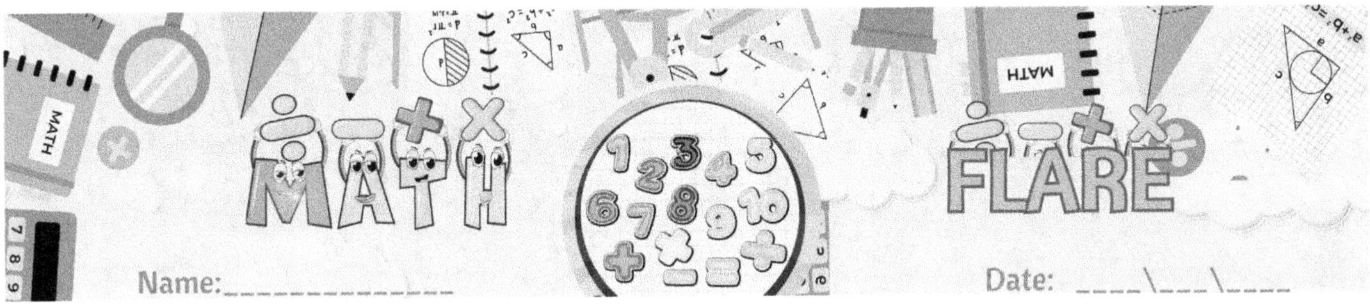

Multiplication (double Digit)

Find the product.

1) 83 × 86

    498
    +664
    7138

2) 21 × 59

3) 91 × 93

4) 27 × 49

5) 23 × 38

6) 18 × 21

7) 61 × 25

8) 28 × 88

9) 31 × 74

10) 98 × 24

11) 41 × 21

12) 75 × 51

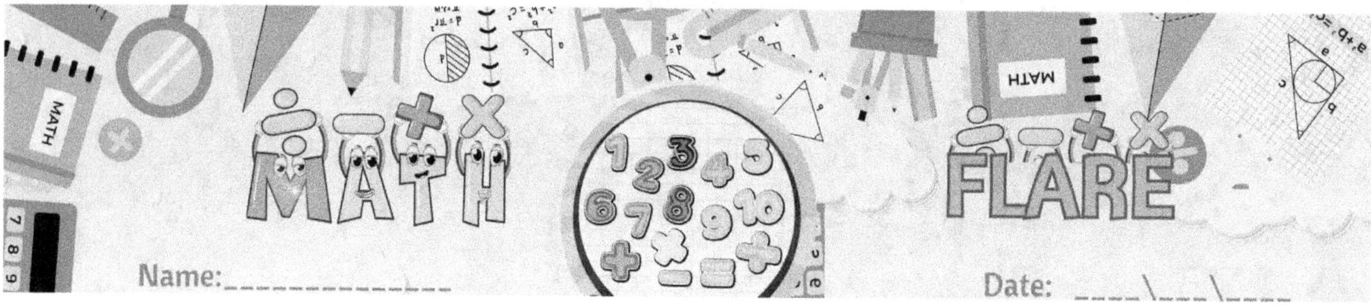

13) 48×97

14) 41×55

15) 28×52

16) 13×93

17) 76×63

18) 63×23

19) 12×49

20) 33×79

21) 44×64

22) 64×12

23) 22×14

24) 54×10

25) 68×56

26) 59×59

27) 16×17

28) 18×72

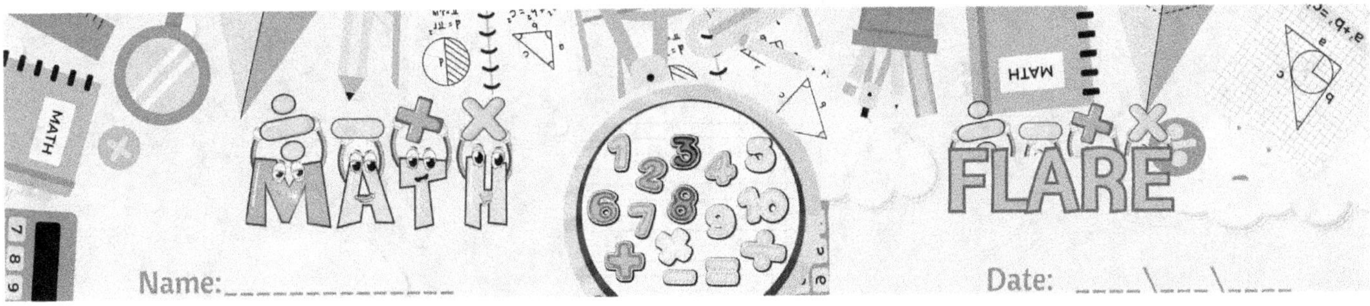

29) $\begin{array}{r} 20 \\ \times\ 70 \\ \hline \end{array}$

30) $\begin{array}{r} 20 \\ \times\ 93 \\ \hline \end{array}$

31) $\begin{array}{r} 62 \\ \times\ 71 \\ \hline \end{array}$

32) $\begin{array}{r} 31 \\ \times\ 70 \\ \hline \end{array}$

33) $\begin{array}{r} 36 \\ \times\ 24 \\ \hline \end{array}$

34) $\begin{array}{r} 44 \\ \times\ 97 \\ \hline \end{array}$

35) $\begin{array}{r} 60 \\ \times\ 15 \\ \hline \end{array}$

36) $\begin{array}{r} 86 \\ \times\ 81 \\ \hline \end{array}$

37) $\begin{array}{r} 51 \\ \times\ 29 \\ \hline \end{array}$

38) $\begin{array}{r} 79 \\ \times\ 76 \\ \hline \end{array}$

39) $\begin{array}{r} 56 \\ \times\ 73 \\ \hline \end{array}$

40) $\begin{array}{r} 39 \\ \times\ 45 \\ \hline \end{array}$

41) $\begin{array}{r} 53 \\ \times\ 41 \\ \hline \end{array}$

42) $\begin{array}{r} 86 \\ \times\ 71 \\ \hline \end{array}$

43) $\begin{array}{r} 92 \\ \times\ 52 \\ \hline \end{array}$

44) $\begin{array}{r} 88 \\ \times\ 69 \\ \hline \end{array}$

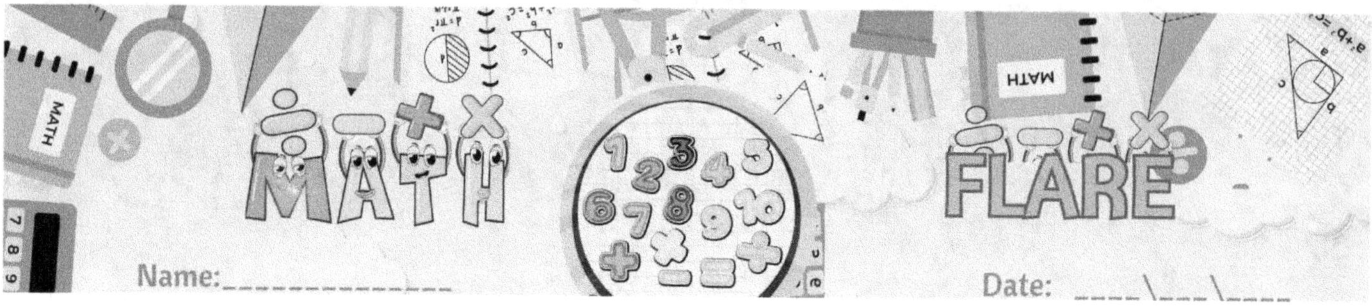

Multiplication (3 Digit)

Find the product.

1) $\begin{array}{r} 552 \\ \times\ 908 \\ \hline 4416 \\ 0000 \\ 4968 \\ \hline 501216 \end{array}$

2) $\begin{array}{r} 125 \\ \times\ 413 \\ \hline \end{array}$

3) $\begin{array}{r} 387 \\ \times\ 389 \\ \hline \end{array}$

4) $\begin{array}{r} 268 \\ \times\ 731 \\ \hline \end{array}$

5) $\begin{array}{r} 441 \\ \times\ 938 \\ \hline \end{array}$

6) $\begin{array}{r} 758 \\ \times\ 985 \\ \hline \end{array}$

7) $\begin{array}{r} 695 \\ \times\ 565 \\ \hline \end{array}$

8) $\begin{array}{r} 490 \\ \times\ 634 \\ \hline \end{array}$

9) $\begin{array}{r} 693 \\ \times\ 772 \\ \hline \end{array}$

10) $\begin{array}{r} 183 \\ \times\ 862 \\ \hline \end{array}$

11) $\begin{array}{r} 371 \\ \times\ 418 \\ \hline \end{array}$

12) $\begin{array}{r} 267 \\ \times\ 461 \\ \hline \end{array}$

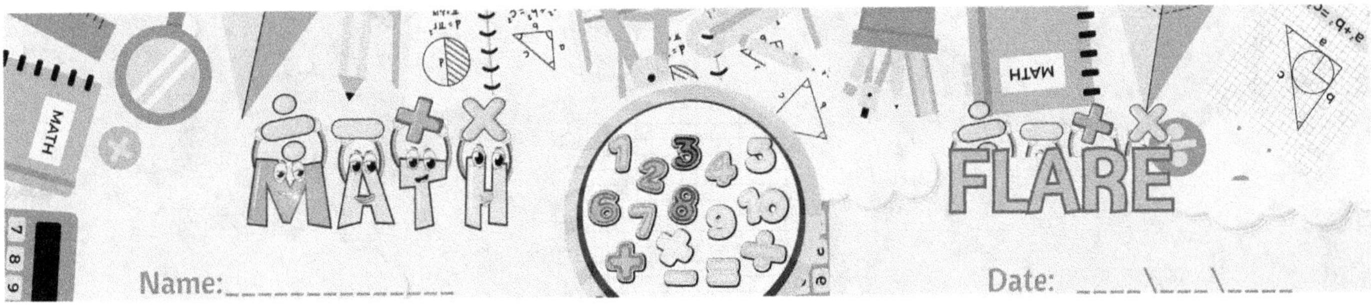

13) 414 × 753

14) 506 × 317

15) 851 × 592

16) 782 × 833

17) 351 × 743

18) 524 × 700

19) 131 × 557

20) 535 × 226

21) 126 × 164

22) 426 × 621

23) 983 × 402

24) 754 × 967

25) 921 × 329

26) 124 × 254

27) 444 × 122

28) 427 × 235

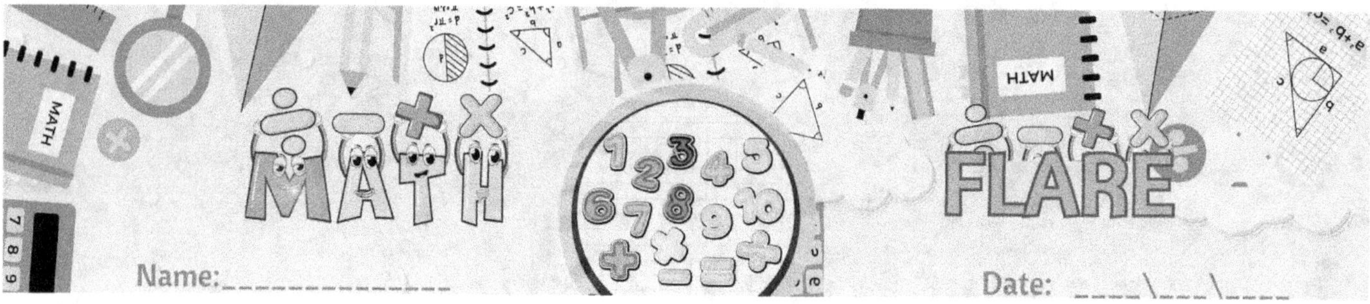

29) 741×663

30) 998×633

31) 883×950

32) 879×847

33) 256×924

34) 734×950

35) 141×788

36) 604×235

37) 337×956

38) 837×307

39) 991×645

40) 477×111

41) 998×538

42) 395×622

43) 569×628

44) 489×329

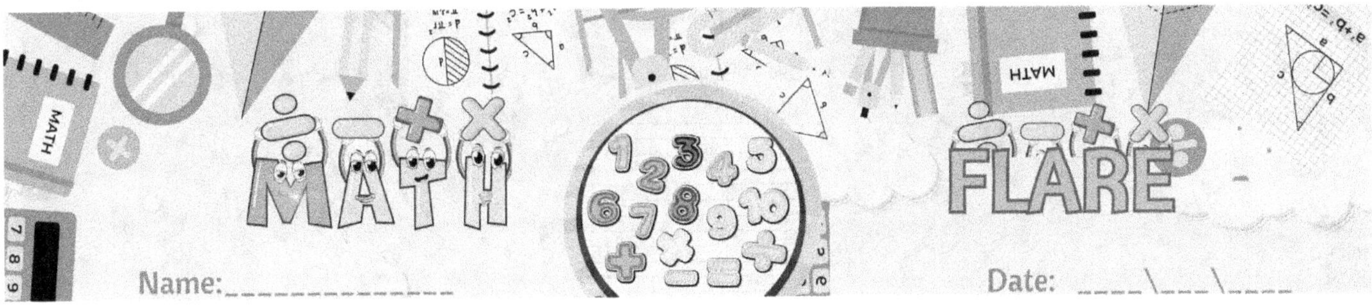

Basic Division

Find the quotient.

1) 4)16 — quotient 4; −16; 0

2) 10)50

3) 6)54

4) 3)6

5) 3)18

6) 5)10

7) 7)56

8) 9)18

9) 7)63

10) 9)45

11) 2)4

12) 3)30

13) 6)24

14) 7)28

15) 4)24

16) 5)25

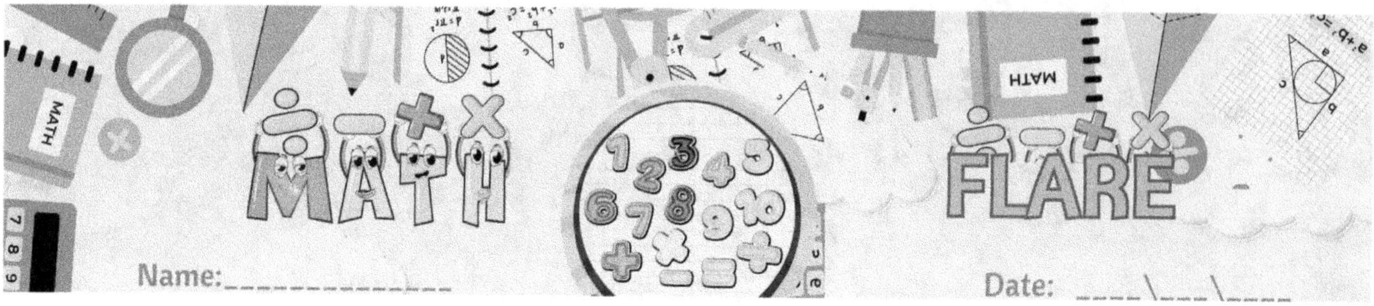

17) $6\overline{)48}$

18) $8\overline{)16}$

19) $1\overline{)5}$

20) $3\overline{)12}$

21) $4\overline{)12}$

22) $6\overline{)18}$

23) $9\overline{)63}$

24) $7\overline{)7}$

25) $1\overline{)3}$

26) $2\overline{)18}$

27) $4\overline{)36}$

28) $5\overline{)45}$

29) $3\overline{)24}$

30) $3\overline{)9}$

31) $8\overline{)40}$

32) $2\overline{)14}$

33) $9\overline{)81}$

34) $5\overline{)35}$

35) $5\overline{)20}$

36) $6\overline{)60}$

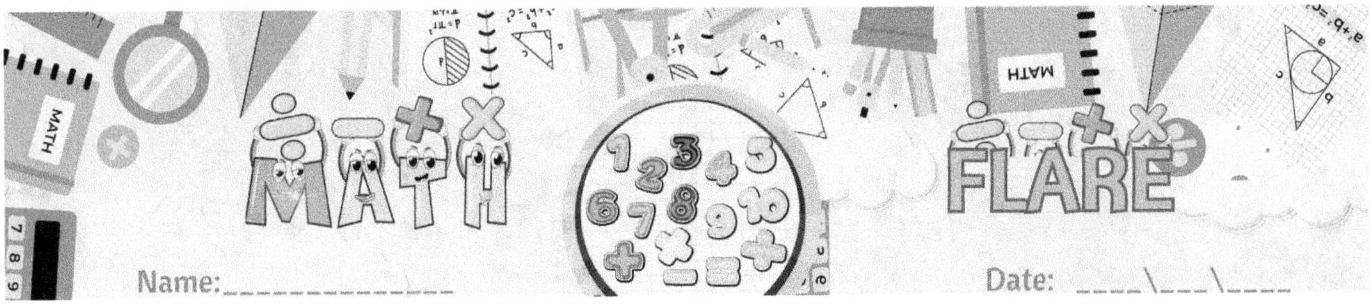

37) $10\overline{)20}$

38) $2\overline{)16}$

39) $8\overline{)24}$

40) $1\overline{)4}$

41) $9\overline{)36}$

42) $2\overline{)10}$

43) $2\overline{)2}$

44) $6\overline{)36}$

45) $8\overline{)64}$

46) $6\overline{)12}$

47) $5\overline{)50}$

48) $3\overline{)3}$

49) $5\overline{)30}$

50) $4\overline{)20}$

51) $6\overline{)6}$

52) $1\overline{)6}$

53) $6\overline{)42}$

54) $5\overline{)15}$

55) $8\overline{)32}$

56) $4\overline{)8}$

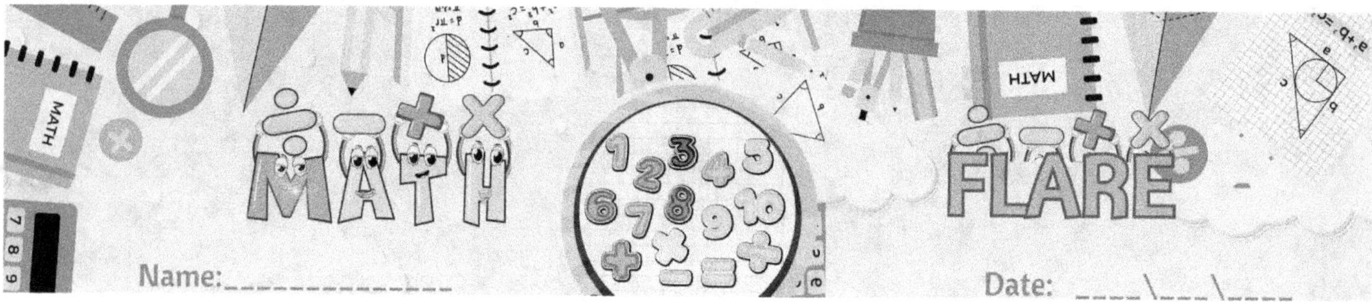

Long Division (within 100)

Find the quotient.

1)
```
     42
12 ) 504
    - 48
      24
    - 24
       0
```

2) 4) 208

3) 7) 441

4) 6) 282

5) 4) 64

6) 11) 1,056

7) 7) 378

8) 5) 495

9) 11) 330

10) 3) 288

11) 6) 474

12) 2) 82

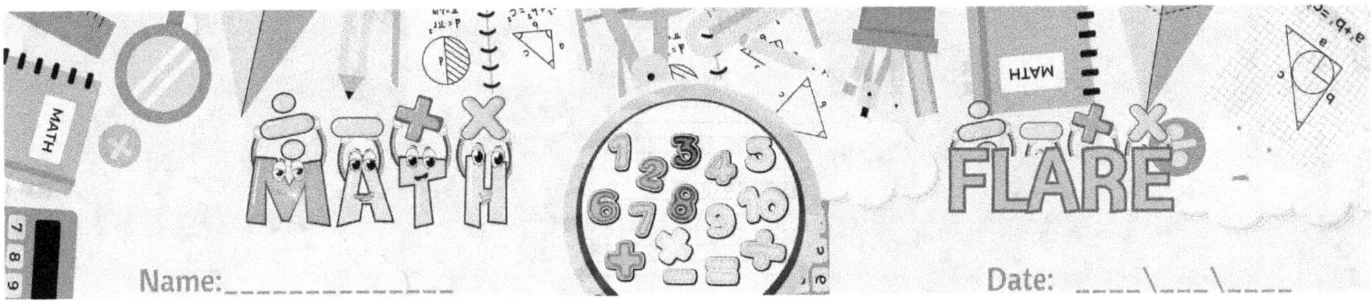

13) $12\overline{)168}$

14) $9\overline{)117}$

15) $4\overline{)384}$

16) $2\overline{)184}$

17) $6\overline{)96}$

18) $2\overline{)124}$

19) $5\overline{)345}$

20) $8\overline{)88}$

21) $10\overline{)130}$

22) $5\overline{)160}$

23) $10\overline{)460}$

24) $8\overline{)168}$

25) $2\overline{)154}$

26) $5\overline{)200}$

27) $2\overline{)86}$

28) $9\overline{)198}$

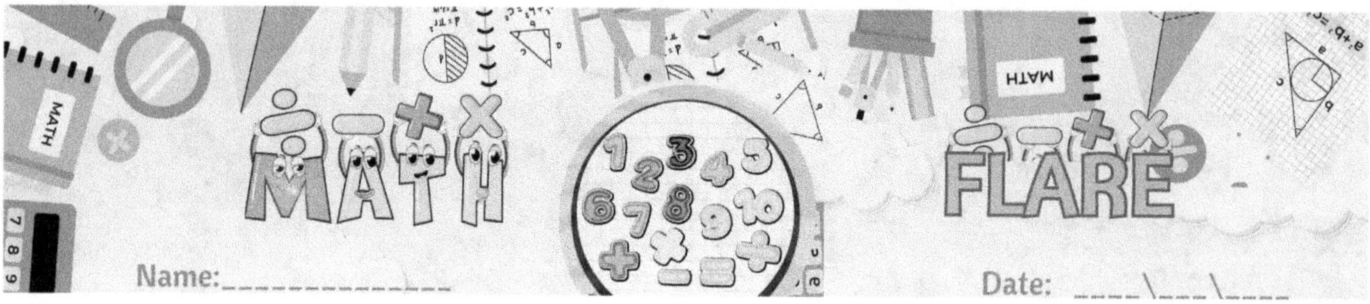

29) $5\overline{)430}$

30) $7\overline{)308}$

31) $11\overline{)363}$

32) $3\overline{)105}$

33) $2\overline{)190}$

34) $7\overline{)287}$

35) $6\overline{)444}$

36) $8\overline{)192}$

37) $3\overline{)93}$

38) $5\overline{)370}$

39) $8\overline{)432}$

40) $6\overline{)306}$

41) $12\overline{)648}$

42) $8\overline{)552}$

43) $10\overline{)20}$

44) $6\overline{)528}$

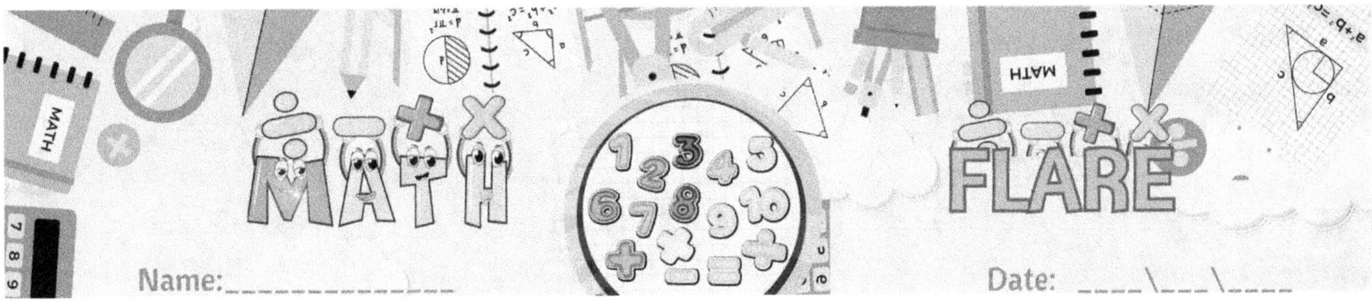

Name:______________ Date: ___________

Long Division (within 1000)

Find the quotient.

1) 6) 2,862

477
- 24
46
- 42
42
- 42
0

2) 4) 640

3) 4) 1,920

4) 19) 703

5) 6) 5,052

6) 19) 4,997

7) 16) 6,256

8) 3) 399

9) 14) 13,398

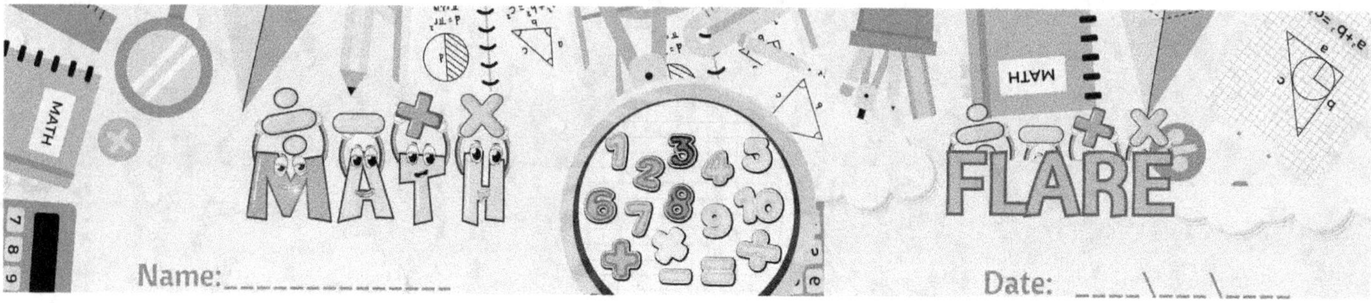

10) $6\overline{)2{,}364}$

11) $16\overline{)9{,}744}$

12) $6\overline{)5{,}940}$

13) $19\overline{)7{,}847}$

14) $7\overline{)4{,}438}$

15) $15\overline{)5{,}895}$

16) $3\overline{)1{,}545}$

17) $19\overline{)10{,}526}$

18) $10\overline{)1{,}760}$

19) $2\overline{)1{,}094}$

20) $19\overline{)12{,}825}$

21) $8\overline{)2{,}976}$

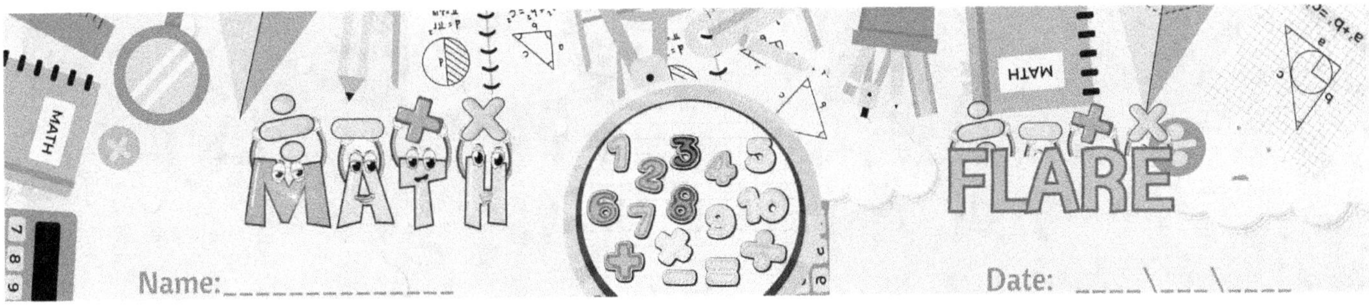

22) $11\overline{)\,8{,}459}$

23) $13\overline{)\,2{,}756}$

24) $15\overline{)\,9{,}015}$

25) $9\overline{)\,4{,}158}$

26) $20\overline{)\,17{,}660}$

27) $15\overline{)\,990}$

28) $2\overline{)\,1{,}304}$

29) $5\overline{)\,850}$

30) $5\overline{)\,3{,}845}$

31) $4\overline{)\,1{,}268}$

32) $7\overline{)\,5{,}936}$

33) $15\overline{)\,6{,}195}$

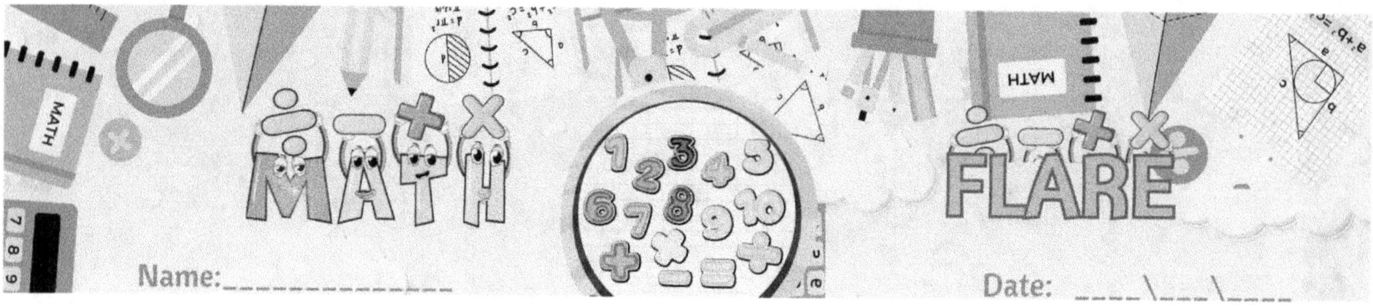

34) $7\overline{)1{,}470}$

35) $18\overline{)16{,}884}$

36) $2\overline{)278}$

37) $1\overline{)595}$

38) $2\overline{)876}$

39) $3\overline{)1{,}431}$

40) $8\overline{)5{,}968}$

41) $14\overline{)10{,}206}$

42) $5\overline{)1{,}425}$

43) $9\overline{)2{,}070}$

44) $16\overline{)13{,}984}$

45) $10\overline{)8{,}210}$

Name:______________ Date: ____________

Multiplication Word Problems

1) Anthony can run four laps in 1 hour. How many laps can Anthony run in 18 hour?

$$\begin{array}{r} 4 \\ \times 18 \\ \hline +32 \\ +4 \\ \hline =72 \end{array}$$

1 hour 4 laps

how many laps can he run in 18 hours?

Anthony can run 72 laps in 18 hours

2) A box contains two bottles of juice, and each bottle contains 19 ounces of juice. How many ounces of juice are there in total?

3) There are 13 flowers in each bouquet. If Isabella has 17 bouquets, how many flowers does Isabella have in all?

Name:________________ Date: ____________

4) Jayden runs 11 miles every day. How many miles will Jayden run in 16 days?

5) There are 18 cars in a parking lot. If each car needs five liters of gasoline, how many liters of gasoline are needed for all the cars?

6) There are 11 pencils in each pack. If Everly buys four packs, how many pencils will Everly have?

7) Naomi has four boxes of lotions. Each box has seven lotions. How many lotions does Naomi have in all?

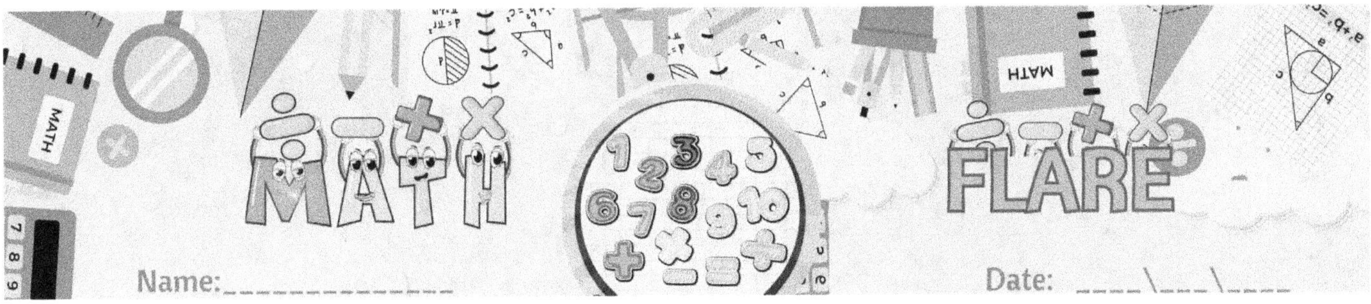

8) Jose earns six dollars per hour. How much will Jose earn after working for 18 hours?

9) There are 14 pencils in each bag. If Avery buys 11 bags, how many pencils will Avery have?

10) Lillian has five vases of flowers. Each vase has four flowers. How many flowers does Lillian have in all?

11) A garden has five rows of flowers and two flowers in each row. How many flowers are there in total?

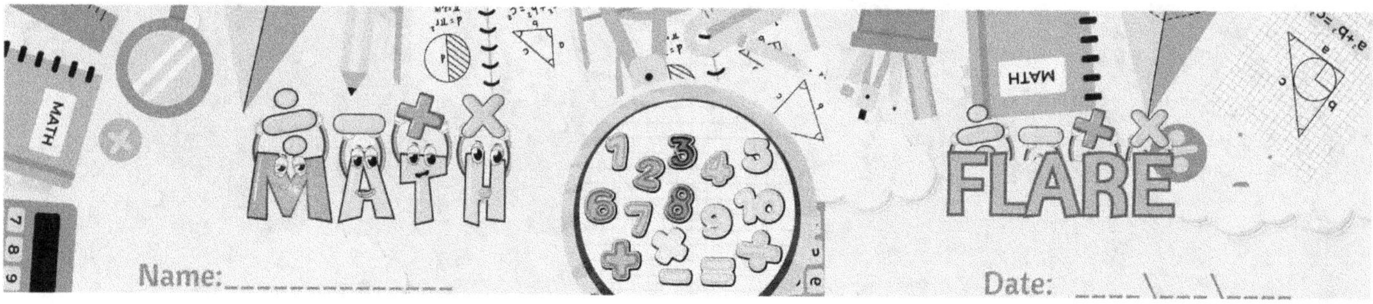

12) There are 14 pages in a book. If 12 books are needed for a class, how many pages are there in total?

13) Isabelle wants to make 11 flower arrangements, and each arrangement requires 14 flowers. How many flowers does Isabelle need in total?

14) Miles can type seven words per minute. How many words can Miles type in 10 minutes?

15) There are four shelves in Carter's bookcase. 20 books can fit on each shelf. How many books can the bookcase hold in total?

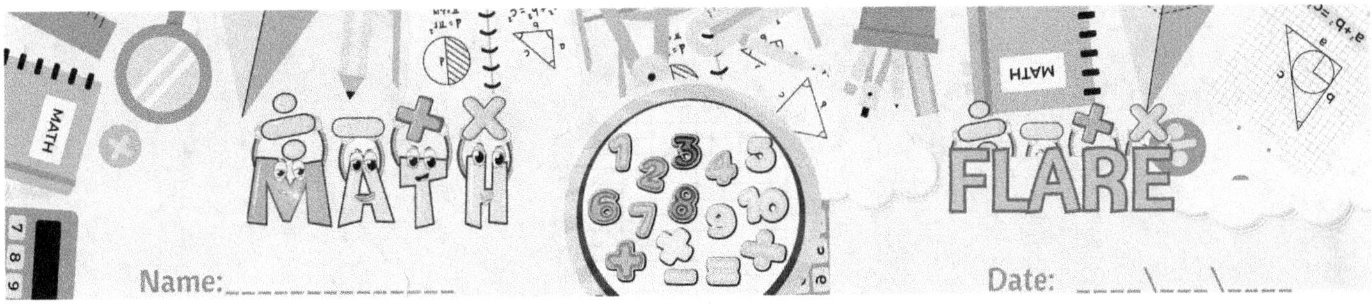

16) Ryan can ride five miles in one hour. How far can he ride in 11 hours?

17) A bookshelf can hold two books. If there are 16 bookshelves in a room, how many books can the room hold in total?

18) There are eight slices of pizza in each box. If Lydia orders 14 boxes, how many slices of pizza will Lydia have?

19) Emily baked three batches of cookies. Each batch had seven cookies. How many cookies did Emily bake in all?

Name:______________ Date: ___________

20) Madelyn has 14 yards of fabric, and each dress requires 14 yards of fabric. How many dresses can Madelyn make?

21) Benjamin can lift 14 kilograms of weight. How many kilograms of weight can he lift in 14 lifts?

22) Ella wants to make 17 pizzas, and each pizza requires 17 cups of cheese. How many cups of cheese does Ella have?

23) A recipe for a cake calls for 11 cups of flour. How many cups of flour are needed to make 10 cakes?

Name:________________ Date: ____________

24) There are 16 shelves in a library. Five books can fit on each shelf. How many books the library have in total?

25) If a car travels at 13 miles per hour for seven hours, how far will it go?

26) Harper baked 16 batches of cakes. Each batch had six cakes. How many cakes did Harper bake in all?

27) Gemma has 20 books. Each book has four pages. How many pages does Gemma have in all?

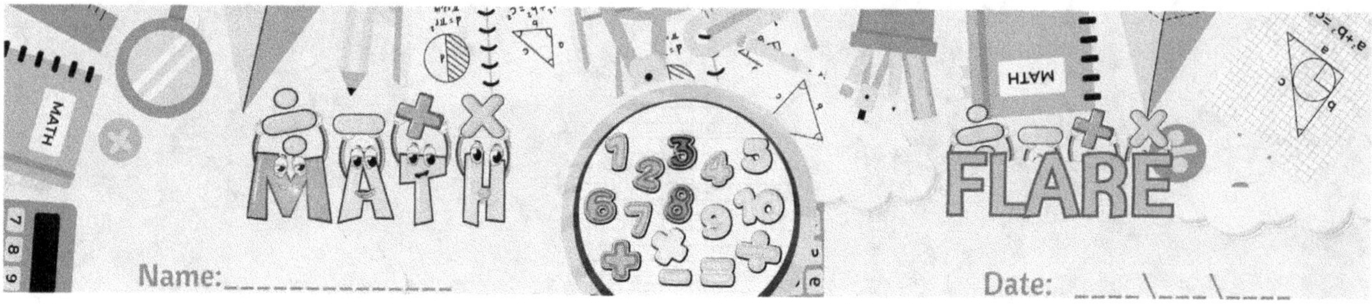

28) Elijah can do six pushups in one minute. How many pushups can Elijah do in three minutes?

29) There are six students in a class. If each student needs 10 pencils, how many pencils are needed for the class in total?

30) If there are 10 students in each classroom and there are 19 classrooms, how many students are there in total?

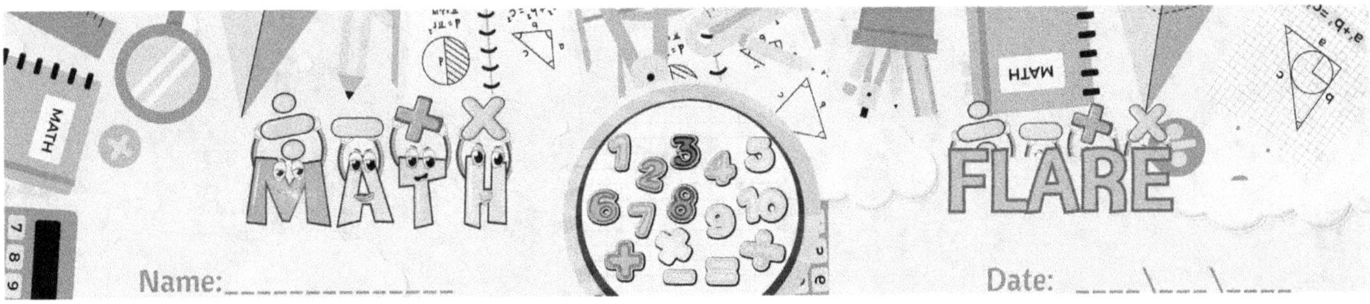

Division Word Problems

1) How many 12 cm pieces of rope can you cut from a rope that is 420 cm long?

```
   35
12)520
  -36
   60
  -60
    0
```

35 pieces can be cut

2) How many 17 cm pieces of pipe can you cut from a pipe that is 340 cm long?

3) Ethan read a book that had 267 pages in three days. If he read the same number of pages each day, how many pages did he read per day?

Name:_______________ Date: ___________

4) A pool is 160 meters long. If it is divided into eight equal parts, how long is each part?

5) Christopher has 1,152 pages of homework to do. If he wants to finish his homework in 12 days, how many pages does he need to do each day?

6) A roll of tape is 276 feet long. If Kinsley needs to cut the tape into 12 pieces that are all the same length, how long will each piece be?

Name:______________ Date: ____________

7) If Olivia has 1,080 pens and wants to distribute them equally to 15 students, how many pens will each student get?

8) You have 192 folders and want to share them equally with six people. How many folders would each person get?

9) A car can travel 176 miles on four gallons of gas. How many miles can it travel on 1 gallon of gas?

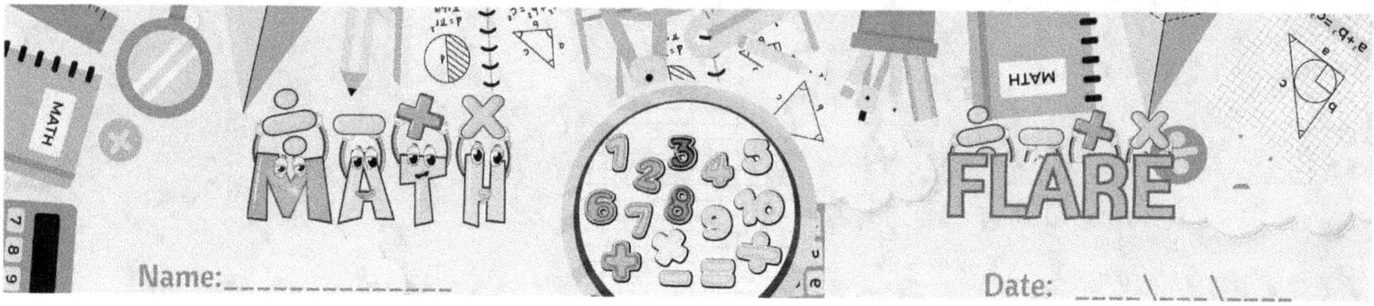

10) Evan has 32 dollars and wants to buy eight thermometers. How much can he spend on each thermometers?

11) If Brooklyn has 852 cups and wants to distribute them equally to 12 students, how many cups will each student get?

12) Isabella has 462 needles and wants to divide them equally among 14 children. How many needles will each child get?

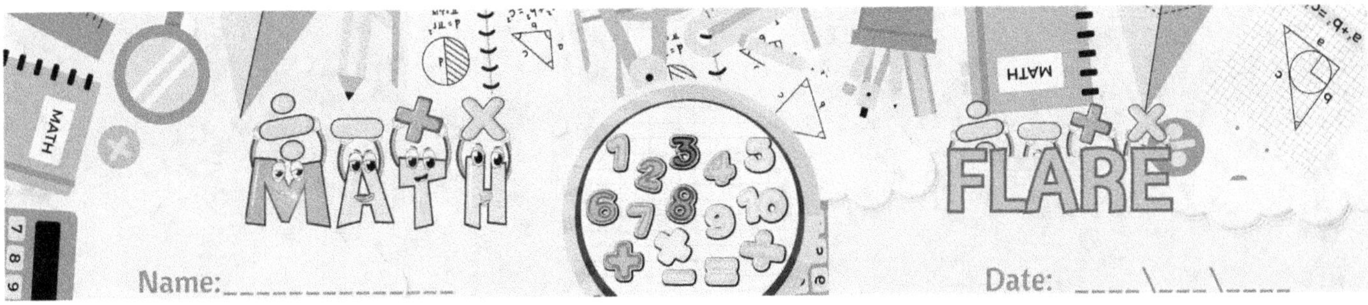

13) Lily has 1,110 toothbrushes. If Lily divides them evenly among 15 children, how many toothbrushes will each child get?

14) Everly has 1,104 cookies and wants to divide them equally into 12 bags. How many cookies will be in each bag?

15) Sophia has $1,539 and she wants to buy 19 watches that cost the same amount. How much does each watches cost?

Name:______________ Date: ____________

16) If a box contains 1,672 chocolates and each person can have 19 chocolates, how many people can be served from that box?

17) It takes Paisley 72 minutes to write 1 page. How many pages can Paisley write in 144 minutes?

18) Nathaniel scored 874 points in 19 games. What is his average score per game?

19) Adalyn is packing 390 cupcakes into boxes. Each box can hold six cupcakes. How many boxes will Adalyn need?

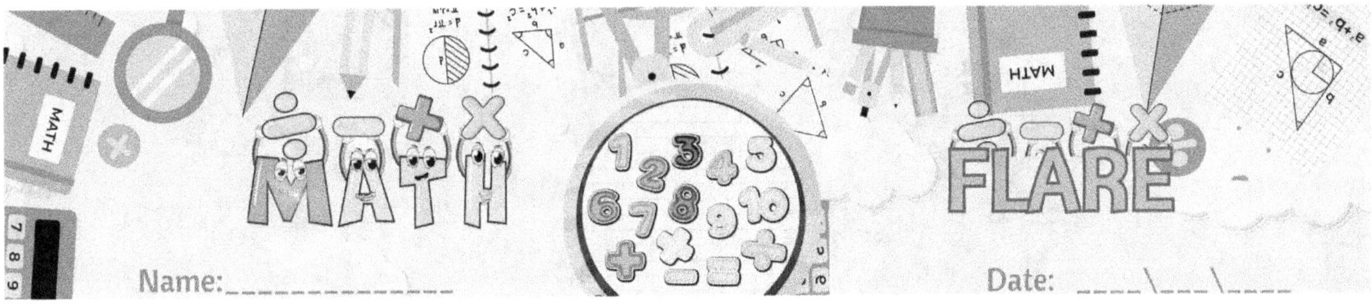

Name:______________ Date: ____________

20) Jose can type 210 words in seven minutes. How many words can he type in 1 minute?

21) If a garden is 186 feet long and it is divided into six equal parts, how long is each part?

22) A box of scalpels has 10 scalpels. If five children each get an equal number of scalpels, how many scalpels will each child get?

23) A box contains 408 candy bars. If each candy bar has 17 calories, how many calories are there in the box?

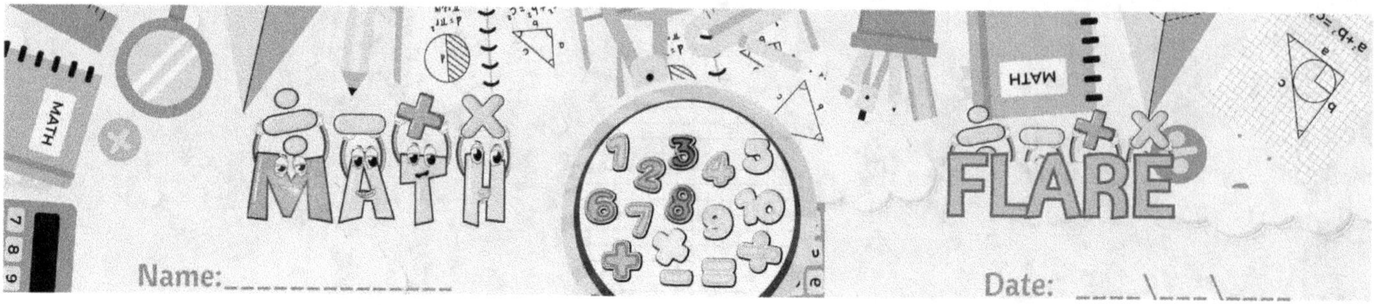

24) A box of vitamins weighs 240 pounds. If one vitamin weighs 12 pounds, how many vitamins are there in the box?

25) At a restaurant, 18 friends decided to divide the bill equally. If each person paid $85, then what was the total bill?

26) Penelope baked 306 cakes for a party. If she wants to divide them into nine equal portions, how many cakes will each portion have?

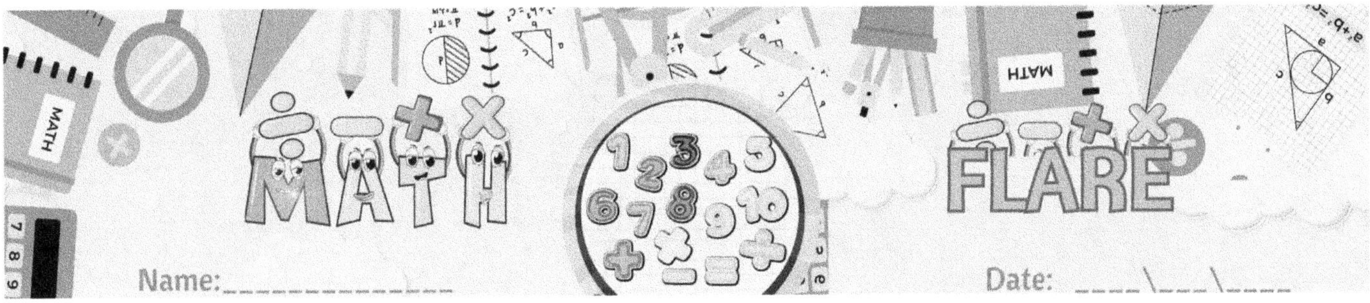

27) If a garden is 1,080 feet wide and it is divided into 12 equal parts, how wide is each part?

28) If a rope is 602 meters long and you want to cut it into seven equal pieces, how long will each piece be?

29) A recipe calls for 735 cups of sugar to make 15 cookies. How much sugar is needed to make 1 cookie?

30) If the pizzas have 380 slices and is divided equally among 10 people, how many slices will each person get?

Chapter. 03

Decimals

Adding Decimals

Adding decimals is like adding whole numbers, but we must align the decimal points carefully. For instance, when adding 49.88 and 45.78:

Step 1: Align the decimal points.

$$\begin{array}{r} 49.88 \\ +\ 45.78 \\ \hline \end{array}$$

Step 2: Start adding from the rightmost digit (the ones place) and move to the left.

Add 8 and 8: 8 + 8 = 16. Write down 6 in the ones place and carry over 1 to the tenths place.

$$\begin{array}{r} 49.88 \\ +\ 45.78 \\ \hline 6 \end{array}$$

Step 3: Add the tenths place.

Add 1 (carried over from the previous step), 8, and 7: 1 + 8 + 7 = 16. Write down 6 in the tenths place and carry over 1 to the hundredths place.

$$\begin{array}{r} 49.88 \\ +\ 45.78 \\ \hline 66 \end{array}$$

Step 4: Continue adding digits to the left until you reach the leftmost digit:

$$\begin{array}{r} 49.88 \\ +\ 45.78 \\ \hline 9566 \end{array}$$

Step 5: Finally, write the sum with the decimal point directly below the decimal points in the original numbers.

$$\begin{array}{r} 49.88 \\ +\ 45.78 \\ \hline 95.66 \end{array}$$

Subtracting Decimals

Subtracting decimals follows a process like adding decimals, except instead of adding the numbers, we subtract them.

Let's solve more problems:

$$\begin{array}{r} 467.52 \\ +\ 758.37 \\ \hline 1{,}225.89 \end{array} \qquad \begin{array}{r} 409.71 \\ -\ 291.47 \\ \hline 118.24 \end{array}$$

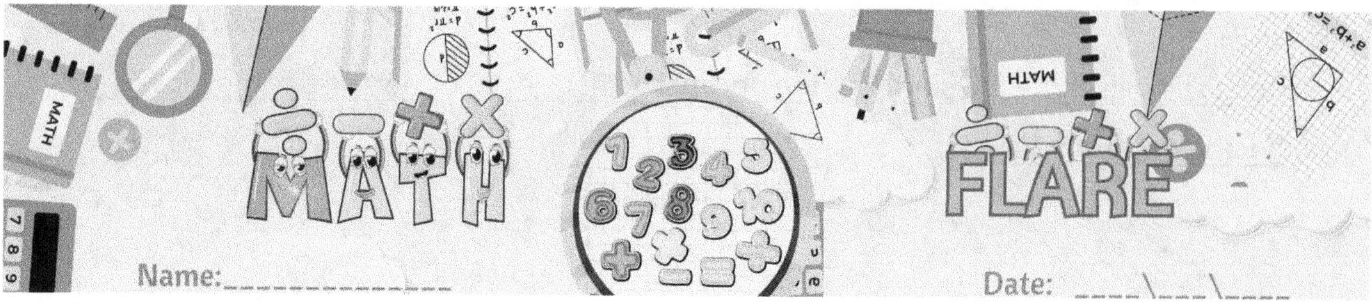

Adding Decimals

Find the sum.

1) $467.52 + 758.37 = 1{,}225.89$

2) $815.81 + 107.35 =$ ______

3) $952.29 + 626.36 =$ ______

4) $150.82 + 994.16 =$ ______

5) $797.59 + 934.85 =$ ______

6) $479.39 + 685.19 =$ ______

7) $183.78 + 134.12 =$ ______

8) $103.98 + 742.25 =$ ______

9) $851.20 + 454.69 =$ ______

10) $753.70 + 308.49 =$ ______

11) $748.43 + 797.23 =$ ______

12) $553.64 + 697.24 =$ ______

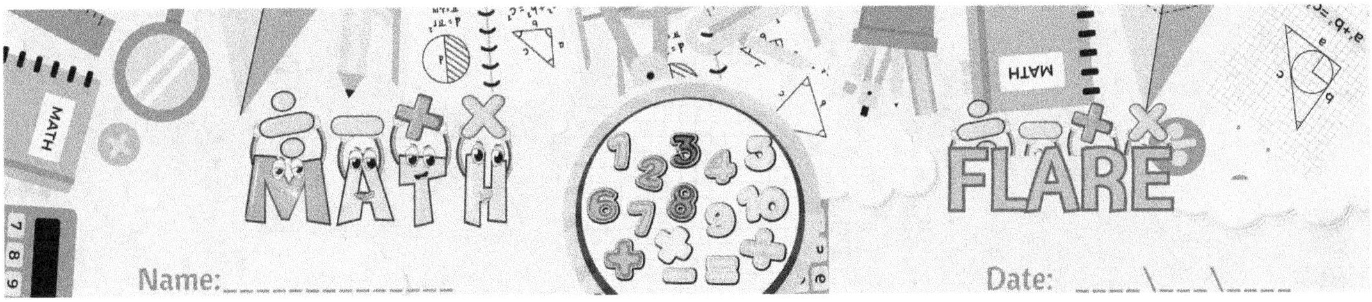

13) 394.11 + 503.08 = ______

14) 972.94 + 357.84 = ______

15) 194.87 + 727.54 = ______

16) 417.75 + 246.23 = ______

17) 402.78 + 725.38 = ______

18) 190.95 + 907.47 = ______

19) 710.90 + 235.04 = ______

20) 614.31 + 964.14 = ______

21) 963.42 + 517.89 = ______

22) 185.55 + 556.40 = ______

23) 733.45 + 147.09 = ______

24) 528.22 + 768.96 = ______

25) 976.49 + 479.14 = ______

26) 667.46 + 142.07 = ______

27) 806.12 + 825.88 = ______

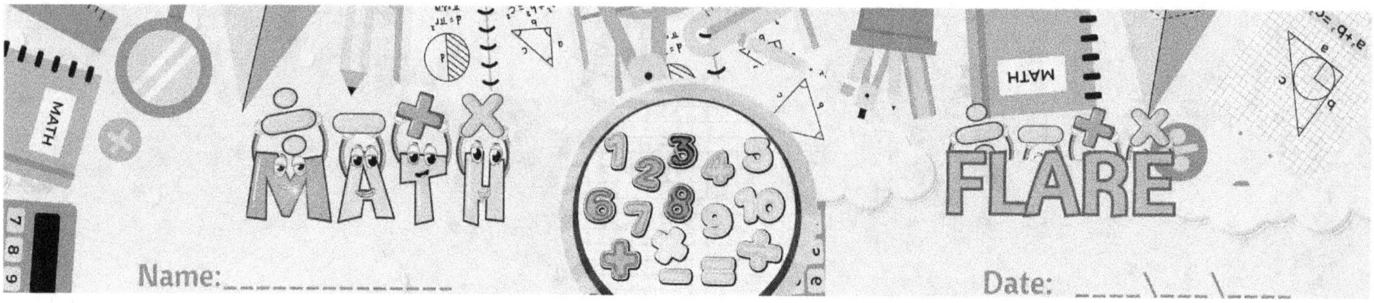

Subtracting Decimals

Find the difference.

1) 409.71 − 291.47 = ______

2) 581.21 − 426.84 = ______

3) 378.95 − 159.71 = ______

4) 567.47 − 139.35 = ______

5) 332.96 − 193.61 = ______

6) 562.45 − 190.94 = ______

7) 198.81 − 111.15 = ______

8) 495.49 − 371.66 = ______

9) 979.02 − 210.17 = ______

10) 804.35 − 189.73 = ______

11) 853.15 − 754.71 = ______

12) 303.81 − 257.46 = ______

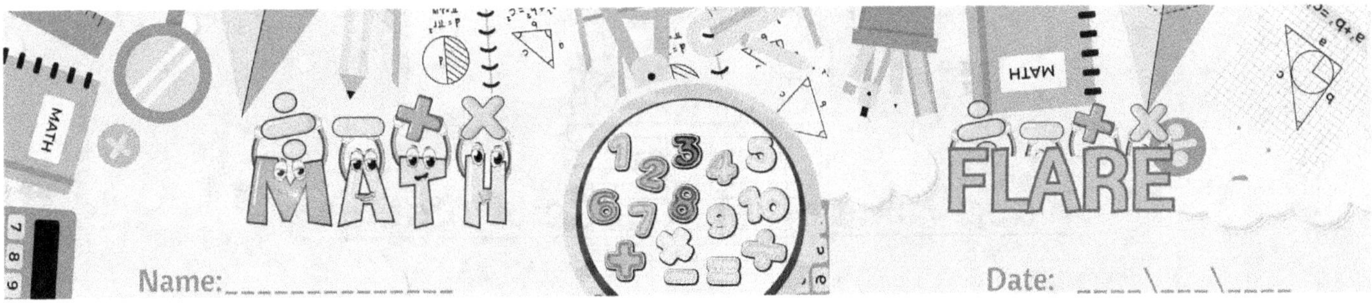

Name:_______________ Date: _________

13) 813.21 − 645.20 = ______

14) 814.85 − 636.50 = ______

15) 387.12 − 327.83 = ______

16) 987.06 − 732.13 = ______

17) 709.93 − 652.56 = ______

18) 874.28 − 409.08 = ______

19) 334.98 − 243.32 = ______

20) 297.93 − 151.78 = ______

21) 870.72 − 266.88 = ______

22) 797.35 − 514.70 = ______

23) 641.61 − 324.81 = ______

24) 504.40 − 136.64 = ______

25) 717.63 − 283.33 = ______

26) 935.26 − 475.24 = ______

27) 905.74 − 874.68 = ______

Chapter. 04

Place Value and Expanded Notations

Place value tells us the value of a digit in a number based on where it's placed.

Imagine we have the number 647.528. It has 6 digits.

Now, each digit holds a special place. Let's break down the number 647.528:

- The digit 6 is in the hundreds place. Its value is $6 \times 100 = 600$.
- The digit 4 is in the tens place. Its value is $4 \times 10 = 40$.
- The digit 7 is in the ones place. Its value is $7 \times 1 = 7$.
- The digit 5 is in the tenths place. Its value is $5 \times \frac{1}{10} = 0.5$.
- The digit 2 is in the hundredths place. Its value is $2 \times \frac{1}{100} = 0.02$.
- The digit 8 is in the thousandths place. Its value is $8 \times \frac{1}{1000} = 0.008$.

When we add these values together, we find the value of the entire number:

$$600 + 40 + 7 + 0.5 + 0.02 + 0.008 = 647.528$$

Let's solve some problems:

Place value of the underlined digit:

600.<u>5</u>28 = 5 tenths

Expanded notations:

891,479 800,000 + 90,000 + 1,000 + 400 + 70 + 9

691,905 6 hundred thousands + 9 ten thousands + 1 thousand + 9 hundreds + 5 ones

988.582 9 hundreds + 8 tens + 8 ones + 5 tenths + 8 hundredths + 2 thousandths

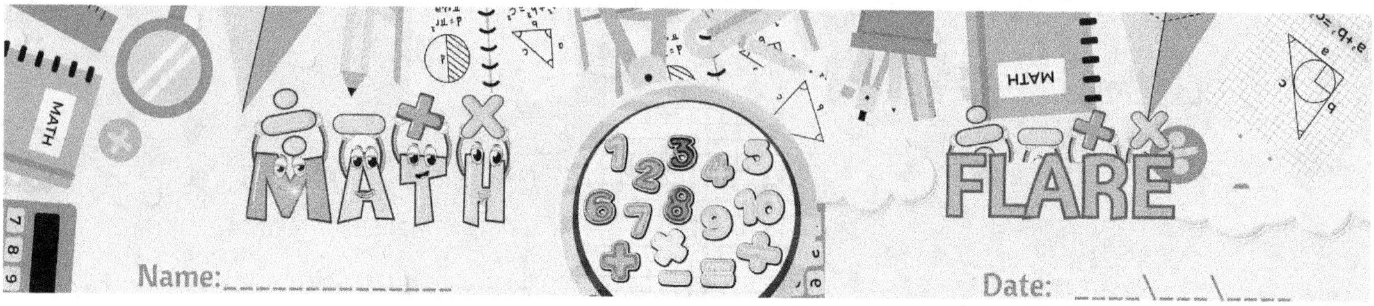

Place Value

Determine the place value of the underlined digit.

1) $600.\underline{5}28$ = 5 tenths

2) $24,\underline{7}57.6$ = ____________________

3) $\underline{1}30,293$ = ____________________

4) $4,61\underline{8}.24$ = ____________________

5) $50,74\underline{8}.6$ = ____________________

6) $6,2\underline{9}3.9$ = ____________________

7) $8\underline{3},790.1$ = ____________________

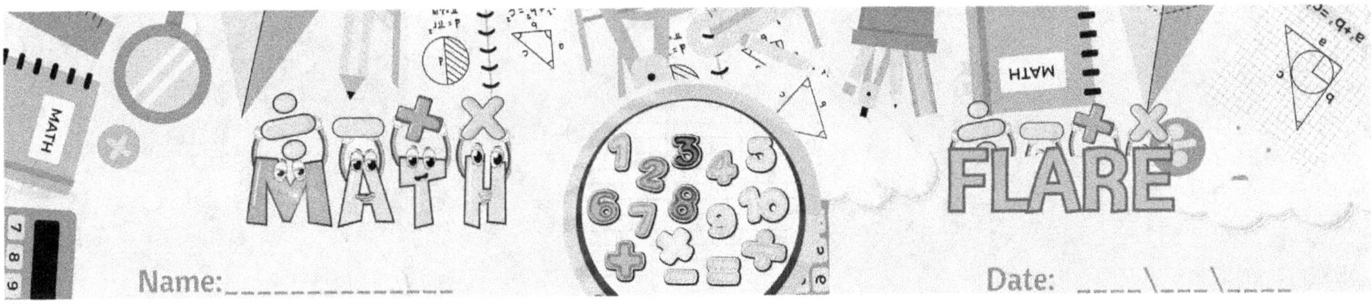

8) 990.326 = ____________________

9) 4,231.89 = ____________________

10) 5,301.51 = ____________________

11) 436.604 = ____________________

12) 16,588.7 = ____________________

13) 59,720.1 = ____________________

14) 45,410.5 = ____________________

15) 289,021 = ____________________

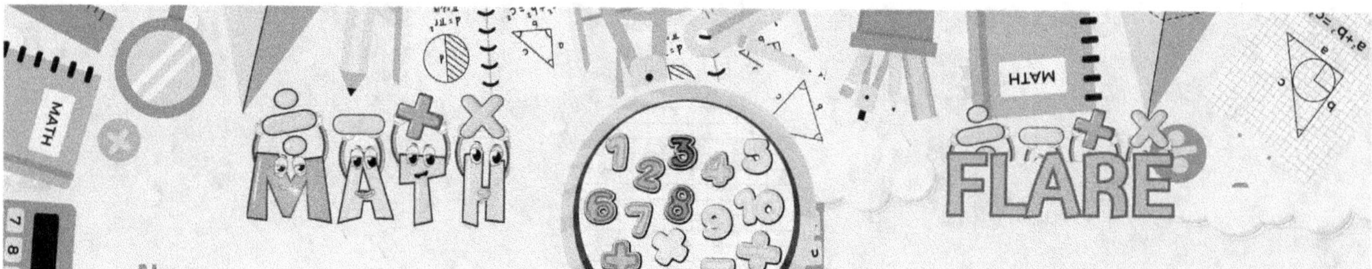

Name:_______________ Date: ____________

16) $6\underline{8}6.518$ = ______________________________

17) $6{,}084.4\underline{4}$ = ______________________________

18) $714{,}\underline{5}37$ = ______________________________

19) $466{,}25\underline{7}$ = ______________________________

20) $3{,}78\underline{0}.9$ = ______________________________

21) $3\underline{8}6{,}451$ = ______________________________

22) $85{,}64\underline{6}.4$ = ______________________________

23) $\underline{1}43.841$ = ______________________________

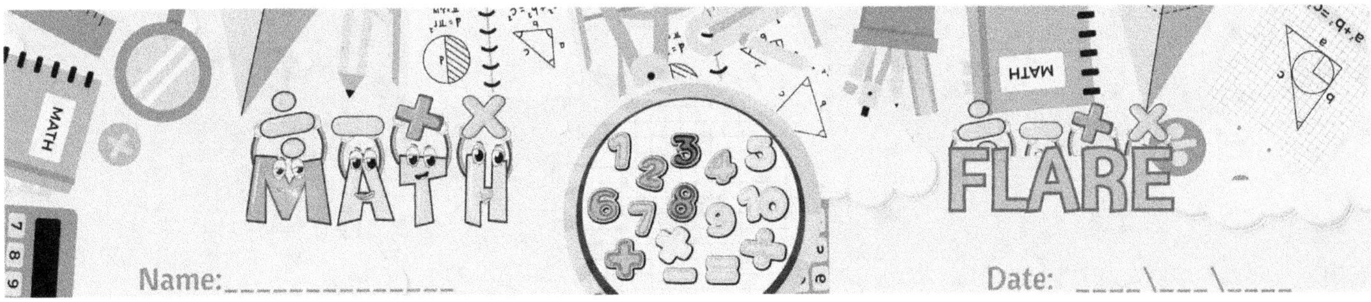

24) $6\underline{8},400.6$ = ______________________________

25) $3\underline{4},829.2$ = ______________________________

26) $\underline{8}10,257$ = ______________________________

27) $8,080.7\underline{8}$ = ______________________________

28) $4,515.8\underline{9}$ = ______________________________

29) $50,662.\underline{7}$ = ______________________________

30) $808.89\underline{5}$ = ______________________________

31) $988.\underline{0}52$ = ______________________________

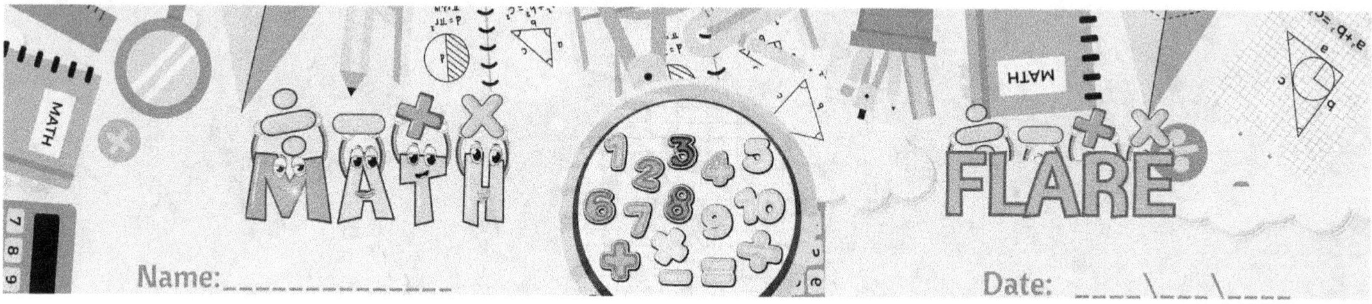

32) <u>3</u>6,314.9 = ______________________________

33) 595.<u>2</u>99 = ______________________________

34) <u>8</u>,613.7 = ______________________________

35) 937,<u>3</u>75 = ______________________________

36) 862,29<u>2</u> = ______________________________

37) <u>5</u>65.476 = ______________________________

38) 4<u>5</u>,639.6 = ______________________________

39) 85<u>0</u>,328 = ______________________________

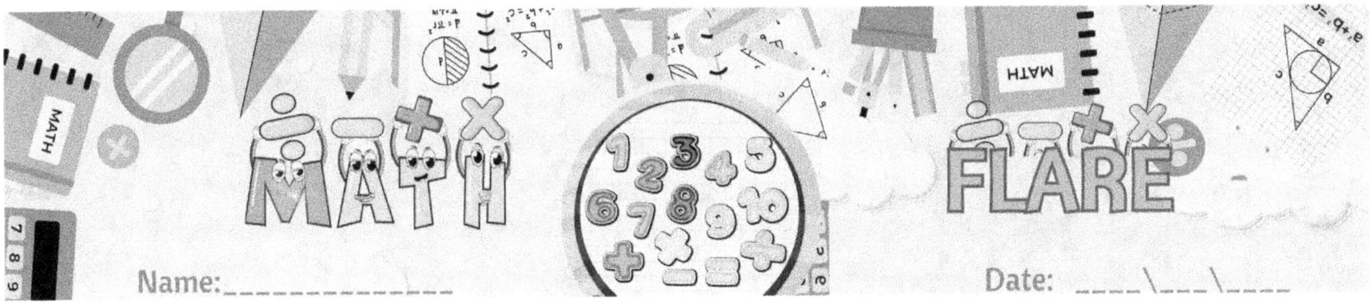

40) 98,004.9 = ______________________________

41) 57,080.8 = ______________________________

42) 2,654.27 = ______________________________

43) 5,168.24 = ______________________________

44) 72,137.1 = ______________________________

45) 10,462.6 = ______________________________

46) 48,484 = ______________________________

47) 6,199.42 = ______________________________

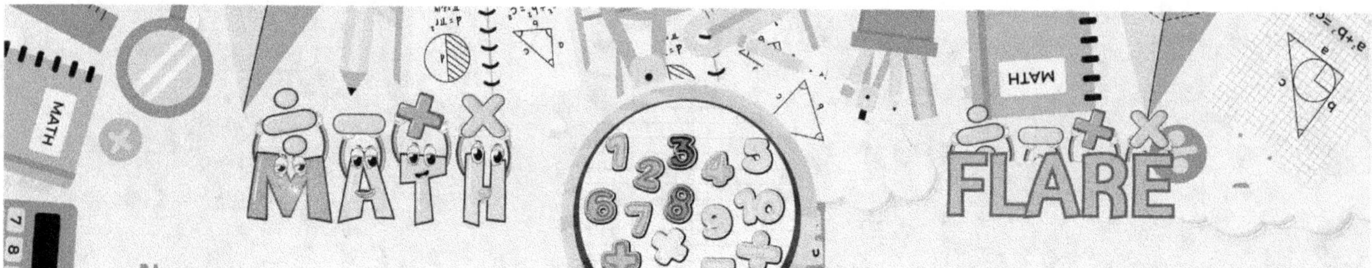

Name:______________ Date: _________

48) $2\underline{2}2,417$ = ______________________________

49) $5\underline{1}6,985$ = ______________________________

50) $\underline{8},467.82$ = ______________________________

51) $3,789.8\underline{8}$ = ______________________________

52) $532.\underline{0}98$ = ______________________________

53) $47,89\underline{3}.8$ = ______________________________

54) $9\underline{1}2.996$ = ______________________________

55) $40,32\underline{9}.7$ = ______________________________

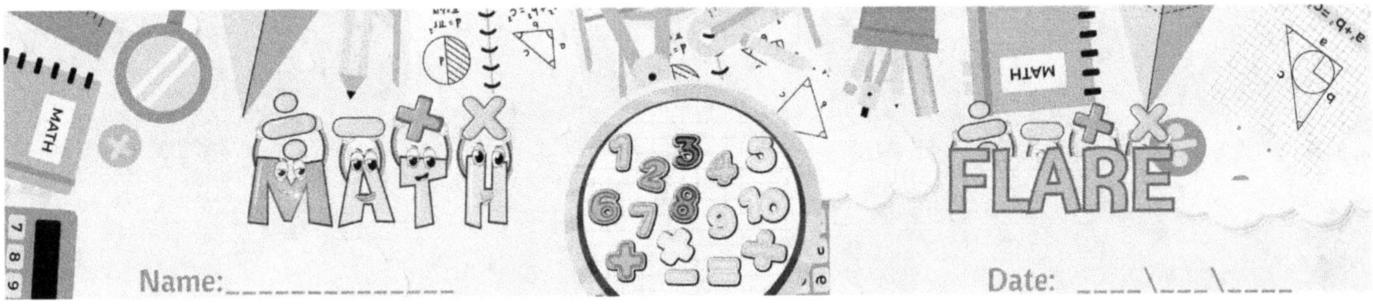

56) 744,06<u>4</u> = ______________________________

57) 20<u>3</u>.735 = ______________________________

58) 446,28<u>6</u> = ______________________________

59) 2,135.<u>3</u>2 = ______________________________

60) 69,722.<u>7</u> = ______________________________

61) 82<u>1</u>.31 = ______________________________

62) 486.31<u>2</u> = ______________________________

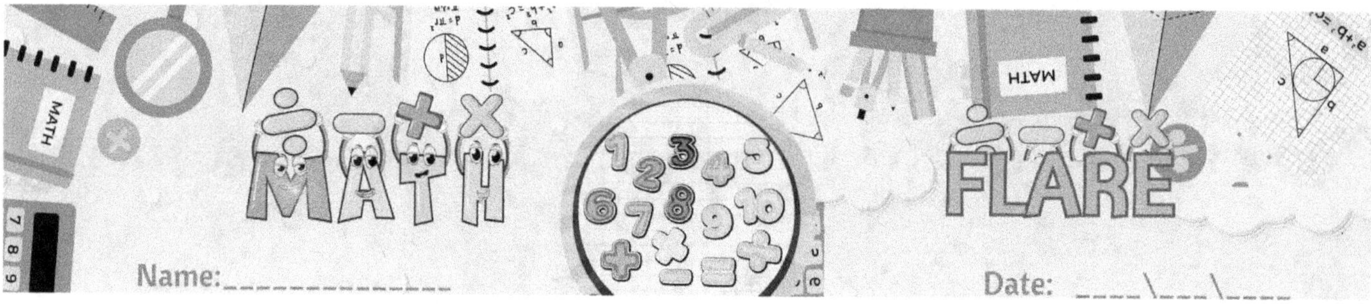

Place Value: Expanded Notation

Provide the expanded notation for each value.

1) 891,479   800,000 + 90,000 + 1,000 + 400 + 70 + 9

2) ________________   500 + 70 + 6 + 0.5 + 0.08 + 0.007

3) ________________   300 + 70 + 5 + 0.8 + 0.001

4) ________________   800 + 80 + 8 + 0.8 + 0.08 + 0.007

5) ________________   900,000 + 70,000 + 7,000 + 200 + 90 + 2

6) ________________   400 + 50 + 2 + 0.2 + 0.08 + 0.003

7) ________________   900 + 90 + 2 + 0.7 + 0.08 + 0.004

8) ________________   7,000 + 400 + 60 + 1 + 0.8 + 0.08

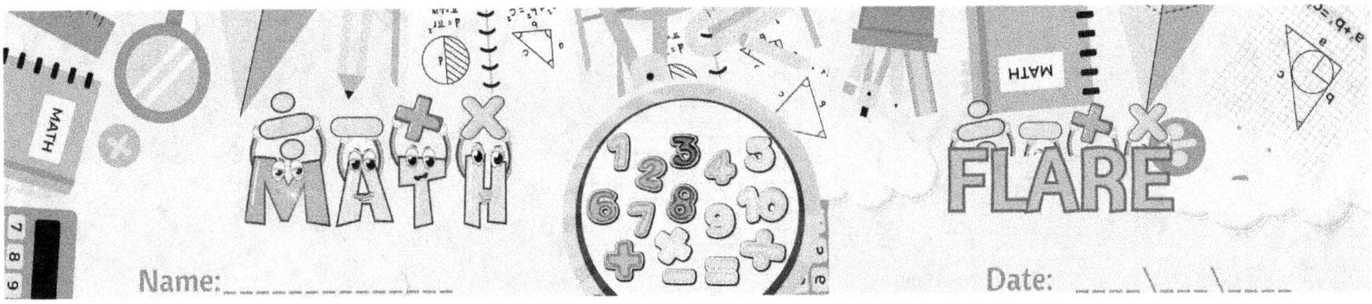

Name:______________ Date: ____________

9) ____________________ 1,000 + 200 + 30 + 0.9

10) ____________________ 600,000 + 30,000 + 2,000 + 700 + 80 + 7

11) ____________________ 700,000 + 50,000 + 7,000 + 800 + 70 + 2

12) ____________________ 8,000 + 100 + 80 + 1 + 0.4 + 0.03

13) ____________________ 200,000 + 90,000 + 3,000 + 100 + 30

14) ____________________ 700,000 + 40,000 + 1,000 + 900 + 20 + 7

15) ____________________ 100,000 + 20,000 + 5,000 + 900 + 60 + 8

16) ____________________ 700 + 6 + 0.3 + 0.05 + 0.004

17) ____________________ 4,000 + 800 + 20 + 2 + 0.7 + 0.01

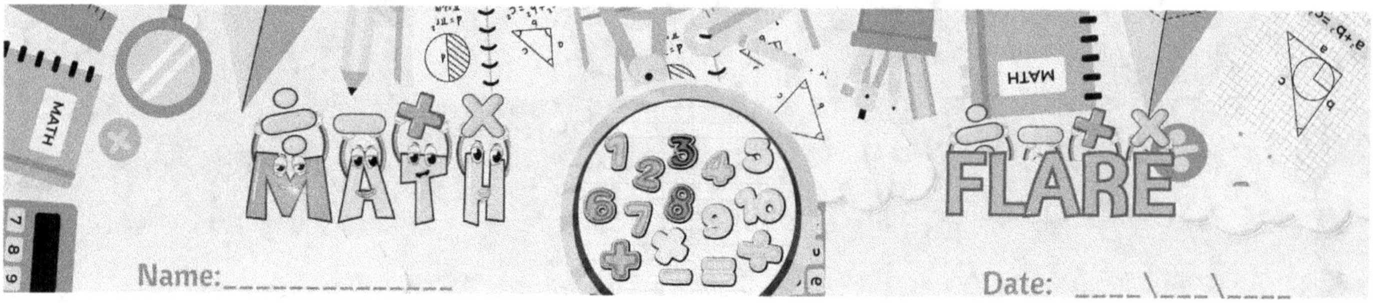

18) ____________________ 50,000 + 2,000 + 200 + 8 + 0.7

19) ____________________ 700 + 20 + 3 + 0.8 + 0.08 + 0.009

20) ____________________ 300 + 10 + 7 + 0.7 + 0.05 + 0.007

21) ____________________ 90,000 + 5,000 + 600 + 70 + 8 + 0.1

22) ____________________ 70,000 + 6,000 + 500 + 20 + 6 + 0.1

23) ____________________ 40,000 + 8,000 + 200 + 90 + 2 + 0.8

24) ____________________ 7,000 + 400 + 20 + 9 + 0.7 + 0.06

25) ____________________ 8,000 + 600 + 70 + 3 + 0.1 + 0.03

26) ____________________ 6,000 + 300 + 80 + 0.6 + 0.09

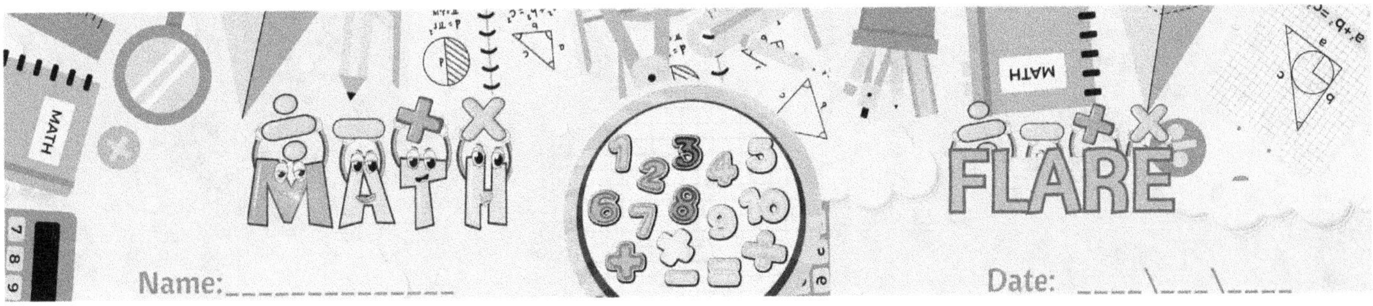

27) ______________ 1,000 + 100 + 80 + 6 + 0.9 + 0.08

28) ______________ 400 + 0.8 + 0.07 + 0.009

29) ______________ 20,000 + 70 + 0.9

30) ______________ 20,000 + 5,000 + 500 + 60 + 7 + 0.5

31) ______________ 70,000 + 700 + 30 + 6 + 0.1

32) ______________ 900,000 + 80,000 + 9,000 + 700 + 50 + 1

33) ______________ 7,000 + 800 + 10 + 4 + 0.2

34) ______________ 100 + 90 + 8 + 0.07 + 0.008

35) ______________ 300,000 + 90,000 + 7,000 + 700 + 60 + 3

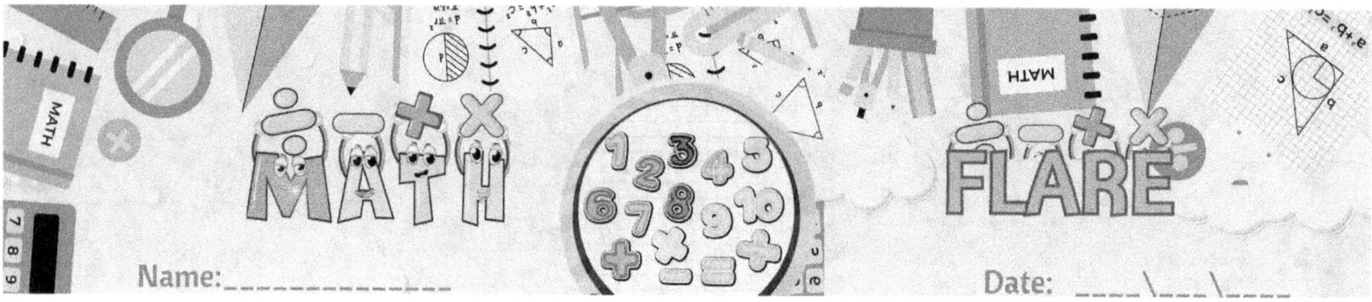

36) ____________ 4,000 + 100 + 10 + 6 + 0.9 + 0.07

37) ____________ 9,000 + 10 + 9 + 0.5 + 0.05

38) ____________ 4,000 + 300 + 40 + 5 + 0.2 + 0.08

39) ____________ 600 + 90 + 0.8 + 0.07 + 0.006

40) ____________ 6,000 + 400 + 90 + 5 + 0.6 + 0.07

41) ____________ 90,000 + 1,000 + 600 + 30 + 9 + 0.7

42) ____________ 90,000 + 6,000 + 400 + 90 + 1 + 0.8

43) ____________ 3,000 + 40 + 3 + 0.7 + 0.09

44) ____________ 100,000 + 90,000

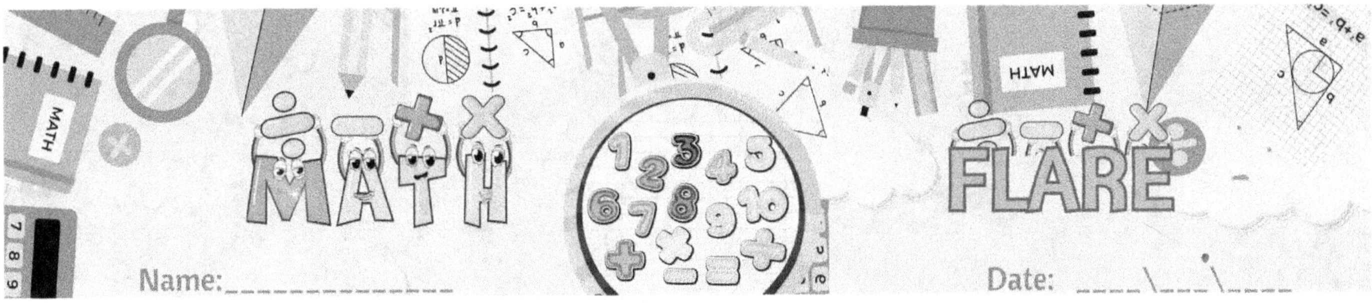

45) ______________ 70,000 + 8,000 + 100 + 40 + 2 + 0.3

46) ______________ 700,000 + 10,000 + 8,000 + 900 + 60 + 6

47) ______________ 900 + 50 + 0.06 + 0.005

48) ______________ 10,000 + 600 + 20 + 8 + 0.1

49) ______________ 9,000 + 200 + 30 + 2 + 0.3 + 0.01

50) ______________ 600 + 90 + 9 + 0.8 + 0.04 + 0.008

51) ______________ 50,000 + 9,000 + 700 + 70 + 0.2

52) ______________ 400 + 20 + 2 + 0.2 + 0.05 + 0.009

53) ______________ 30,000 + 1,000 + 20 + 1 + 0.4

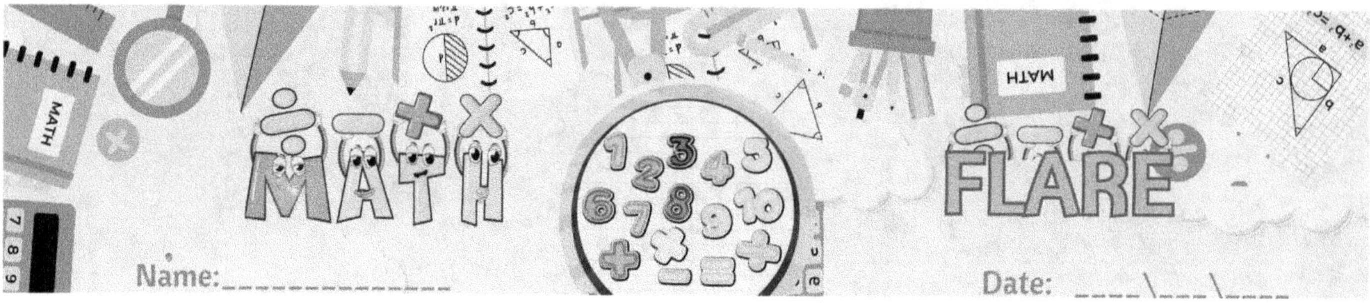

54) ____________________ 10,000 + 8,000 + 500 + 20 + 0.9

55) ____________________ 9,000 + 300 + 10 + 2 + 0.8 + 0.03

56) ____________________ 20,000 + 2,000 + 600 + 20 + 1 + 0.8

57) ____________________ 10,000 + 9,000 + 300 + 60 + 5 + 0.9

58) ____________________ 60,000 + 3,000 + 200 + 80 + 2 + 0.3

59) ____________________ 1,000 + 200 + 10 + 5 + 0.7 + 0.05

60) ____________________ 40,000 + 3,000 + 900 + 20 + 2 + 0.3

61) ____________________ 40,000 + 3,000 + 300 + 50 + 8 + 0.5

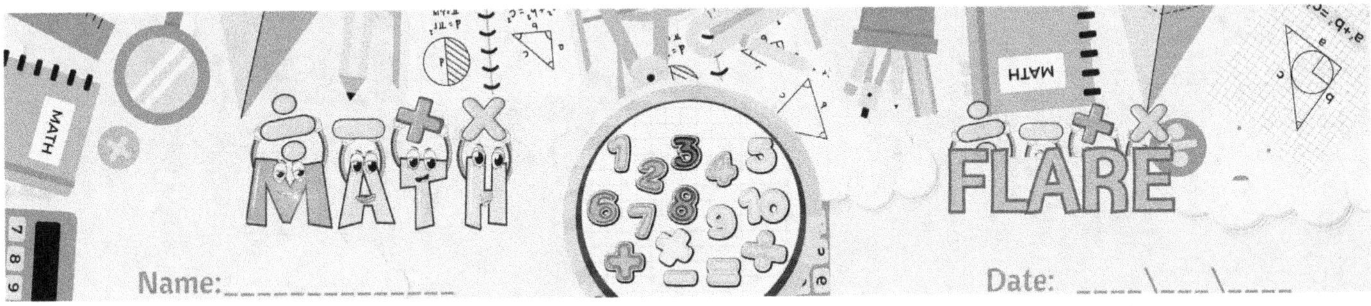

Place Value: Expanded Notation

Provide the expanded notation for each value.

1) 691,905 — 6 hundred thousands + 9 ten thousands + 1 thousand + 9 hundreds + 5 ones

2) ________________ 6 hundred thousands + 4 ten thousands + 5 thousands + 4 hundreds + 7 tens + 9 ones

3) ________________ 8 thousands + 6 hundreds + 7 tens + 4 ones + 1 tenth + 4 hundredths

4) ________________ 9 hundreds + 2 tens + 5 ones + 4 tenths + 2 hundredths + 4 thousandths

5) ________________ 7 hundred thousands + 6 ten thousands + 8 thousands + 1 hundred + 2 tens

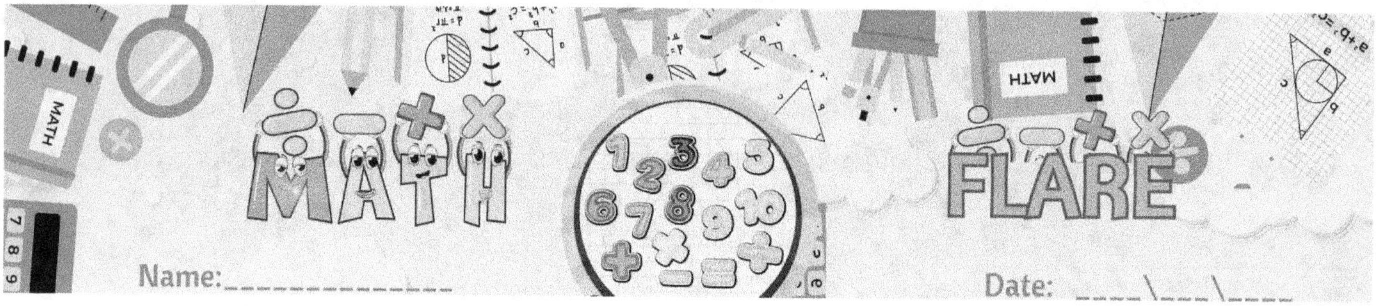

Name:______________ Date: ____________

6) ____________________ 1 ten thousand + 3 thousands + 6 hundreds + 7 tens + 2 ones + 3 tenths

7) ____________________ 1 hundred + 9 tens + 5 ones + 5 hundredths + 2 thousandths

8) ____________________ 4 thousands + 4 hundreds + 4 tens + 1 one + 6 tenths + 4 hundredths

9) ____________________ 7 ten thousands + 1 thousand + 4 hundreds + 2 tens + 6 ones + 9 tenths

10) ____________________ 8 hundred thousands + 4 thousands + 3 hundreds + 9 tens + 7 ones

11) ____________________ 1 thousand + 4 hundreds + 7 tens + 7 ones + 4 tenths + 3 hundredths

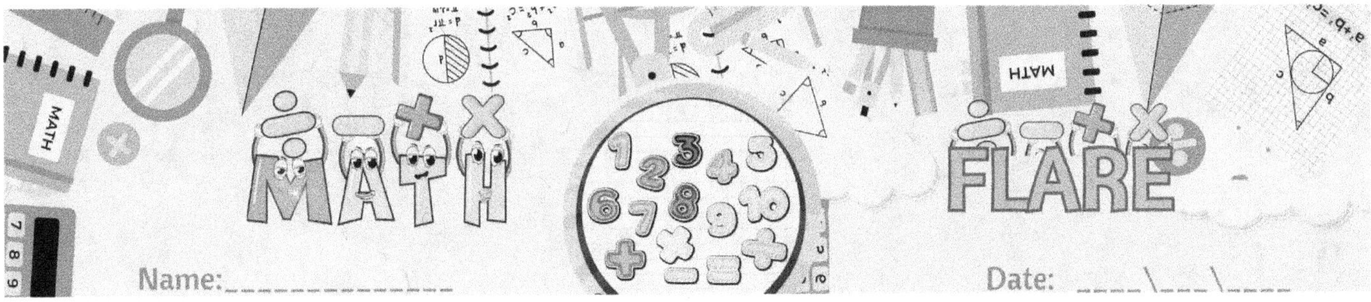

12) __________________ 8 ten thousands + 3 thousands + 1 hundred + 2 tens + 1 one

13) __________________ 1 ten thousand + 7 thousands + 4 hundreds + 3 tens + 2 ones + 2 tenths

14) __________________ 4 hundred thousands + 1 thousand + 3 hundreds + 5 tens + 9 ones

15) __________________ 9 thousands + 9 hundreds + 1 ten + 8 ones + 6 tenths + 1 hundredth

16) __________________ 5 ten thousands + 6 thousands + 8 tens + 8 ones + 2 tenths

17) __________________ 3 hundred thousands + 9 ten thousands + 2 thousands + 9 hundreds + 2 tens + 8 ones

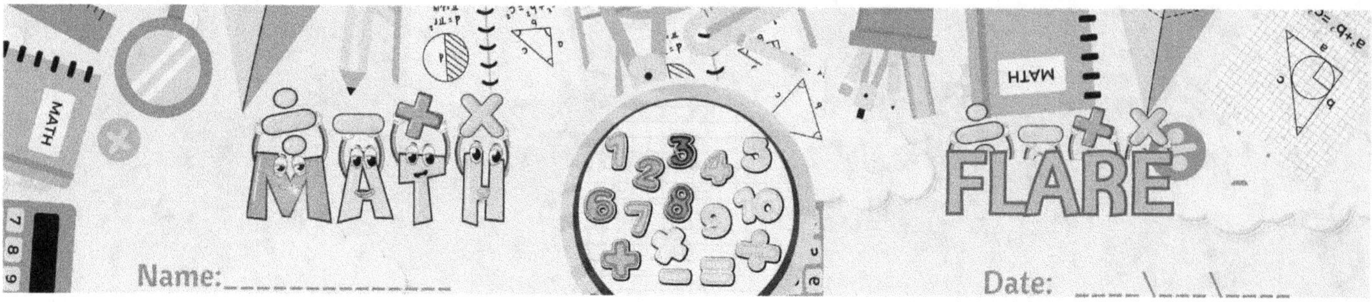

18) ____________________ 9 thousands + 6 hundreds + 1 ten + 5 ones + 5 tenths + 3 hundredths

19) ____________________ 2 hundreds + 4 tens + 8 ones + 3 tenths + 4 hundredths + 7 thousandths

20) ____________________ 6 ten thousands + 8 thousands + 8 hundreds + 3 tenths

21) ____________________ 1 hundred thousand + 1 ten thousand + 2 thousands + 4 hundreds + 1 ten + 8 ones

22) ____________________ 4 ten thousands + 7 thousands + 7 hundreds + 6 tens + 4 ones + 7 tenths

23) ____________________ 5 thousands + 8 ones + 6 tenths

Name:______________ Date: ____________

24) ____________________ 6 hundred thousands + 5 ten thousands + 7 thousands + 9 hundreds + 7 tens + 2 ones

25) ____________________ 3 hundreds + 8 tens + 5 ones + 1 tenth + 3 thousandths

26) ____________________ 7 ten thousands + 7 thousands + 9 hundreds + 5 tens + 3 ones + 7 tenths

27) ____________________ 6 thousands + 9 hundreds + 6 tens + 2 ones + 1 tenth

28) ____________________ 2 ten thousands + 6 thousands + 6 hundreds + 7 tens + 9 ones + 4 tenths

29) ____________________ 2 hundred thousands + 7 ten thousands + 1 thousand + 5 hundreds + 4 tens + 5 ones

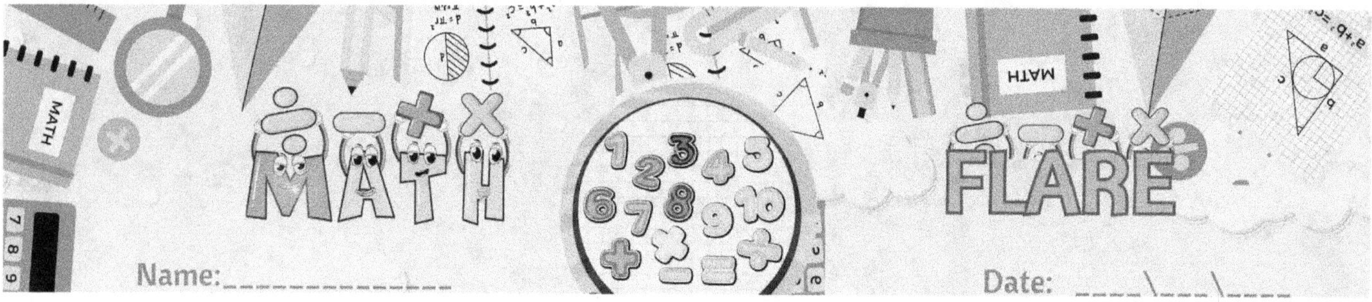

30) ____________________ 3 ten thousands + 1 thousand + 8 hundreds + 3 ones + 8 tenths

31) ____________________ 3 ten thousands + 6 thousands + 9 hundreds + 1 ten + 3 ones + 2 tenths

32) ____________________ 4 ten thousands + 1 thousand + 2 hundreds + 9 tens + 5 ones + 4 tenths

33) ____________________ 3 hundred thousands + 5 ten thousands + 1 thousand + 6 hundreds + 5 tens + 4 ones

34) ____________________ 3 ten thousands + 1 thousand + 5 hundreds + 9 tens + 8 ones + 2 tenths

35) ____________________ 3 hundred thousands + 2 ten thousands + 4 thousands + 4 hundreds + 9 tens + 2 ones

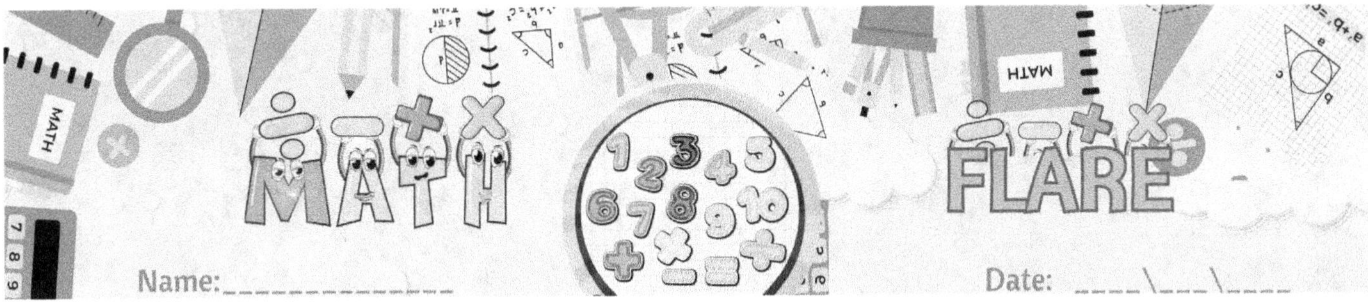

36) ____________________ 4 ten thousands + 1 thousand + 9 hundreds + 4 tens + 4 ones

37) ____________________ 4 ten thousands + 3 thousands + 6 hundreds + 9 tens + 6 ones + 4 tenths

38) ____________________ 2 ten thousands + 6 thousands + 4 hundreds + 5 tens + 7 ones + 4 tenths

39) ____________________ 1 hundred thousand + 1 ten thousand + 3 thousands + 3 hundreds + 2 ones

40) ____________________ 6 thousands + 8 hundreds + 2 tens + 2 ones + 4 tenths + 3 hundredths

41) ____________________ 8 ten thousands + 5 thousands + 5 hundreds + 1 one + 3 tenths

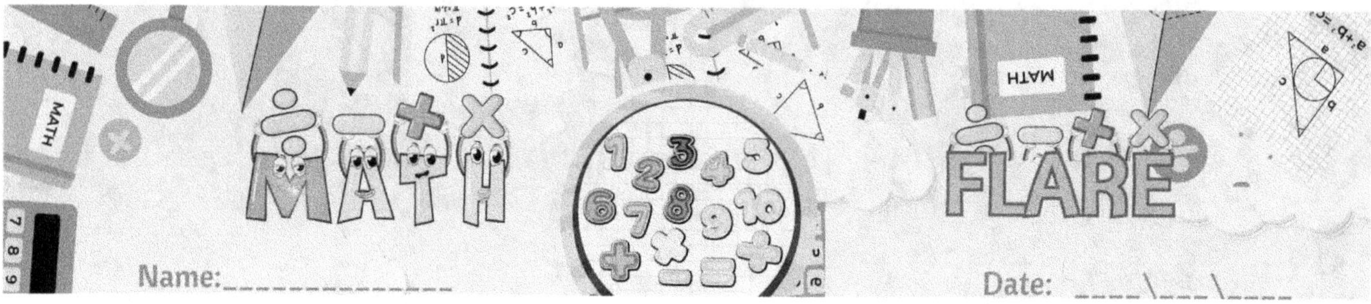

42) ____________________ 6 hundred thousands + 6 ten thousands + 2 thousands + 1 hundred + 1 ten + 6 ones

43) ____________________ 3 thousands + 8 tens + 9 ones + 6 tenths + 2 hundredths

44) ____________________ 8 thousands + 9 hundreds + 5 tens + 4 ones + 5 tenths

45) ____________________ 5 thousands + 4 hundreds + 9 tens + 9 ones + 5 tenths + 9 hundredths

46) ____________________ 5 hundreds + 9 tens + 1 one + 4 hundredths + 8 thousandths

47) ____________________ 2 hundreds + 3 tens + 5 ones + 8 tenths + 9 hundredths + 2 thousandths

Name:______________ Date: ___________

48) ______________________ 7 hundreds + 8 tens + 3 ones + 8 tenths + 5 hundredths

49) ______________________ 9 ten thousands + 3 thousands + 9 hundreds + 4 tens + 2 ones

50) ______________________ 6 hundred thousands + 6 ten thousands + 5 thousands + 3 hundreds + 3 tens + 4 ones

51) ______________________ 8 hundred thousands + 7 hundreds + 3 tens + 1 one

52) ______________________ 6 hundreds + 7 tens + 1 one + 2 tenths + 6 hundredths + 9 thousandths

53) ______________________ 8 hundreds + 7 tens + 3 ones + 2 tenths + 2 hundredths + 7 thousandths

Name:______________ Date: ____________

54) ____________________ 7 hundred thousands + 5 ten thousands + 1 thousand + 2 hundreds + 1 ten + 8 ones

55) ____________________ 4 hundreds + 2 tens + 1 one + 1 tenth + 6 hundredths + 7 thousandths

56) ____________________ 3 thousands + 1 hundred + 4 tens + 2 ones + 5 tenths + 8 hundredths

57) ____________________ 2 thousands + 4 hundreds + 4 tens + 6 ones + 1 tenth + 9 hundredths

58) ____________________ 3 ten thousands + 9 hundreds + 4 tens + 4 ones + 2 tenths

59) ____________________ 6 hundred thousands + 4 ten thousands + 3 hundreds + 2 tens + 2 ones

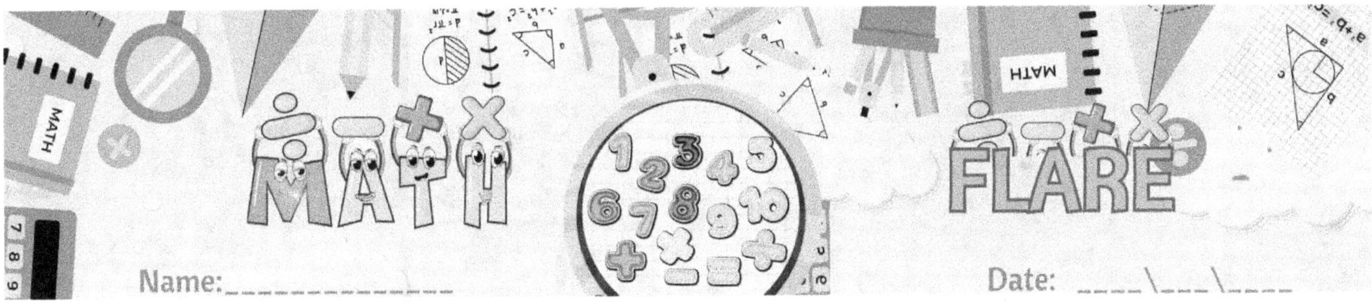

Place Value: Expanded Notation

Provide the expanded notation for each value.

1) 988.582 9 hundreds + 8 tens + 8 ones + 5 tenths + 8 hundredths + 2 thousandths

2) 440.511

3) 928,257

4) 272,618

5) 49,623.2

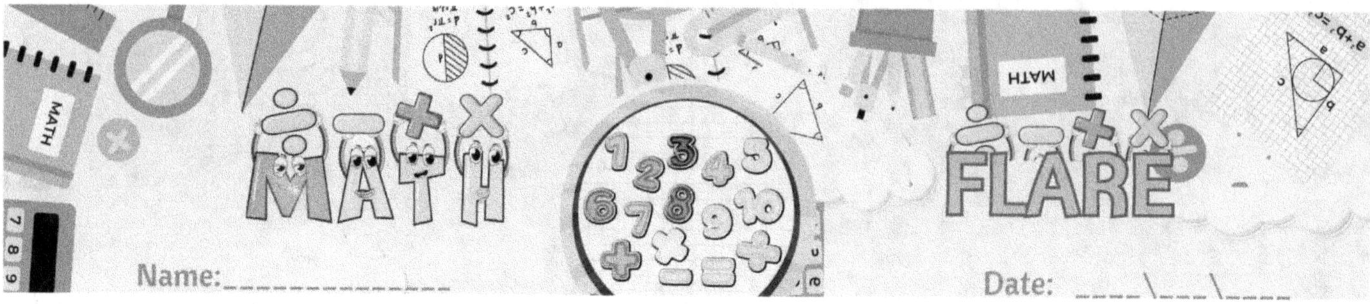

6) 535,265 ______________________________

____

7) 734.788 ______________________________

____

8) 5,795.56 ______________________________

____

9) 858,339 ______________________________

____

10) 1,768.66 ______________________________

____

11) 67,242.1 ______________________________

____

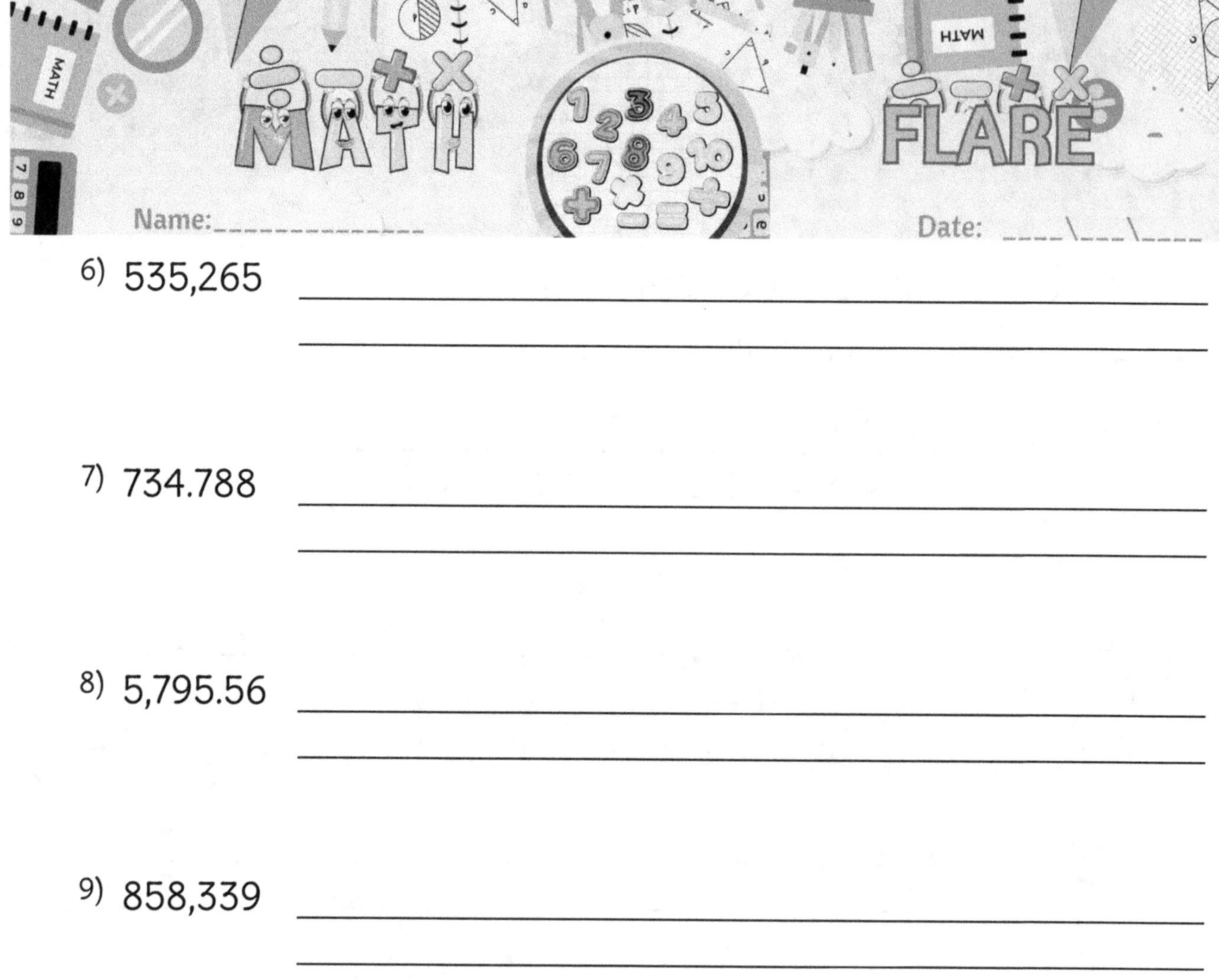

Name:______________ Date: _________

12) 223.918 ______________________

13) 2,283.53 ______________________

14) 948.251 ______________________

15) 5,661.02 ______________________

16) 832,989 ______________________

17) 450,301 ______________________

Name:______________ Date: ____________

18) 268,685 ______________________________

____

19) 605.408 ______________________________

____

20) 20,801.2 ______________________________

____

21) 794.054 ______________________________

____

22) 64,364.5 ______________________________

____

23) 912,360 ______________________________

____

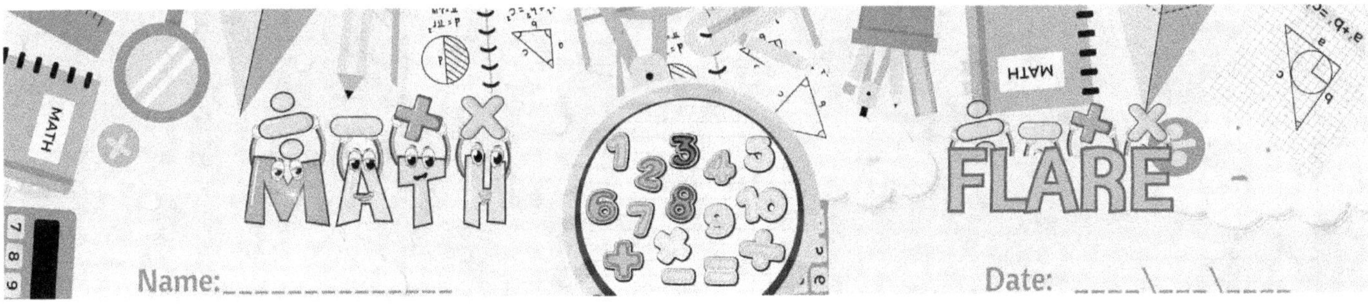

24) 3,273.73

25) 606,210

26) 51,730.6

27) 697.862

28) 539.726

29) 60,043.5

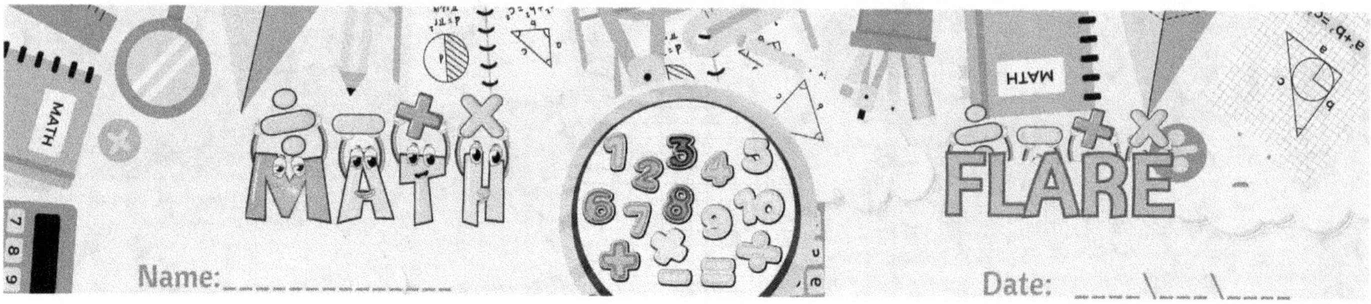

30) 89,481.4

31) 110.234

32) 274.821

33) 22,752.1

34) 62,425.2

35) 124.719

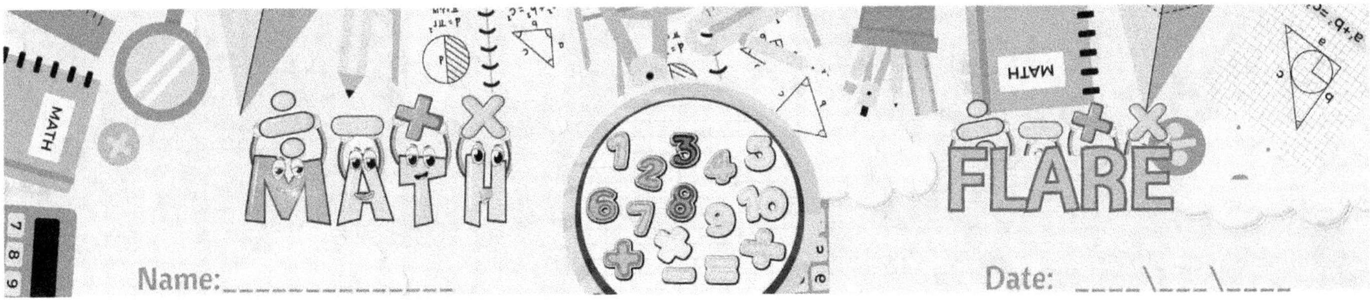

Name:_____________ Date: ___________

36) 341.732 ______________________________

____

37) 9,267.55 ______________________________

____

38) 4,894.98 ______________________________

____

39) 812.729 ______________________________

____

40) 4,601.85 ______________________________

____

41) 8,151.71 ______________________________

____

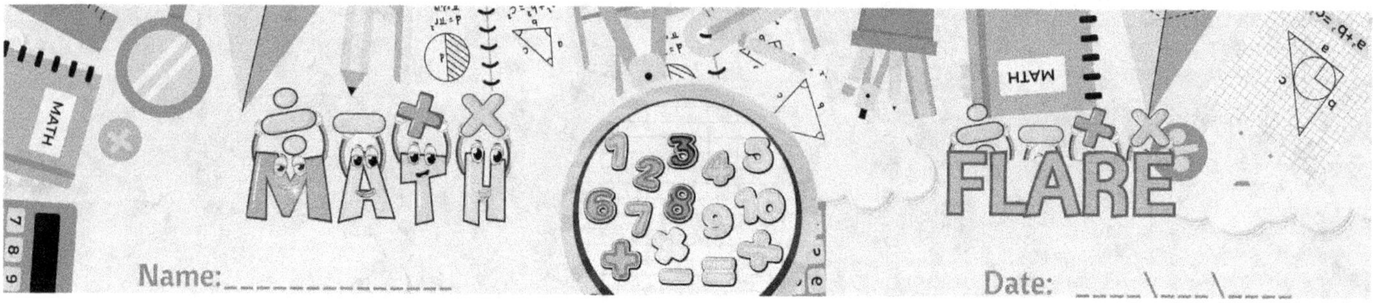

42) 111.492

43) 377.552

44) 706,983

45) 366,999

46) 54,141.6

47) 67,237.7

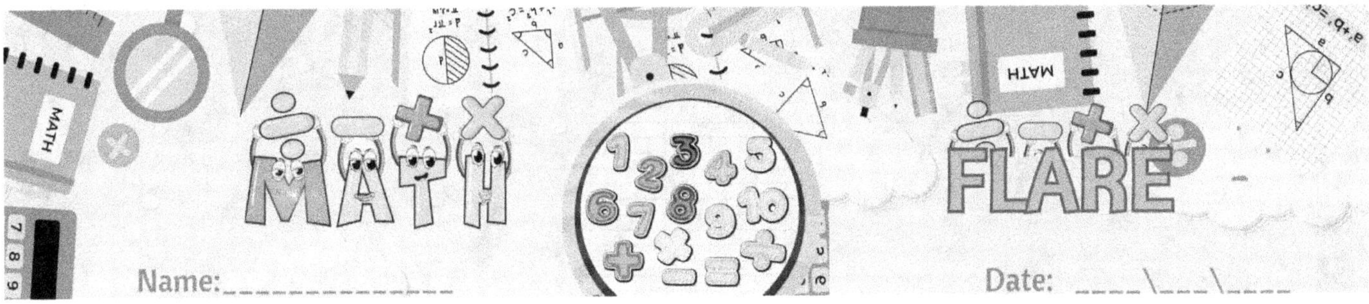

48) 72,301.8 ______________________________

____

49) 407,125 ______________________________

____

50) 918.228 ______________________________

____

51) 970.866 ______________________________

____

52) 1,455.74 ______________________________

____

53) 639.210 ______________________________

____

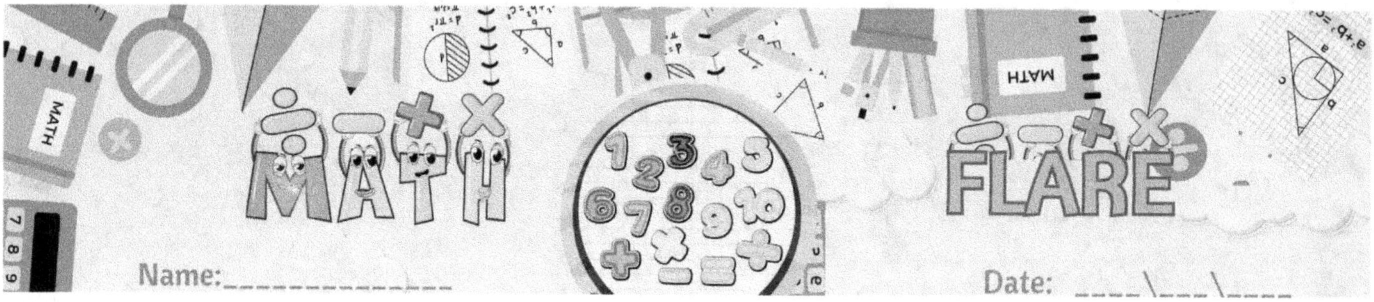

54) 201,430

55) 846,267

56) 444.937

57) 52,815.1

58) 7,008.84

59) 6,664.07

Chapter. 05

Fractions

Fractions represent parts of a whole. They consist of a numerator (the number on top) and a denominator (the number on the bottom).

For example: we have an orange, and we divide it into 5 equal slices. Each slice represents $\frac{1}{5}$ of the orange. Now, if we take 3 of those slices, we have taken $\frac{3}{5}$ of the orange.

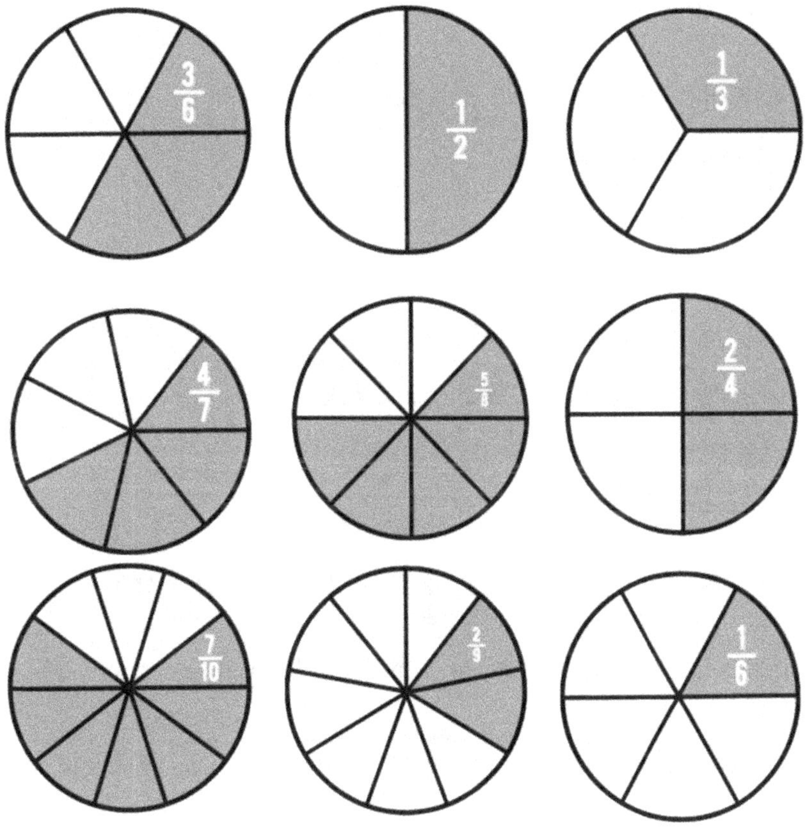

Let's solve a problem:

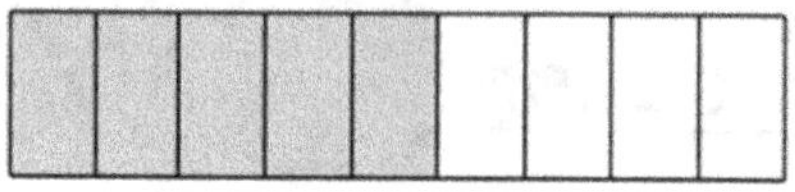 = $\frac{5}{9}$

Comparing Fractions

When comparing fractions, we consider the size of their denominators. Generally, the larger the denominator, the smaller the fraction.

For example:

$\frac{1}{3}$ is smaller than $\frac{1}{2}$ because the denominator 3 is larger than the denominator 2.

If the denominators are the same, we can compare the numerators to determine which fraction is larger.

Let's solve a problem:

$$\frac{56}{60} < \frac{57}{60}$$

Convert Fractions to Decimals

To transform a fraction into a decimal, we divide the numerator by the denominator.

For instance, $\frac{1}{4}$ equals 0.25 because when we divide 1 by 4, we get 0.25.

In certain cases, the resulting decimal repeats infinitely, like $\frac{1}{3}$, which equals 0.3333... In such instances, we round the decimal to a specific number of decimal places.

Let's solve a problem:

$$\frac{52}{100} = 0.52$$

Fractions Addition (Common Denominator)

To add fractions with a common denominator, we add their numerators together and keep the denominator the same.

For example: if we want to add $\frac{3}{5}$ and $\frac{2}{5}$ both fractions have the same denominator of 5. Therefore, to add them, we simply add their numerators:

$$\frac{3}{5}+\frac{2}{5}=\frac{3+2}{5}=\frac{5}{5}$$

Let's solve a problem:

$$\frac{1}{9}+\frac{7}{9}=\frac{1+7}{9}=\frac{8}{9}$$

Fractions Subtraction (Common Denominator)

To subtract fractions with a common denominator, we find the difference between their numerators and keep the denominator the same.

For example:

$$\frac{3}{5}-\frac{2}{5}=\frac{3-2}{5}=\frac{1}{5}$$

Let's solve a problem:

$$\frac{5}{8}-\frac{2}{8}=\frac{5-2}{8}=\frac{3}{8}$$

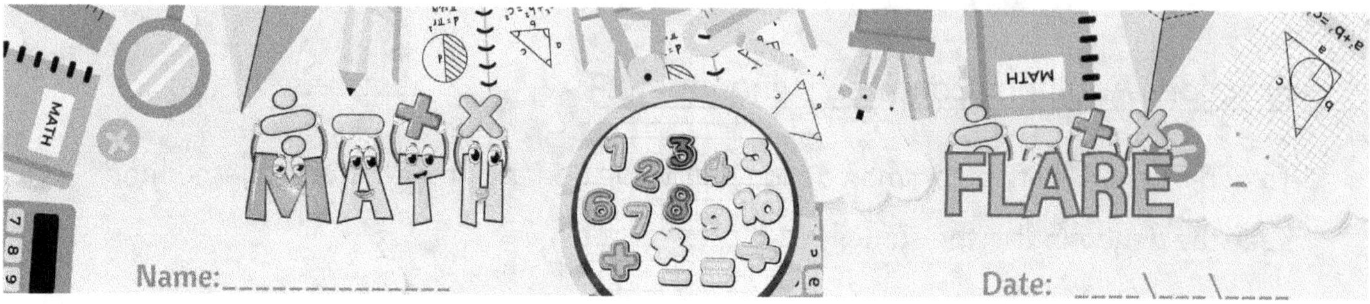

Fraction Identification

Identify fractions of each set of boxes.

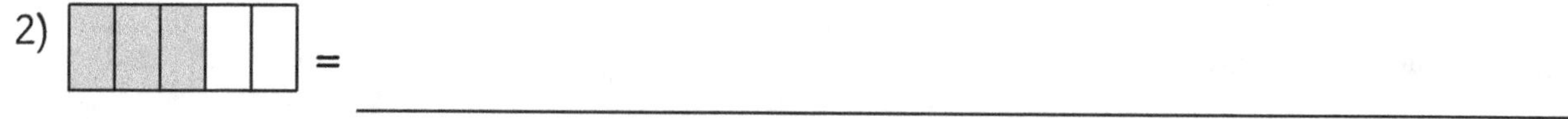

1) 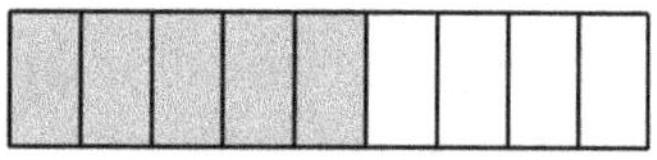 = $\frac{5}{9}$ ______________________

2) 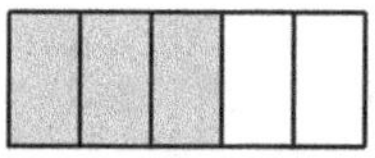 = ______________________

3) 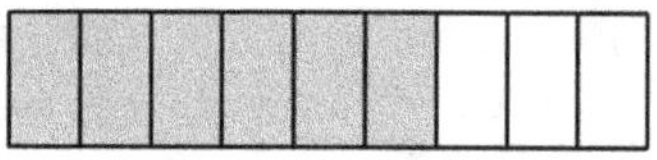 = ______________________

4) 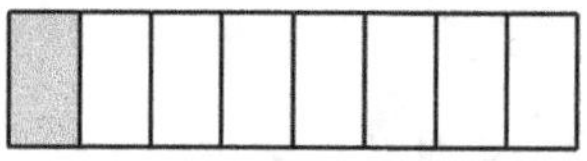 = ______________________

5) 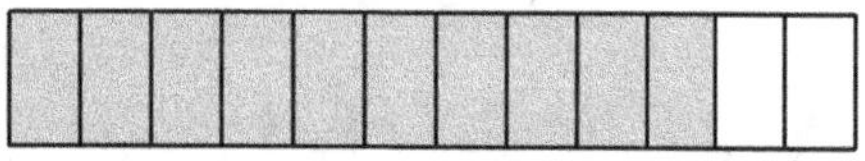 = ______________________

6) 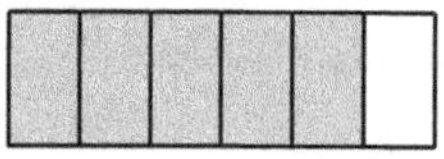 = ______________________

7)  = ______________________

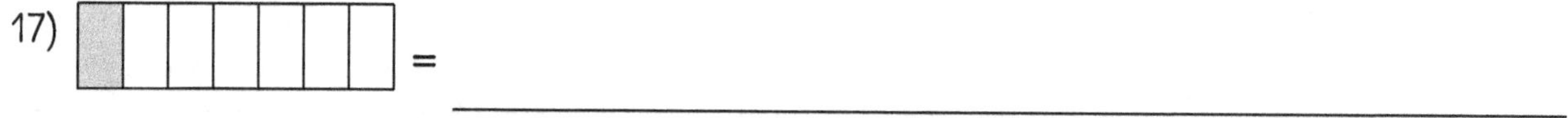

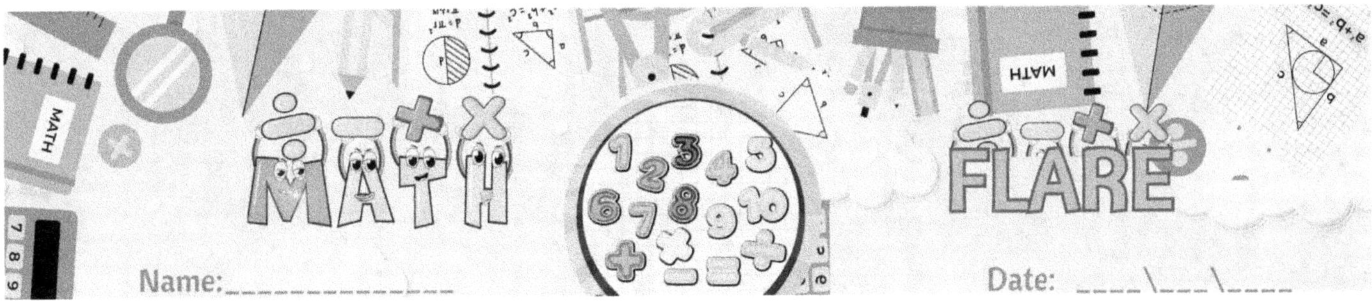

8) 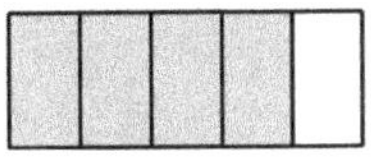 = ______________________

9) 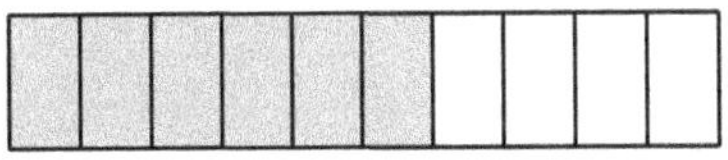 = ______________________

10) 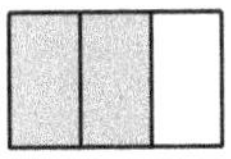 = ______________________

11) 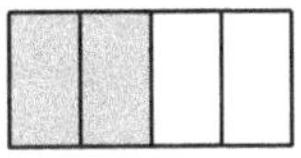 = ______________________

12) 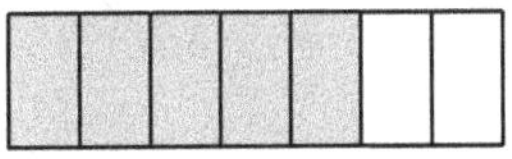 = ______________________

13) 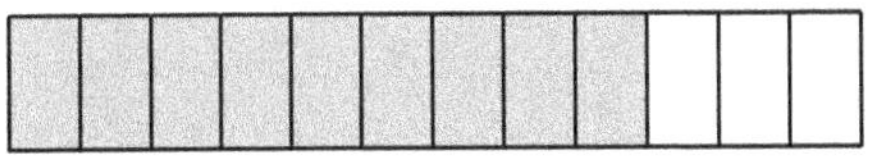 = ______________________

14) 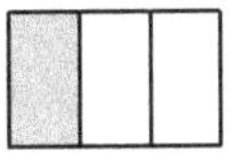 = ______________________

15) 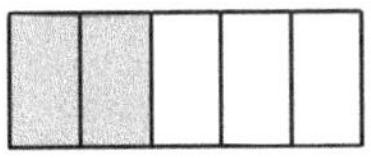 = ______________________

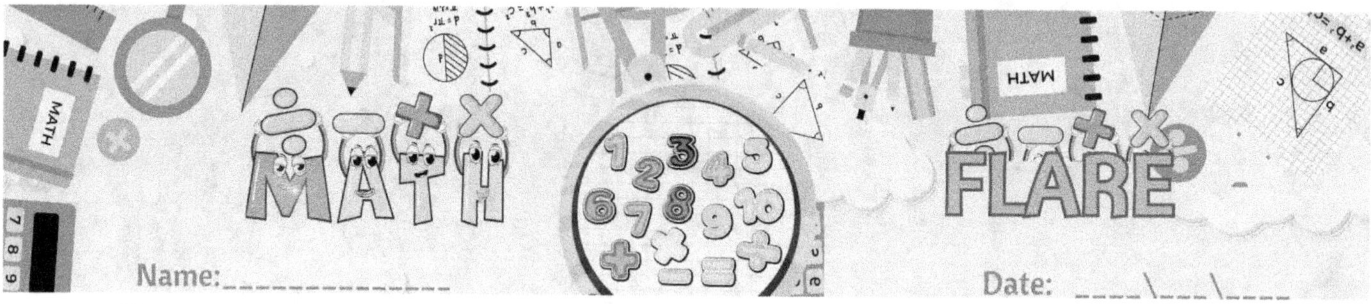

16) 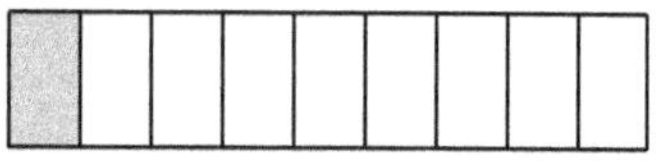 = ______________________

17) 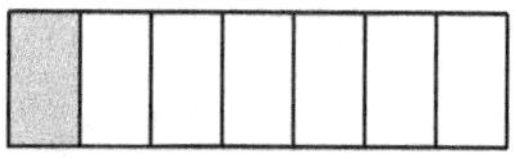 = ______________________

18) 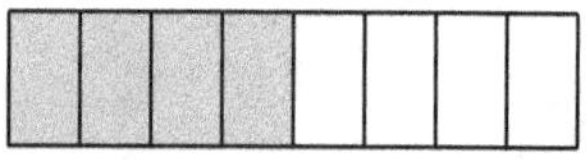 = ______________________

19) 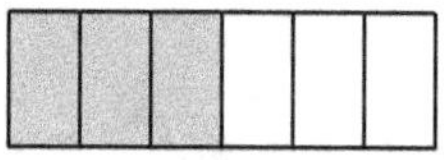 = ______________________

20) 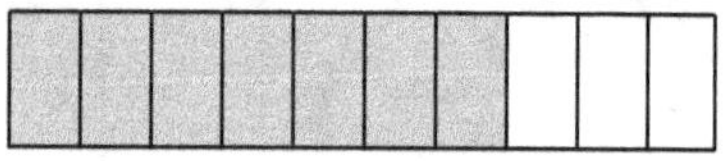 = ______________________

21) 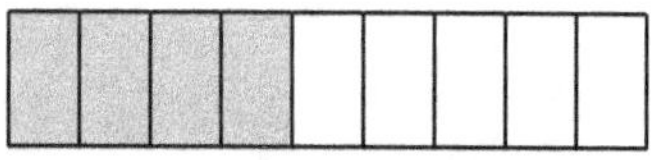 = ______________________

22) 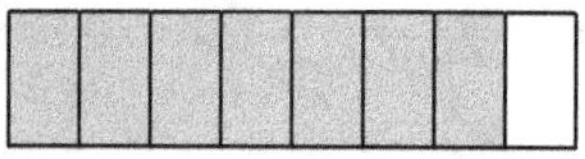 = ______________________

23) 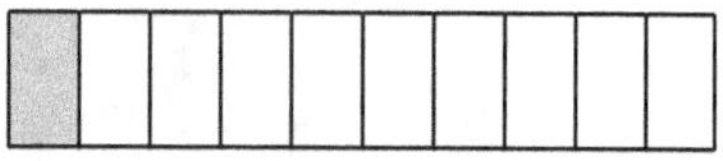 = ______________________

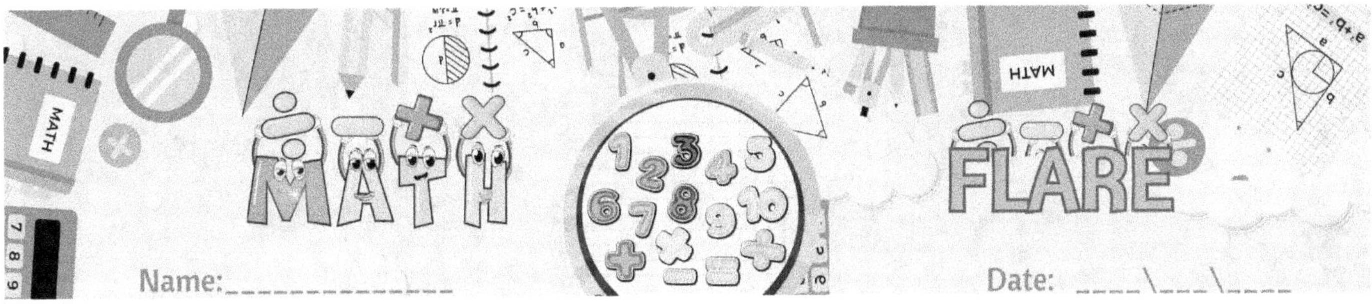

24) 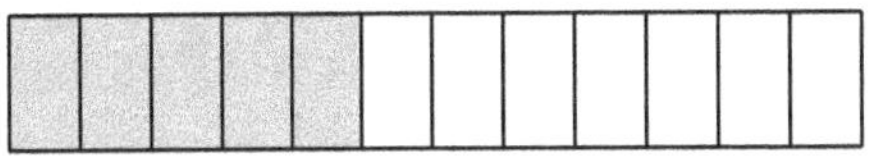 = ______________________

25) 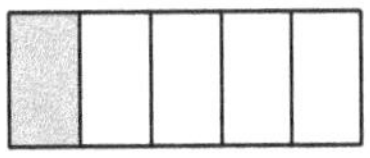 = ______________________

26) 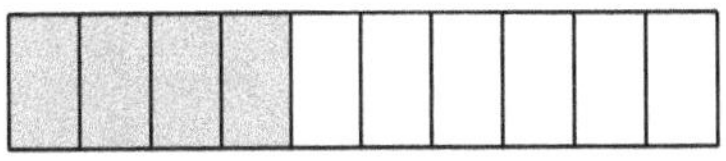 = ______________________

27) 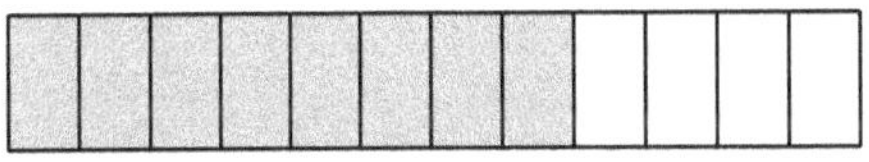 = ______________________

28) 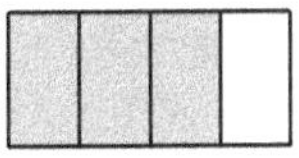 = ______________________

29) 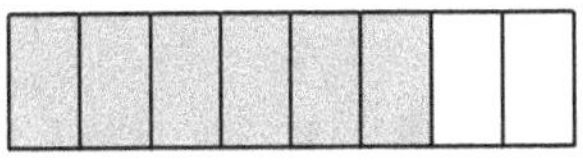 = ______________________

30) 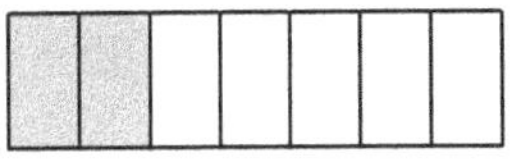 = ______________________

31) 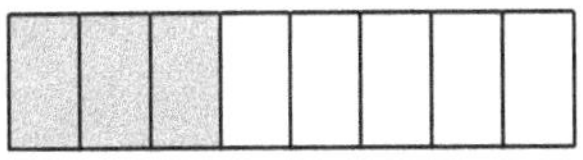 = ______________________

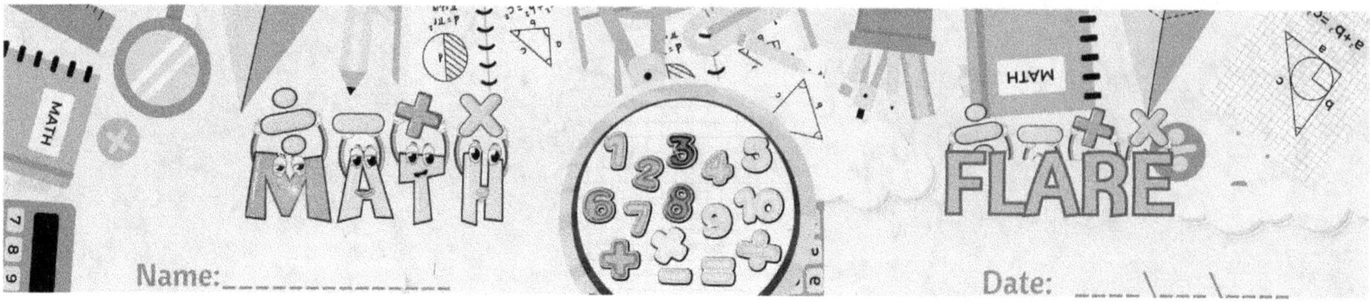

32) 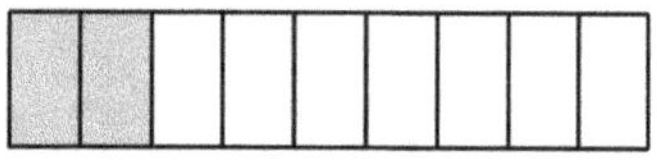 = ____________________

33) 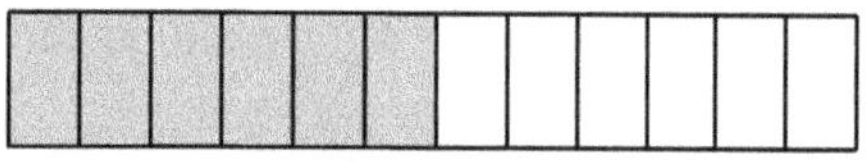 = ____________________

34) 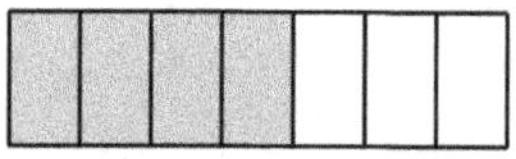 = ____________________

35) 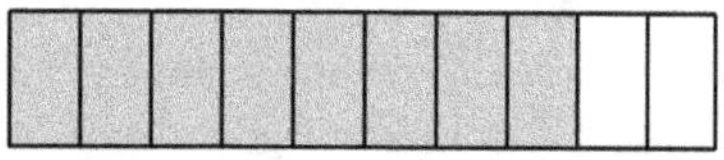 = ____________________

36) 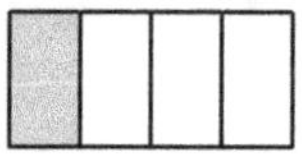 = ____________________

37) 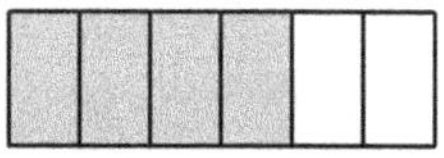 = ____________________

38) 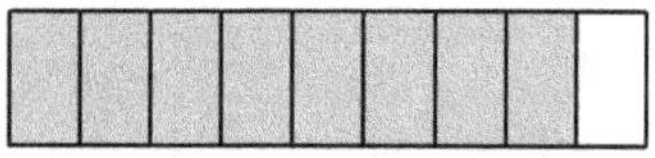 = ____________________

39) 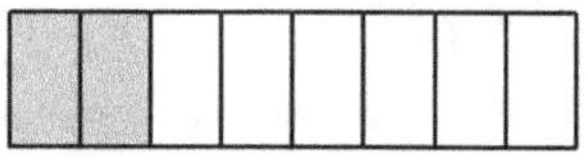 = ____________________

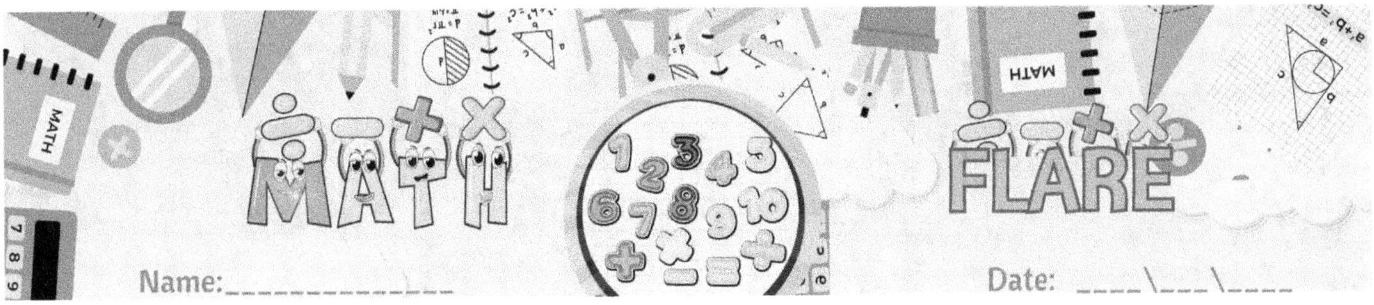

Compare the Fractions

Put the signs < , >, or =

1) $\frac{32}{46}$ > $\frac{13}{46}$

2) $\frac{5}{6}$ ___ $\frac{3}{6}$

3) $\frac{63}{70}$ ___ $\frac{33}{70}$

4) $\frac{20}{96}$ ___ $\frac{64}{96}$

5) $\frac{32}{72}$ ___ $\frac{103}{72}$

6) $\frac{2}{4}$ ___ $\frac{3}{4}$

7) $\frac{40}{85}$ ___ $\frac{21}{85}$

8) $\frac{1}{8}$ ___ $\frac{1}{8}$

9) $\frac{56}{70}$ ___ $\frac{6}{70}$

10) $\frac{39}{16}$ ___ $\frac{5}{16}$

11) $\frac{18}{22}$ ___ $\frac{58}{22}$

12) $\frac{2}{21}$ ___ $\frac{34}{21}$

13) $\frac{44}{96}$ ___ $\frac{45}{96}$

14) $\frac{35}{55}$ ___ $\frac{27}{55}$

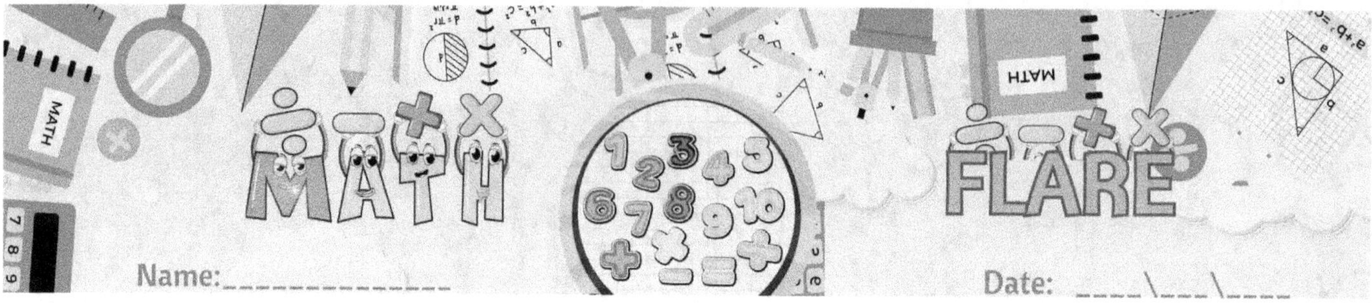

15) $\frac{2}{7}$ ___ $\frac{6}{7}$

16) $\frac{15}{13}$ ___ $\frac{7}{13}$

17) $\frac{1}{12}$ ___ $\frac{13}{12}$

18) $\frac{110}{160}$ ___ $\frac{102}{160}$

19) $\frac{44}{56}$ ___ $\frac{166}{56}$

20) $\frac{13}{6}$ ___ $\frac{2}{6}$

21) $\frac{88}{40}$ ___ $\frac{106}{40}$

22) $\frac{66}{25}$ ___ $\frac{21}{25}$

23) $\frac{10}{18}$ ___ $\frac{15}{18}$

24) $\frac{9}{4}$ ___ $\frac{2}{4}$

25) $\frac{4}{36}$ ___ $\frac{33}{36}$

26) $\frac{20}{19}$ ___ $\frac{5}{19}$

27) $\frac{99}{100}$ ___ $\frac{173}{100}$

28) $\frac{3}{90}$ ___ $\frac{243}{90}$

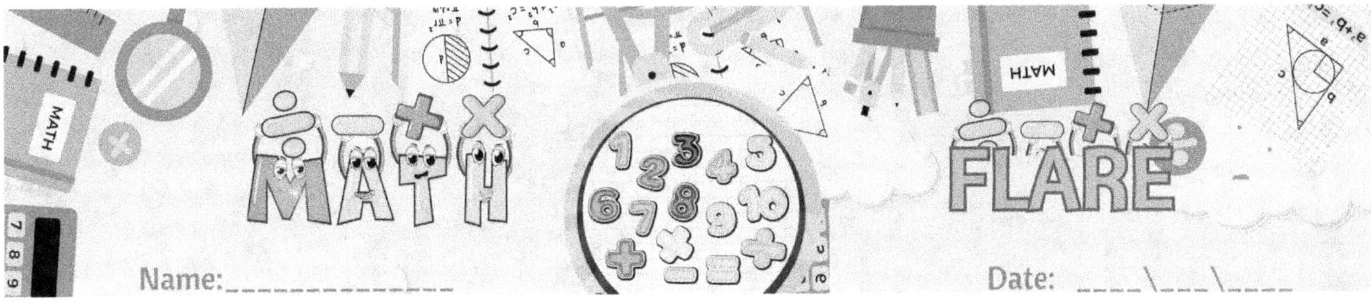

Name:_______________ Date: ____________

29) $\frac{6}{46}$ ___ $\frac{129}{46}$

30) $\frac{10}{15}$ ___ $\frac{9}{15}$

31) $\frac{36}{102}$ ___ $\frac{26}{102}$

32) $\frac{17}{36}$ ___ $\frac{79}{36}$

33) $\frac{7}{10}$ ___ $\frac{4}{10}$

34) $\frac{33}{60}$ ___ $\frac{34}{60}$

35) $\frac{3}{2}$ ___ $\frac{1}{2}$

36) $\frac{91}{75}$ ___ $\frac{124}{75}$

37) $\frac{92}{50}$ ___ $\frac{26}{50}$

38) $\frac{28}{20}$ ___ $\frac{16}{20}$

39) $\frac{4}{6}$ ___ $\frac{1}{6}$

40) $\frac{4}{5}$ ___ $\frac{4}{5}$

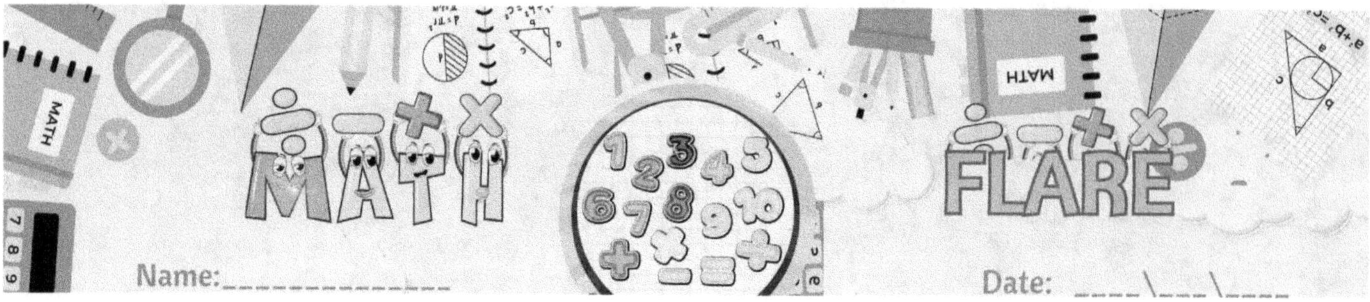

Convert Fractions to Decimals

Write decimal equivalent of the fractions.

1) $\frac{52}{100}$ = 0.52

2) $\frac{6}{12}$ = ______

3) $\frac{1}{8}$ = ______

4) $\frac{17}{18}$ = ______

5) $\frac{3}{16}$ = ______

6) $\frac{26}{50}$ = ______

7) $\frac{13}{22}$ = ______

8) $\frac{8}{13}$ = ______

9) $\frac{14}{17}$ = ______

10) $\frac{30}{32}$ = ______

11) $\frac{14}{20}$ = ______

12) $\frac{1}{6}$ = ______

MATH FLARE

Name:_______________ Date: ____________

13) $\frac{2}{3}$ = ____________________

14) $\frac{13}{15}$ = ____________________

15) $\frac{16}{36}$ = ____________________

16) $\frac{1}{4}$ = ____________________

17) $\frac{19}{60}$ = ____________________

18) $\frac{61}{75}$ = ____________________

19) $\frac{2}{5}$ = ____________________

20) $\frac{5}{11}$ = ____________________

21) $\frac{1}{2}$ = ____________________

22) $\frac{10}{21}$ = ____________________

23) $\frac{55}{70}$ = ____________________

24) $\frac{28}{30}$ = ____________________

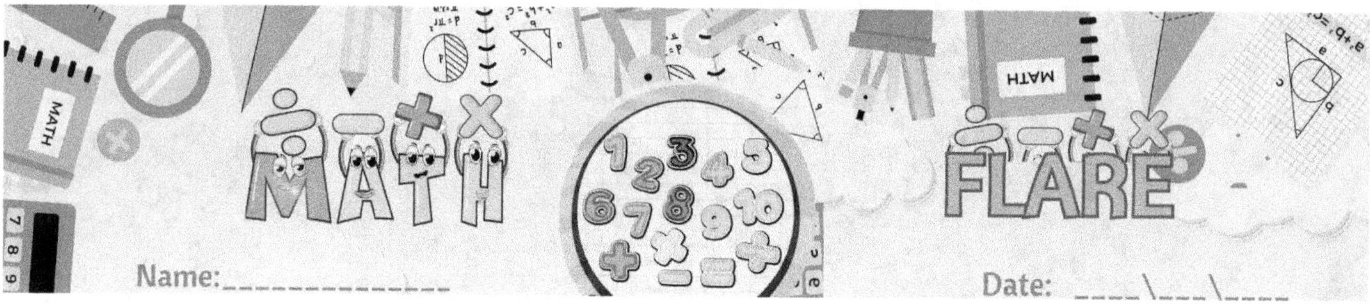

25) $\frac{6}{40}$ = ________________

26) $\frac{2}{10}$ = ________________

27) $\frac{6}{25}$ = ________________

28) $\frac{4}{14}$ = ________________

29) $\frac{1}{9}$ = ________________

30) $\frac{7}{23}$ = ________________

31) $\frac{6}{19}$ = ________________

32) $\frac{1}{24}$ = ________________

33) $\frac{6}{7}$ = ________________

34) $\frac{16}{19}$ = ________________

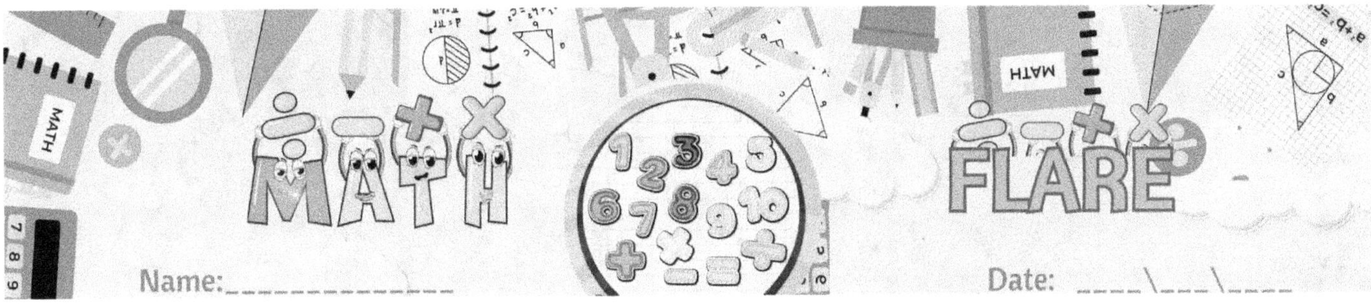

Fractions Addition (Common Denominator)

Find the sum.

1) $\frac{2}{5} + \frac{1}{5} =$ $\frac{2+1}{5} = \frac{3}{5}$

2) $\frac{2}{4} + \frac{1}{4} =$ ______

3) $\frac{1}{6} + \frac{1}{6} =$ ______

4) $\frac{4}{12} + \frac{7}{12} =$ ______

5) $\frac{4}{10} + \frac{1}{10} =$ ______

6) $\frac{1}{5} + \frac{1}{5} =$ ______

7) $\frac{2}{7} + \frac{4}{7} =$ ______

8) $\frac{4}{9} + \frac{4}{9} =$ ______

9) $\frac{1}{2} + \frac{1}{2} =$ ______

10) $\frac{5}{8} + \frac{2}{8} =$ ______

11) $\frac{1}{3} + \frac{1}{3} =$ ______

12) $\frac{1}{11} + \frac{2}{11} =$ ______

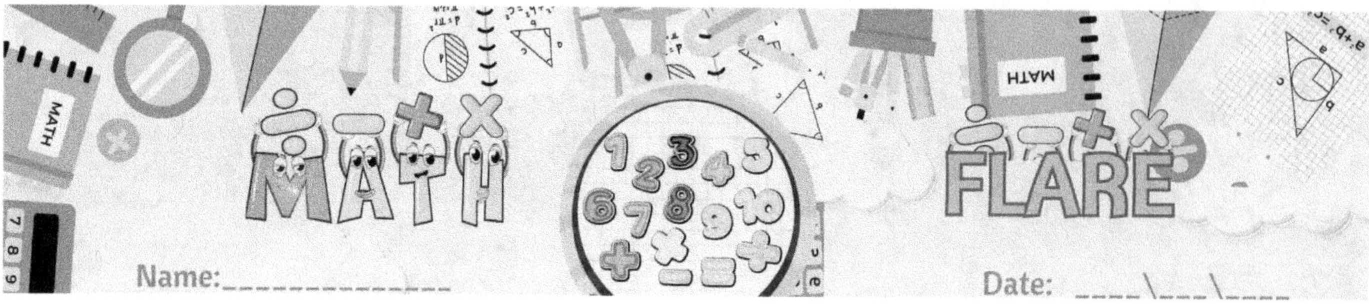

13) $\frac{1}{5} + \frac{3}{5} =$ ______________________

14) $\frac{4}{8} + \frac{2}{8} =$ ______________________

15) $\frac{4}{11} + \frac{1}{11} =$ ______________________

16) $\frac{1}{7} + \frac{2}{7} =$ ______________________

17) $\frac{1}{10} + \frac{8}{10} =$ ______________________

18) $\frac{2}{6} + \frac{3}{6} =$ ______________________

19) $\frac{7}{9} + \frac{1}{9} =$ ______________________

20) $\frac{1}{8} + \frac{3}{8} =$ ______________________

21) $\frac{3}{7} + \frac{3}{7} =$ ______________________

22) $\frac{3}{11} + \frac{6}{11} =$ ______________________

23) $\frac{4}{12} + \frac{1}{12} =$ ______________________

24) $\frac{3}{5} + \frac{1}{5} =$ ______________________

25) $\frac{2}{10} + \frac{6}{10} =$ ______________________

26) $\frac{4}{8} + \frac{1}{8} =$ ______________________

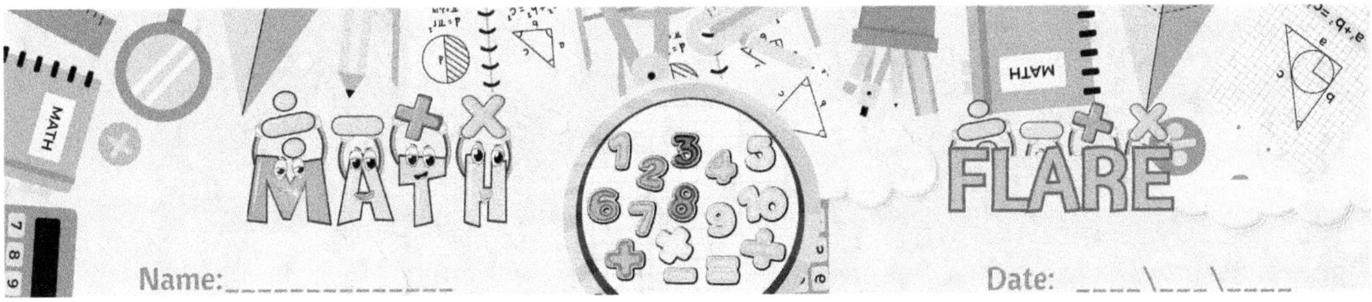

27) $\frac{8}{12} + \frac{3}{12} =$ ____________

28) $\frac{2}{6} + \frac{2}{6} =$ ____________

29) $\frac{2}{5} + \frac{2}{5} =$ ____________

30) $\frac{3}{11} + \frac{4}{11} =$ ____________

31) $\frac{1}{4} + \frac{2}{4} =$ ____________

32) $\frac{1}{10} + \frac{2}{10} =$ ____________

33) $\frac{4}{9} + \frac{3}{9} =$ ____________

34) $\frac{1}{6} + \frac{3}{6} =$ ____________

35) $\frac{1}{4} + \frac{1}{4} =$ ____________

36) $\frac{6}{10} + \frac{1}{10} =$ ____________

37) $\frac{5}{12} + \frac{3}{12} =$ ____________

38) $\frac{3}{11} + \frac{1}{11} =$ ____________

39) $\frac{1}{8} + \frac{2}{8} =$ ____________

40) $\frac{4}{7} + \frac{2}{7} =$ ____________

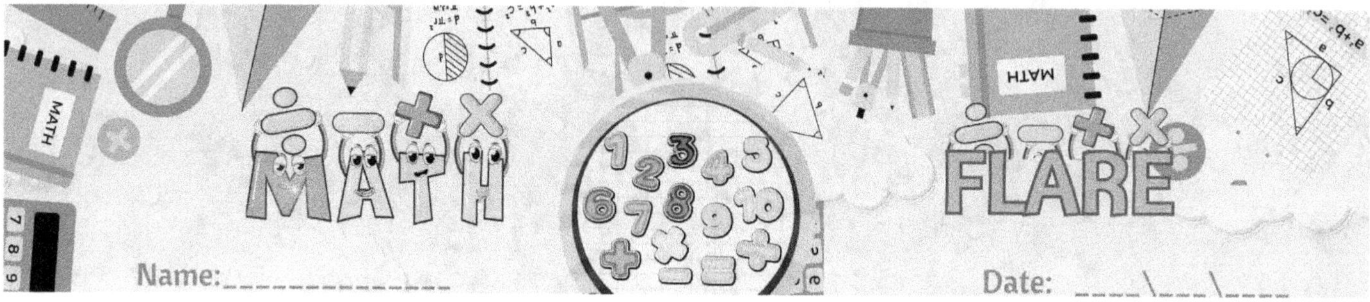

41) $\frac{1}{5} + \frac{2}{5} =$ ____________________

42) $\frac{4}{10} + \frac{4}{10} =$ ____________________

43) $\frac{5}{11} + \frac{4}{11} =$ ____________________

44) $\frac{3}{9} + \frac{5}{9} =$ ____________________

45) $\frac{6}{12} + \frac{1}{12} =$ ____________________

46) $\frac{1}{8} + \frac{5}{8} =$ ____________________

47) $\frac{1}{10} + \frac{1}{10} =$ ____________________

48) $\frac{1}{8} + \frac{1}{8} =$ ____________________

49) $\frac{8}{12} + \frac{2}{12} =$ ____________________

50) $\frac{3}{9} + \frac{3}{9} =$ ____________________

51) $\frac{7}{11} + \frac{2}{11} =$ ____________________

52) $\frac{1}{6} + \frac{4}{6} =$ ____________________

53) $\frac{1}{7} + \frac{1}{7} =$ ____________________

54) $\frac{5}{7} + \frac{1}{7} =$ ____________________

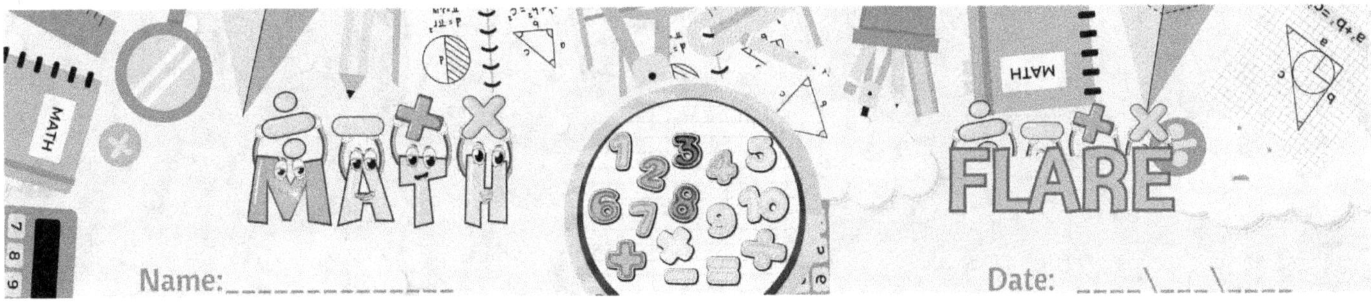

55) $\frac{1}{10} + \frac{4}{10} =$ ____________________

56) $\frac{3}{11} + \frac{7}{11} =$ ____________________

57) $\frac{2}{8} + \frac{3}{8} =$ ____________________

58) $\frac{3}{9} + \frac{1}{9} =$ ____________________

59) $\frac{9}{12} + \frac{1}{12} =$ ____________________

60) $\frac{8}{10} + \frac{1}{10} =$ ____________________

61) $\frac{2}{12} + \frac{2}{12} =$ ____________________

62) $\frac{2}{9} + \frac{3}{9} =$ ____________________

63) $\frac{8}{11} + \frac{1}{11} =$ ____________________

64) $\frac{2}{7} + \frac{3}{7} =$ ____________________

65) $\frac{3}{10} + \frac{3}{10} =$ ____________________

66) $\frac{1}{11} + \frac{5}{11} =$ ____________________

67) $\frac{6}{9} + \frac{2}{9} =$ ____________________

68) $\frac{3}{12} + \frac{3}{12} =$ ____________________

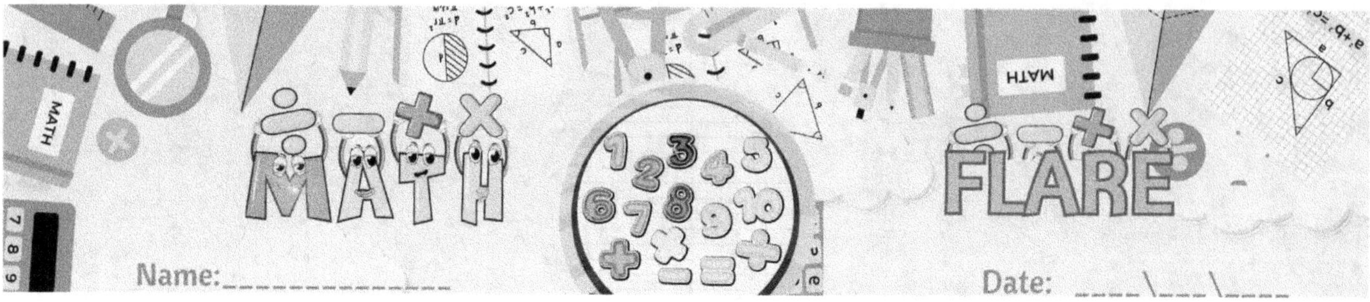

69) $\frac{1}{8} + \frac{4}{8} =$ ______________________

70) $\frac{3}{6} + \frac{1}{6} =$ ______________________

71) $\frac{4}{9} + \frac{1}{9} =$ ______________________

72) $\frac{2}{8} + \frac{1}{8} =$ ______________________

73) $\frac{7}{12} + \frac{1}{12} =$ ______________________

74) $\frac{3}{7} + \frac{2}{7} =$ ______________________

75) $\frac{7}{10} + \frac{1}{10} =$ ______________________

76) $\frac{2}{11} + \frac{8}{11} =$ ______________________

77) $\frac{5}{9} + \frac{1}{9} =$ ______________________

78) $\frac{2}{10} + \frac{1}{10} =$ ______________________

79) $\frac{4}{8} + \frac{3}{8} =$ ______________________

80) $\frac{3}{12} + \frac{4}{12} =$ ______________________

81) $\frac{2}{6} + \frac{1}{6} =$ ______________________

82) $\frac{1}{10} + \frac{7}{10} =$ ______________________

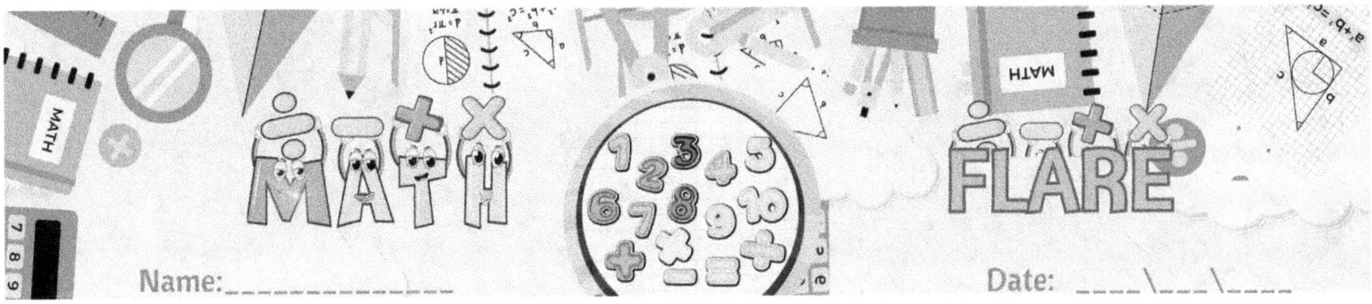

Fractions Subtraction: (Common Denominator)

Find the difference.

1) $\frac{10}{11} - \frac{5}{11} = \frac{10-5}{11} = \frac{5}{11}$

2) $\frac{3}{4} - \frac{1}{4} =$ ____________________

3) $\frac{4}{5} - \frac{2}{5} =$ ____________________

4) $\frac{10}{12} - \frac{7}{12} =$ ____________________

5) $\frac{2}{3} - \frac{1}{3} =$ ____________________

6) $\frac{4}{8} - \frac{2}{8} =$ ____________________

7) $\frac{8}{10} - \frac{1}{10} =$ ____________________

8) $\frac{2}{6} - \frac{1}{6} =$ ____________________

9) $\frac{3}{7} - \frac{1}{7} =$ ____________________

10) $\frac{3}{4} - \frac{2}{4} =$ ____________________

11) $\frac{4}{5} - \frac{1}{5} =$ ____________________

12) $\frac{7}{8} - \frac{5}{8} =$ ____________________

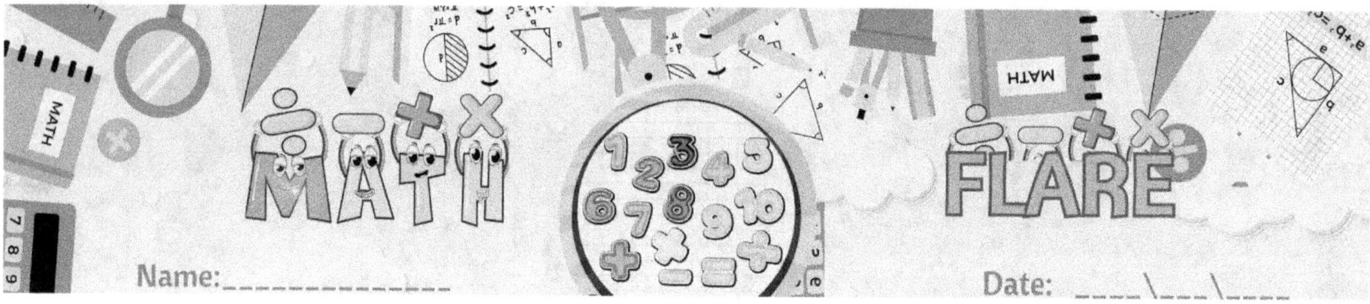

13) $\frac{2}{7} - \frac{1}{7} =$ ____________

14) $\frac{6}{12} - \frac{2}{12} =$ ____________

15) $\frac{6}{10} - \frac{4}{10} =$ ____________

16) $\frac{8}{9} - \frac{4}{9} =$ ____________

17) $\frac{5}{6} - \frac{1}{6} =$ ____________

18) $\frac{5}{11} - \frac{1}{11} =$ ____________

19) $\frac{10}{11} - \frac{8}{11} =$ ____________

20) $\frac{5}{7} - \frac{4}{7} =$ ____________

21) $\frac{4}{6} - \frac{3}{6} =$ ____________

22) $\frac{5}{9} - \frac{4}{9} =$ ____________

23) $\frac{5}{12} - \frac{2}{12} =$ ____________

24) $\frac{6}{8} - \frac{1}{8} =$ ____________

25) $\frac{4}{5} - \frac{3}{5} =$ ____________

26) $\frac{5}{10} - \frac{1}{10} =$ ____________

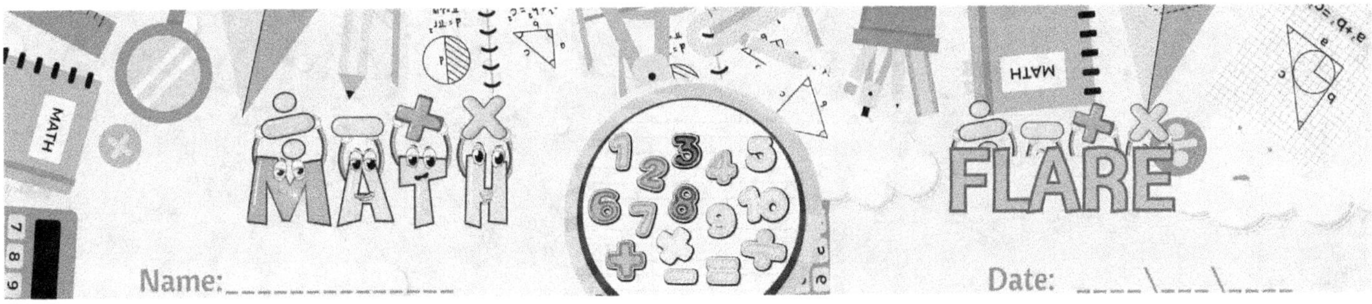

27) $\frac{5}{8} - \frac{4}{8} =$ ____________

28) $\frac{6}{10} - \frac{5}{10} =$ ____________

29) $\frac{6}{8} - \frac{5}{8} =$ ____________

30) $\frac{5}{6} - \frac{4}{6} =$ ____________

31) $\frac{3}{7} - \frac{2}{7} =$ ____________

32) $\frac{8}{9} - \frac{7}{9} =$ ____________

33) $\frac{11}{12} - \frac{4}{12} =$ ____________

34) $\frac{10}{12} - \frac{4}{12} =$ ____________

35) $\frac{9}{11} - \frac{6}{11} =$ ____________

36) $\frac{5}{10} - \frac{3}{10} =$ ____________

37) $\frac{8}{9} - \frac{6}{9} =$ ____________

38) $\frac{6}{7} - \frac{5}{7} =$ ____________

39) $\frac{5}{6} - \frac{3}{6} =$ ____________

40) $\frac{5}{9} - \frac{3}{9} =$ ____________

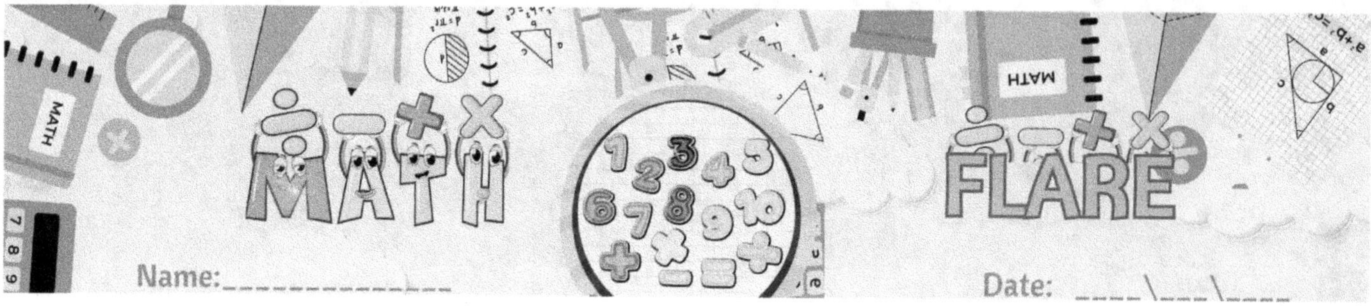

41) $\frac{6}{7} - \frac{3}{7} =$ ______

42) $\frac{7}{12} - \frac{3}{12} =$ ______

43) $\frac{4}{8} - \frac{3}{8} =$ ______

44) $\frac{4}{6} - \frac{2}{6} =$ ______

45) $\frac{9}{10} - \frac{8}{10} =$ ______

46) $\frac{4}{12} - \frac{3}{12} =$ ______

47) $\frac{6}{9} - \frac{5}{9} =$ ______

48) $\frac{3}{5} - \frac{2}{5} =$ ______

49) $\frac{10}{11} - \frac{9}{11} =$ ______

50) $\frac{2}{4} - \frac{1}{4} =$ ______

51) $\frac{3}{8} - \frac{2}{8} =$ ______

52) $\frac{9}{10} - \frac{5}{10} =$ ______

53) $\frac{5}{7} - \frac{2}{7} =$ ______

54) $\frac{8}{9} - \frac{3}{9} =$ ______

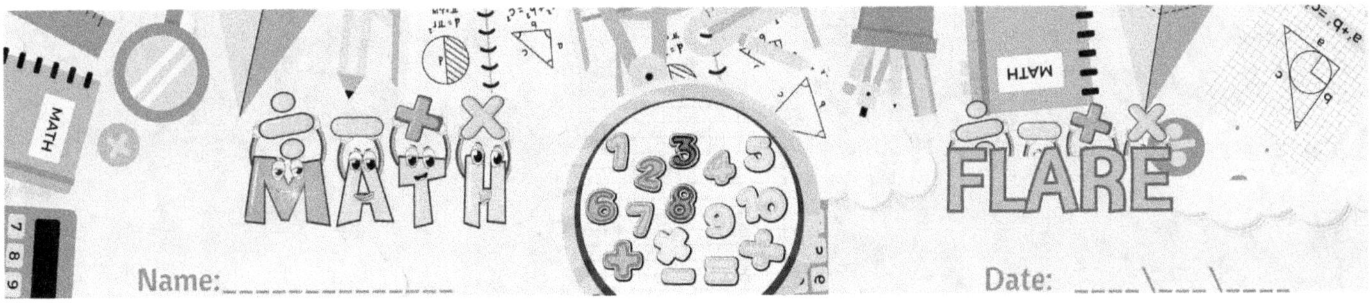

55) $\frac{10}{11} - \frac{4}{11} =$ ____________

56) $\frac{7}{8} - \frac{3}{8} =$ ____________

57) $\frac{7}{10} - \frac{5}{10} =$ ____________

58) $\frac{11}{12} - \frac{1}{12} =$ ____________

59) $\frac{7}{9} - \frac{4}{9} =$ ____________

60) $\frac{2}{5} - \frac{1}{5} =$ ____________

61) $\frac{6}{11} - \frac{1}{11} =$ ____________

62) $\frac{4}{7} - \frac{2}{7} =$ ____________

63) $\frac{9}{12} - \frac{8}{12} =$ ____________

64) $\frac{10}{12} - \frac{8}{12} =$ ____________

65) $\frac{8}{10} - \frac{4}{10} =$ ____________

66) $\frac{4}{11} - \frac{3}{11} =$ ____________

67) $\frac{7}{8} - \frac{6}{8} =$ ____________

68) $\frac{11}{12} - \frac{5}{12} =$ ____________

69) $\frac{6}{9} - \frac{2}{9} =$ ______________________

70) $\frac{9}{12} - \frac{6}{12} =$ ______________________

71) $\frac{5}{11} - \frac{4}{11} =$ ______________________

72) $\frac{4}{9} - \frac{2}{9} =$ ______________________

73) $\frac{9}{10} - \frac{6}{10} =$ ______________________

74) $\frac{8}{12} - \frac{7}{12} =$ ______________________

75) $\frac{3}{6} - \frac{2}{6} =$ ______________________

76) $\frac{3}{11} - \frac{1}{11} =$ ______________________

77) $\frac{4}{7} - \frac{1}{7} =$ ______________________

78) $\frac{8}{9} - \frac{5}{9} =$ ______________________

79) $\frac{8}{11} - \frac{3}{11} =$ ______________________

80) $\frac{7}{12} - \frac{6}{12} =$ ______________________

81) $\frac{5}{8} - \frac{1}{8} =$ ______________________

82) $\frac{7}{9} - \frac{2}{9} =$ ______________________

Chapter. 06

Geometry

Area and Perimeter

The area of a shape represents the amount of space it occupies. The perimeter of a shape is the total distance around its outer edge.

Area of Rectangle

For a square, since all four sides are equal, we only need to know the length of one side to find its area. We can calculate the area of a square by multiplying the length of one side by itself (squared). So, if the length of one side of the square is 's', then the area (A) is given by:

$A = s \times s$

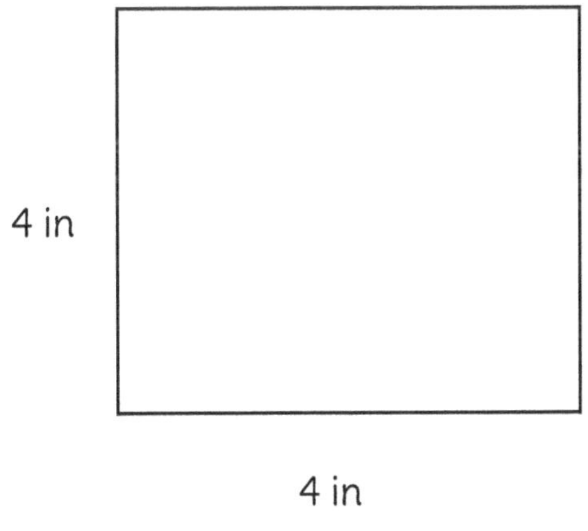

$A = 4 \times 4$

$A = 16$

Perimeter of Rectangle

For a square, since all four sides are equal, we can find the perimeter by adding up the lengths of all four sides. If 's' represents the length of one side, then the perimeter (P) is given by:

$$P = 4 \times s$$

$$P = 4 \times 4$$

$$P = 16$$

Area of Triangle:

The area of a triangle represents the amount of space enclosed within its three sides. The formula for calculating the area of a triangle depends on the type of triangle. For a general triangle, we use the formula:

$$A = \frac{1}{2} \times \text{base} \times \text{height}$$

Where:

- A represents the area of the triangle.
- The base is the length of any one side of the triangle.
- The height is the perpendicular distance from the base to the opposite vertex.

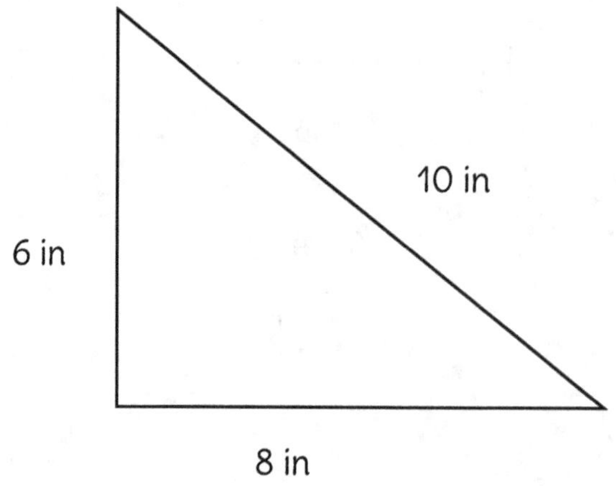

$$A = \frac{1}{2} \times \text{base} \times \text{height}$$

$$A = \frac{1}{2} \times 6 \times 8$$

$$A = \frac{1}{2} \times 48$$

$$A = 24$$

Perimeter of Triangle:

The perimeter of a triangle is the total length of its three sides. To find the perimeter, we simply add the lengths of all three sides together:

$$P = \text{side1} + \text{side2} + \text{side3}$$

$$P = 6 + 8 + 10$$

$$P = 24$$

Equilateral Triangle

An equilateral triangle is a triangle in which all three sides are equal in length. To find the area and perimeter of an equilateral triangle, we can use the following formulas:

- Area (A): $\frac{\sqrt{3}}{4} \times a^2$ where a is the length of one side of the equilateral triangle.
- Perimeter (P): $P = 3a$ where a is the length of one side of the equilateral triangle.

Let's solve a problem:

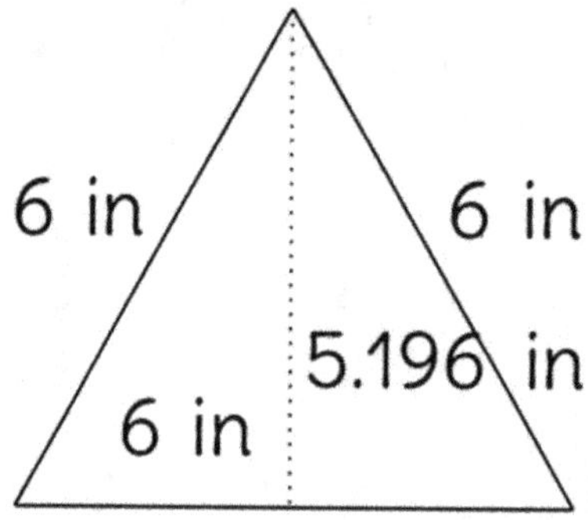

Area of Equilateral Triangle:

Area (A): $\frac{\sqrt{3}}{4} \times (6)^2$

Area (A): $\frac{\sqrt{3}}{4} \times 36$

Area (A): $\frac{36\sqrt{3}}{4}$

Area (A): $\frac{36(1.73)}{4}$

Area (A): $\frac{62.35}{4}$

Area (A): 15.59 in^2

Perimeter of Equilateral Triangle:

$P = 3a$

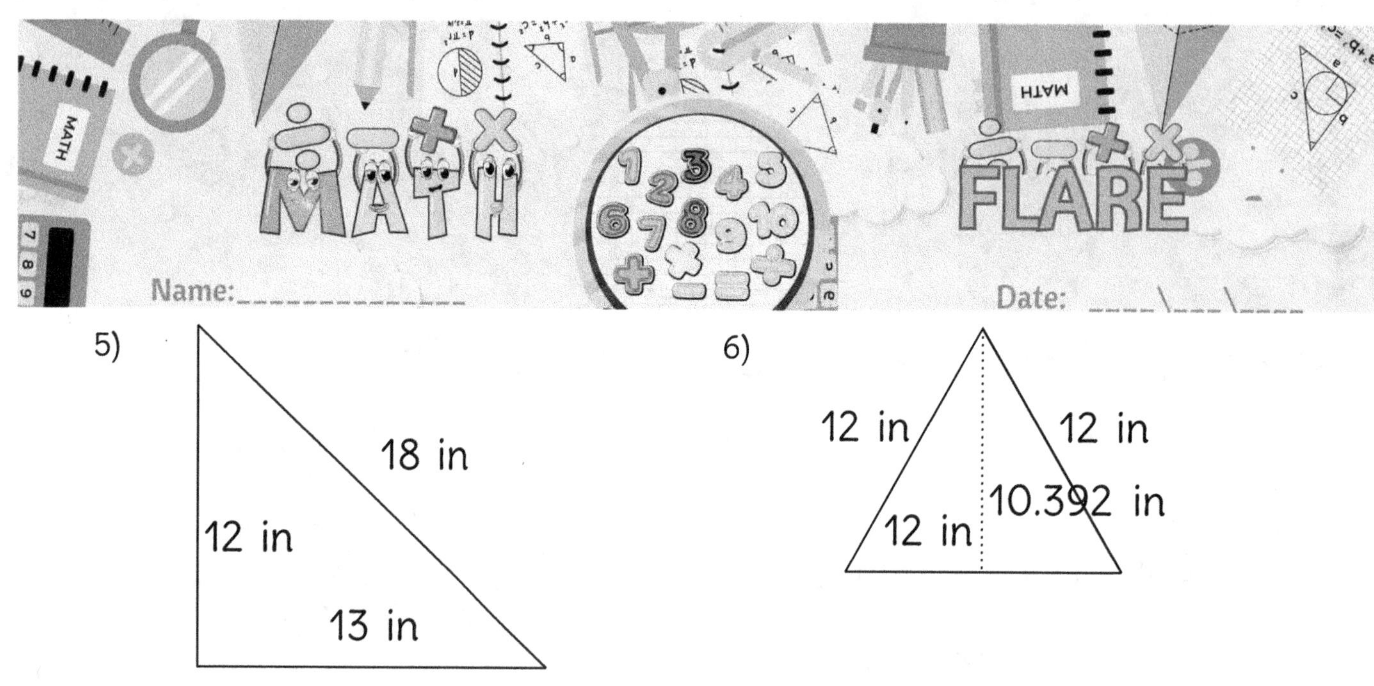

$P = 3(6) = 18$

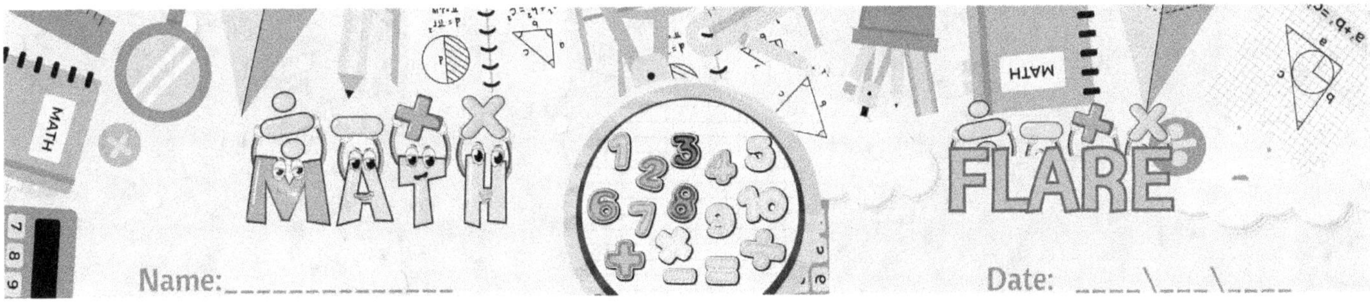

Name:_______________ Date: ___________

Area and Perimeter: Rectangles and Triangles

1)

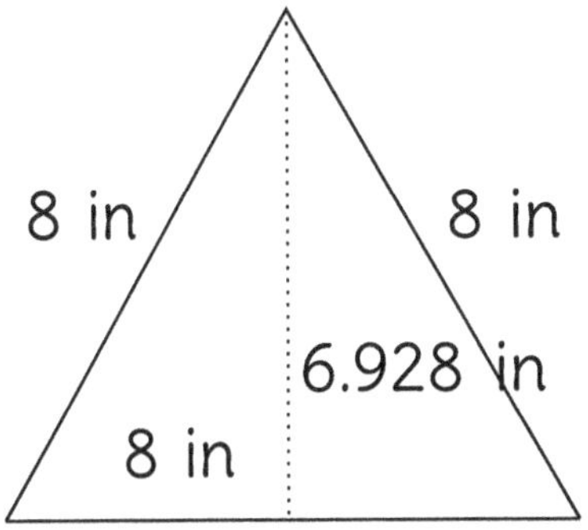

P = 24 in A = 27.71 in^2

2)

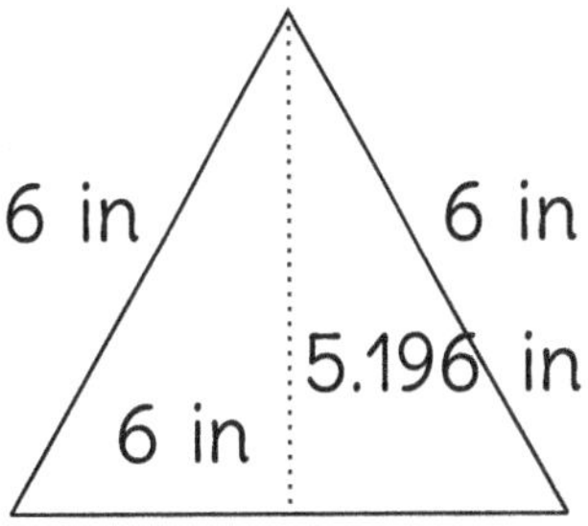

3)

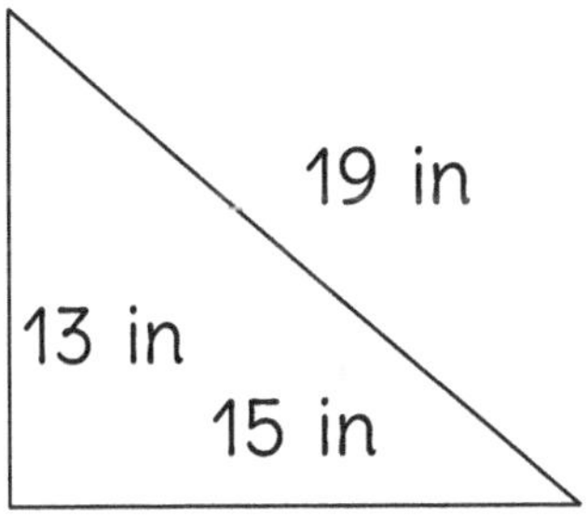

4)

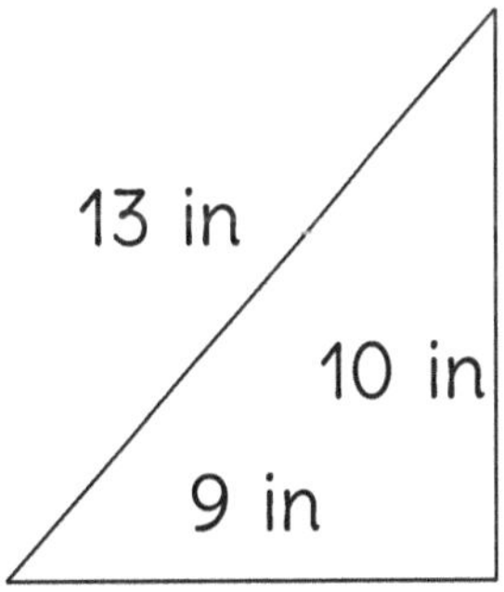

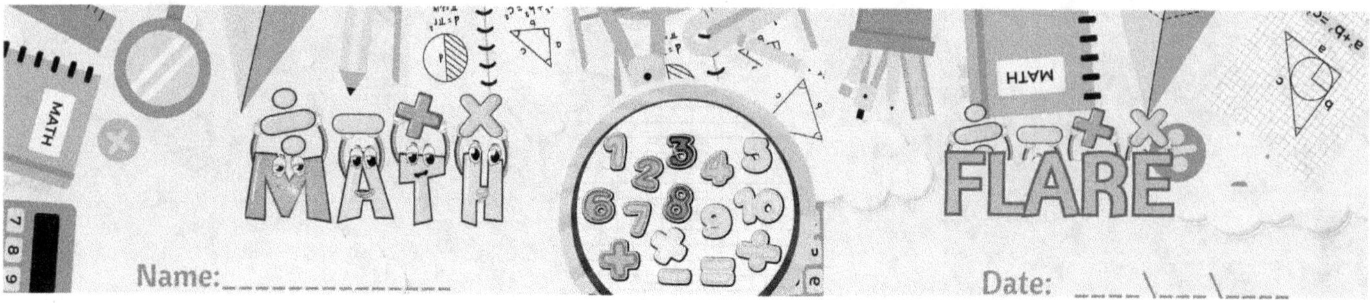
MATH
FLARE
Name:______________
Date: ____________

5)

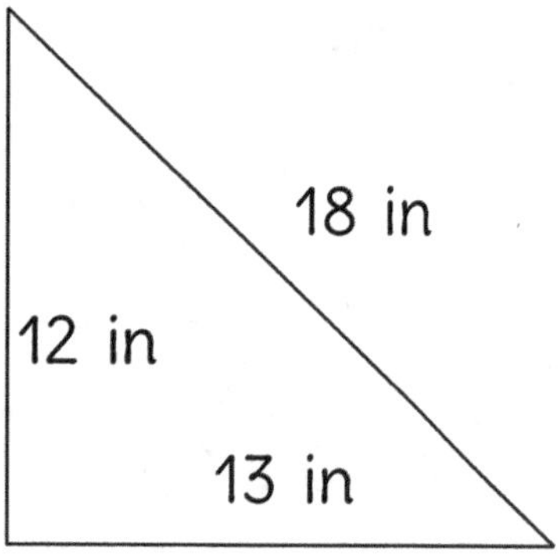
18 in
12 in
13 in

6)

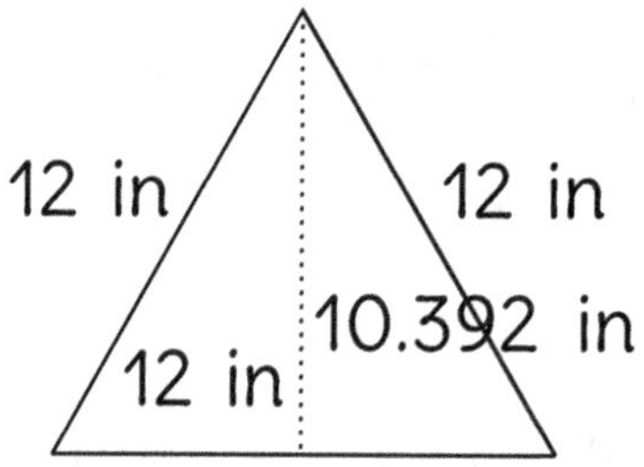
12 in
12 in
10.392 in
12 in

7)

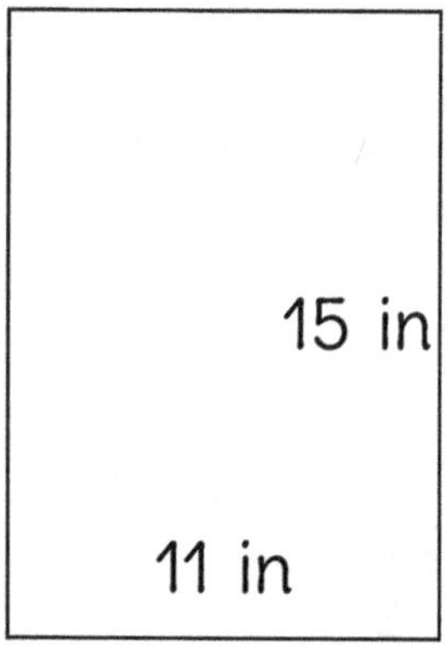
15 in
11 in

8)

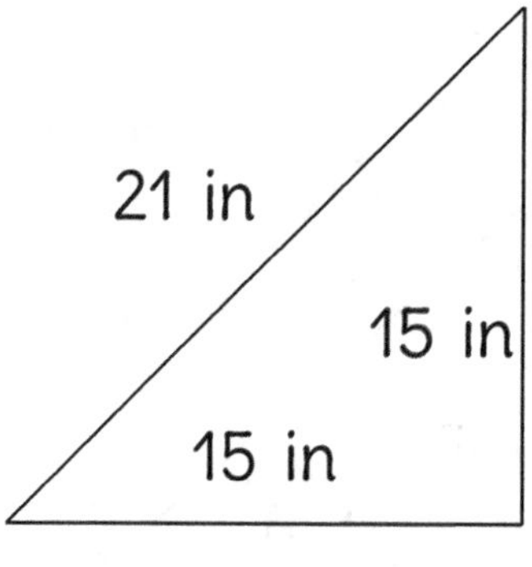
21 in
15 in
15 in

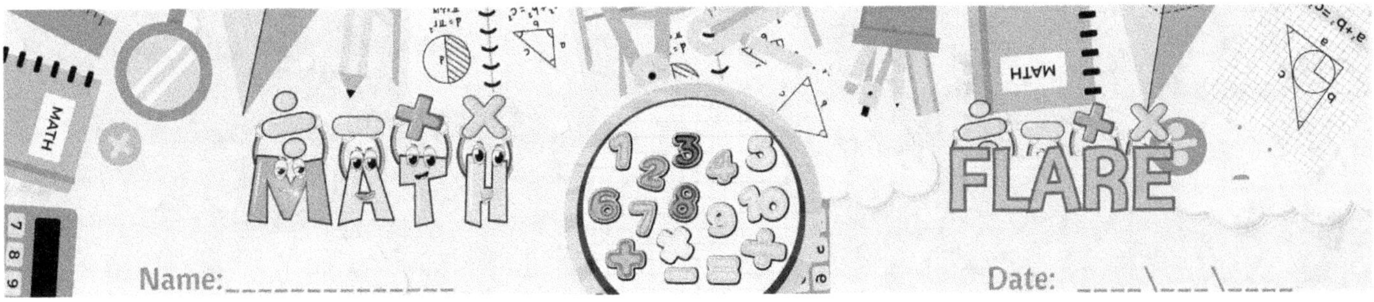
MATH
FLARE
Name:
Date:

9)

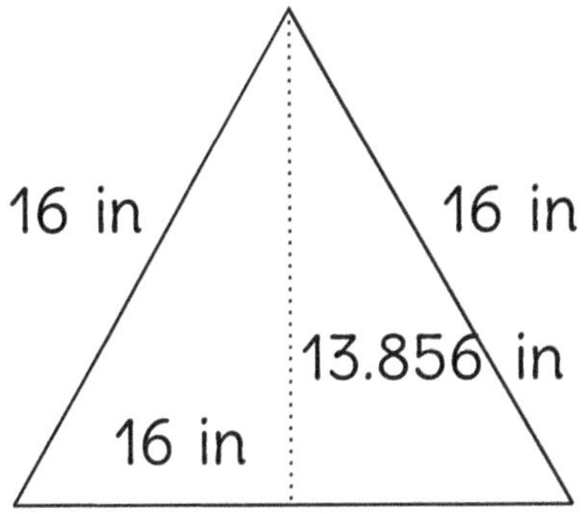
16 in
16 in
13.856 in
16 in

10)

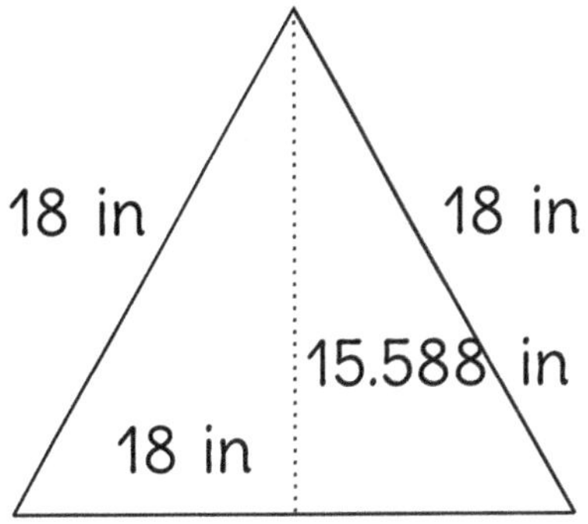
18 in
18 in
15.588 in
18 in

11)

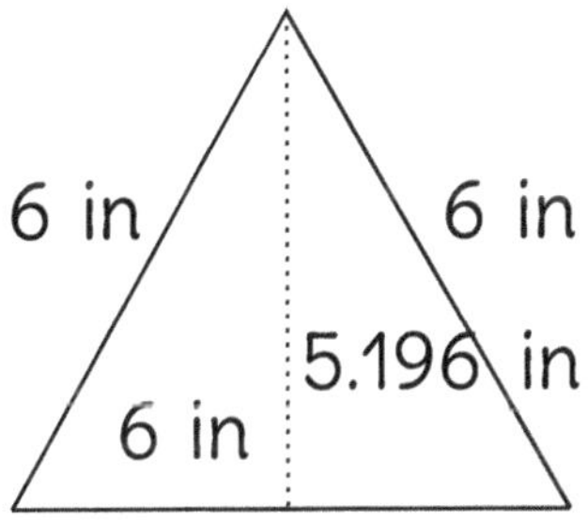
6 in
6 in
5.196 in
6 in

12)

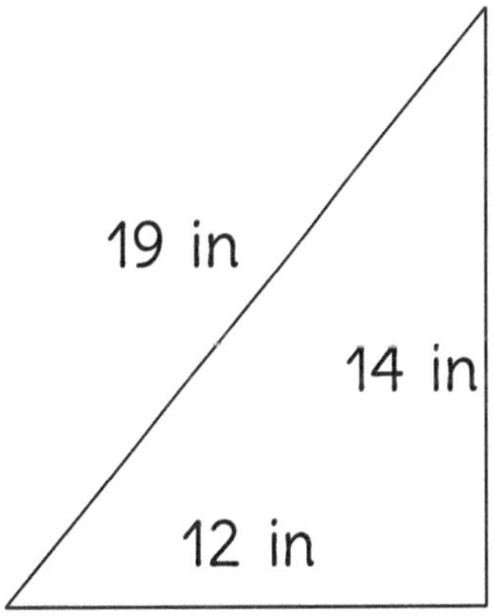
19 in
14 in
12 in

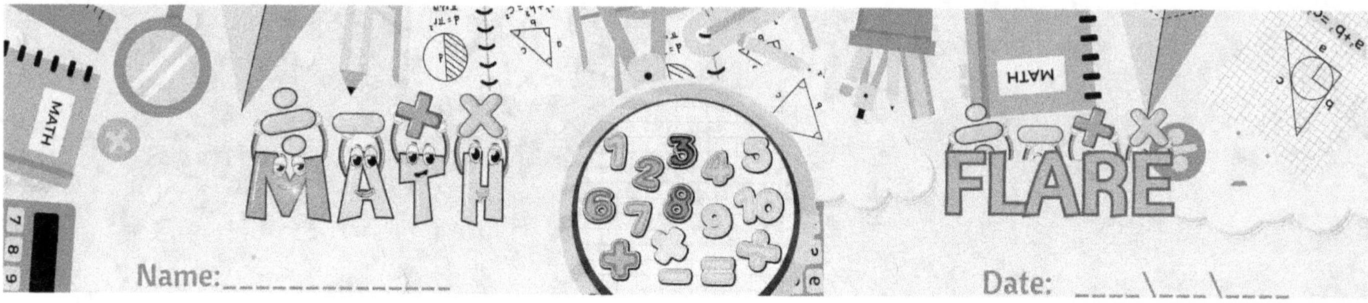
MATH
FLARE
Name:
Date:

13)

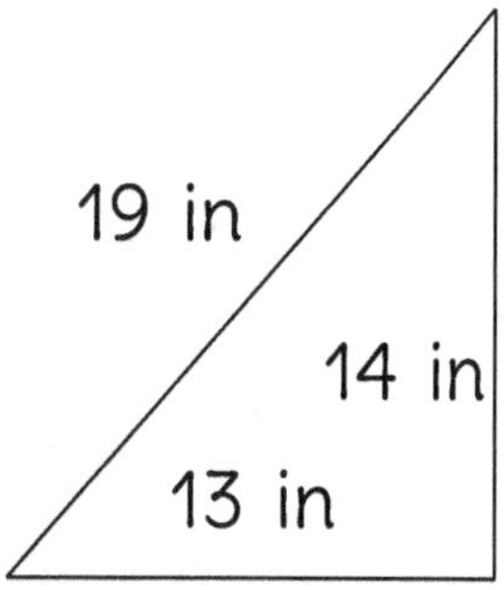
19 in
14 in
13 in

14)

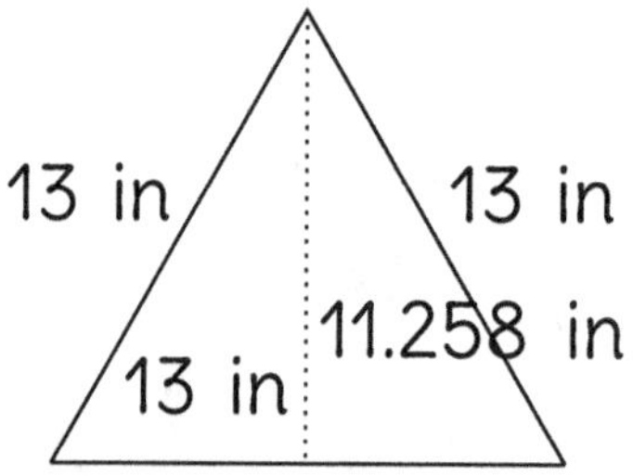
13 in
13 in
11.258 in
13 in

15)

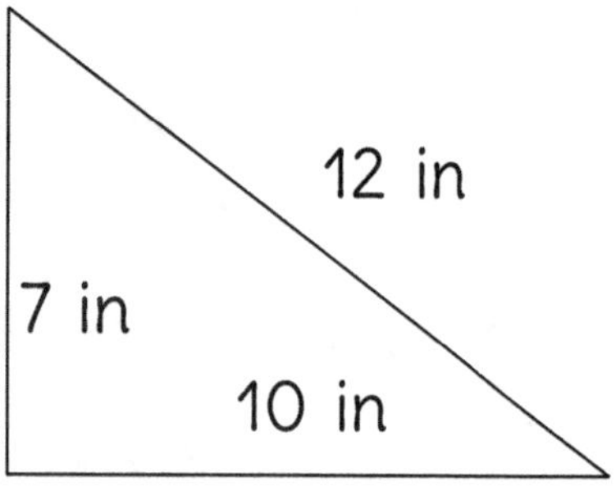
12 in
7 in
10 in

16)

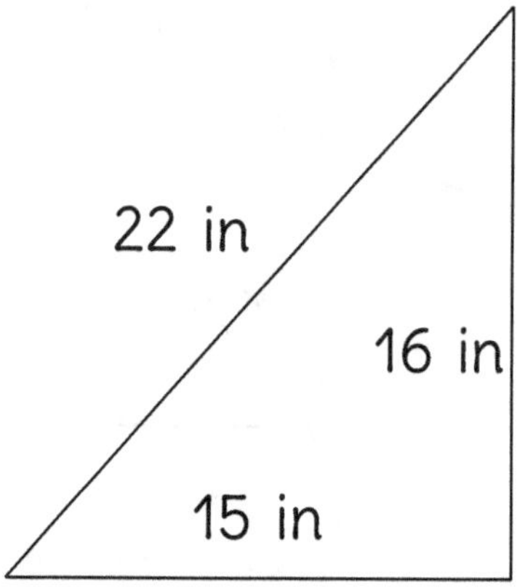
22 in
16 in
15 in

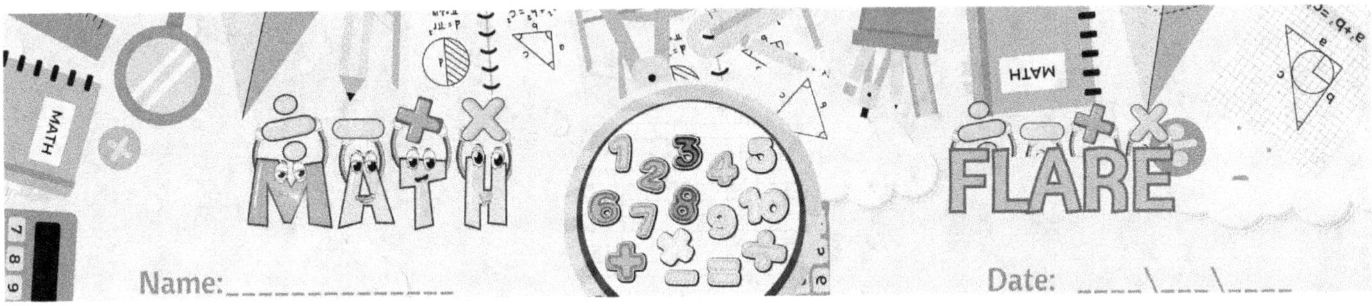
MATH
FLARE
Name:
Date:

17)

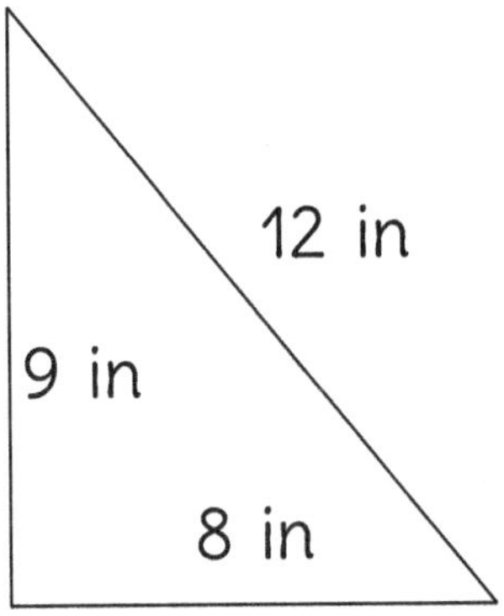
12 in
9 in
8 in

18)

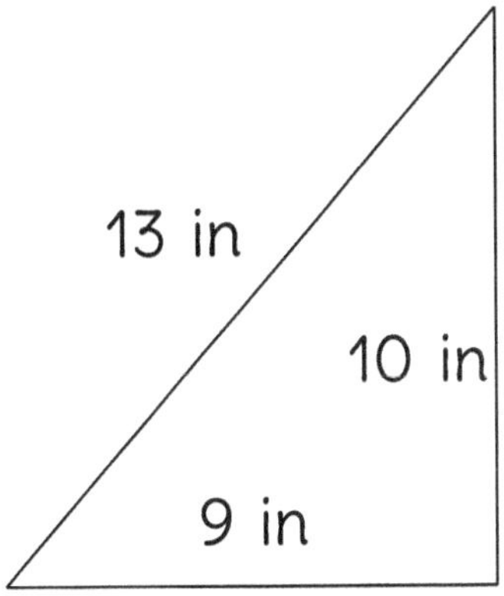
13 in
10 in
9 in

19)

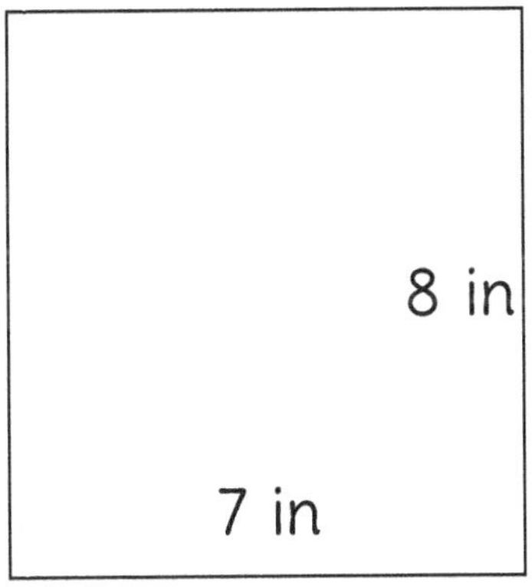
8 in
7 in

20)

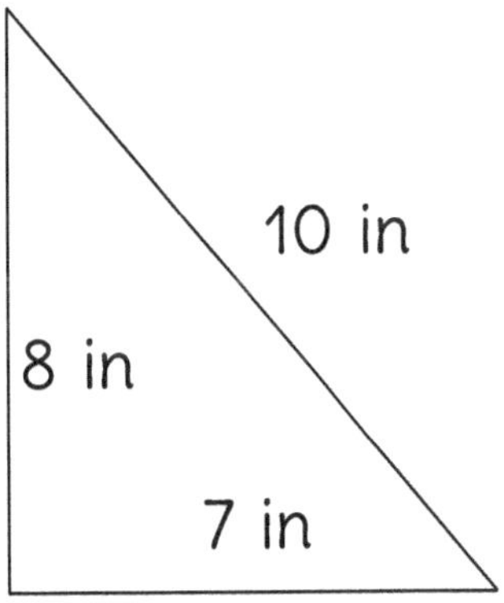
10 in
8 in
7 in

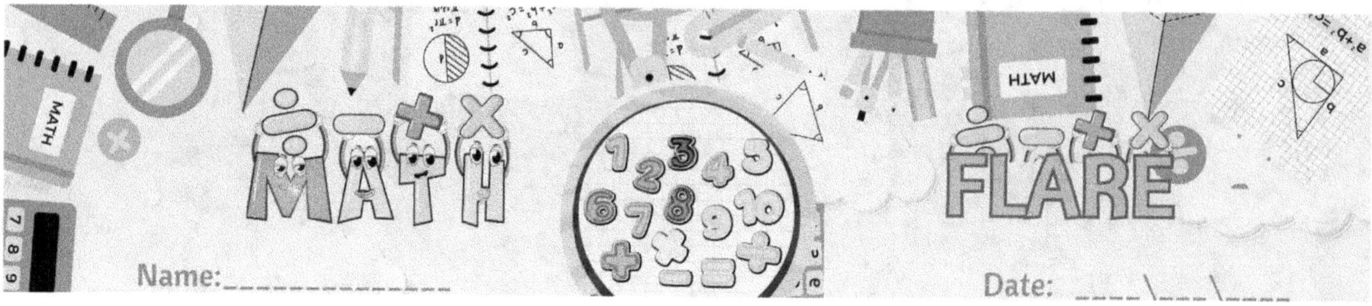
MATH
FLARE
Name:
Date:

21)

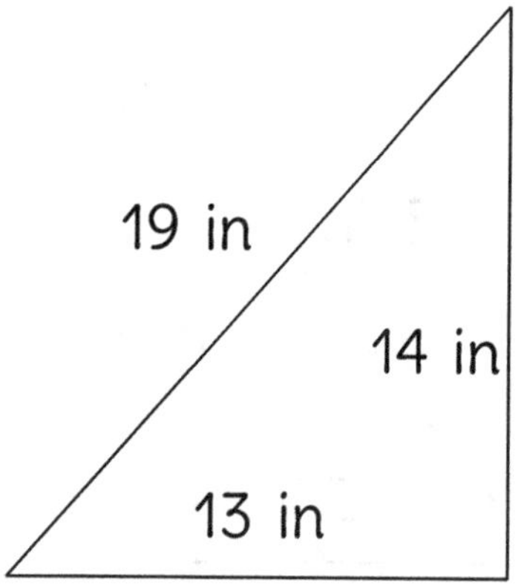
19 in
14 in
13 in

22)

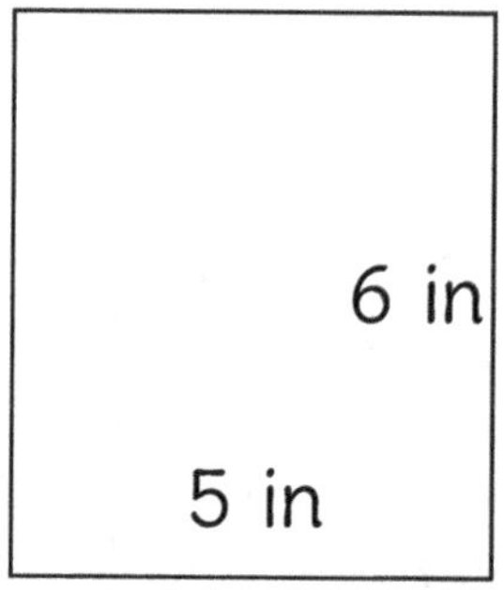
6 in
5 in

23)

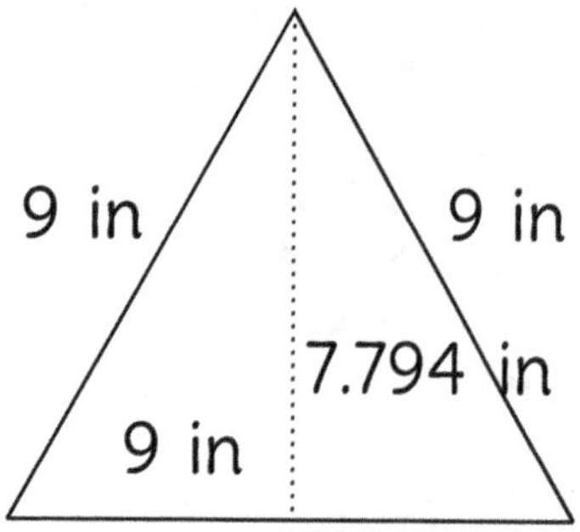
9 in
9 in
7.794 in
9 in

24)

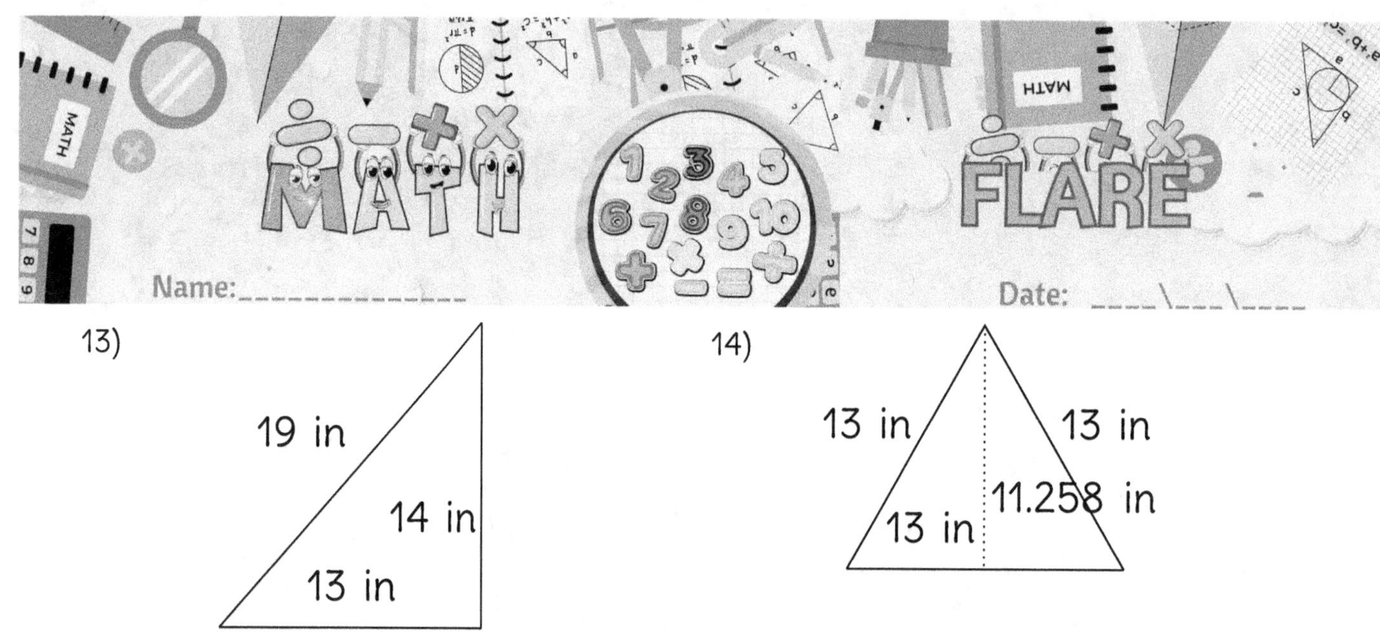

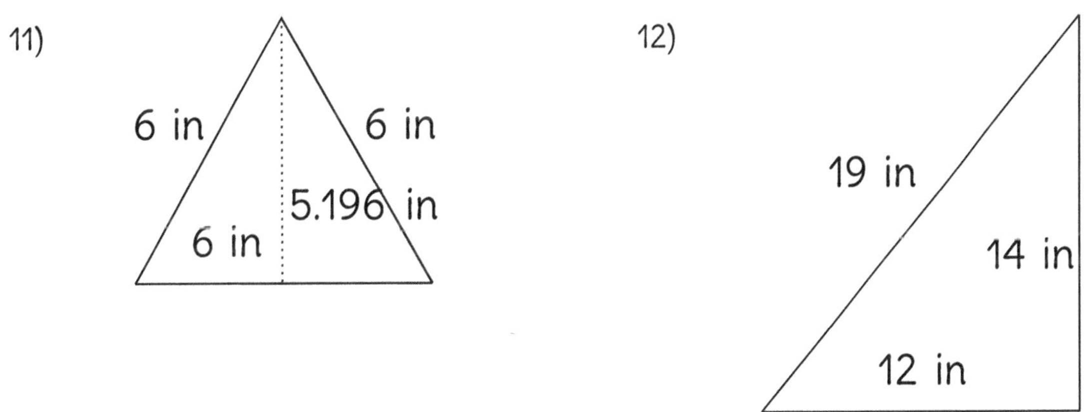

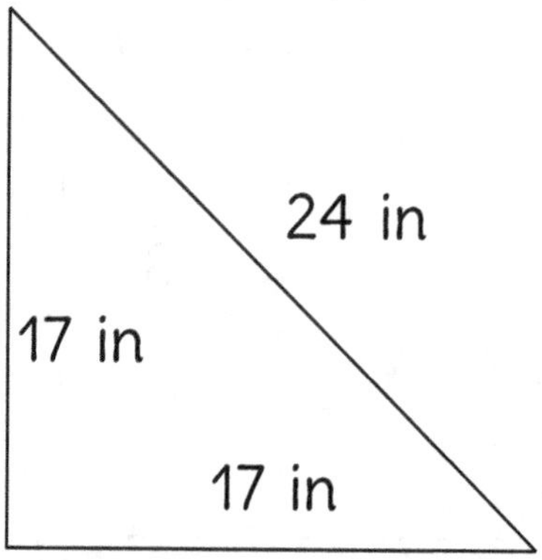
24 in
17 in
17 in

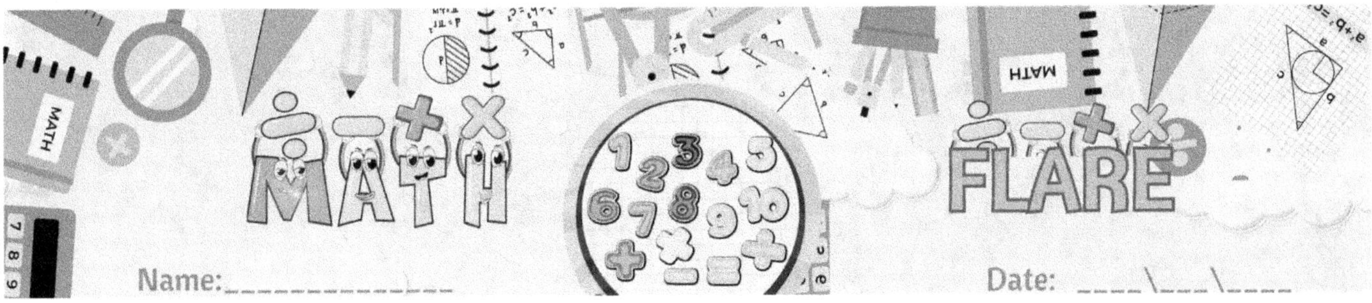
MATH
FLARE
Name:
Date:

25)

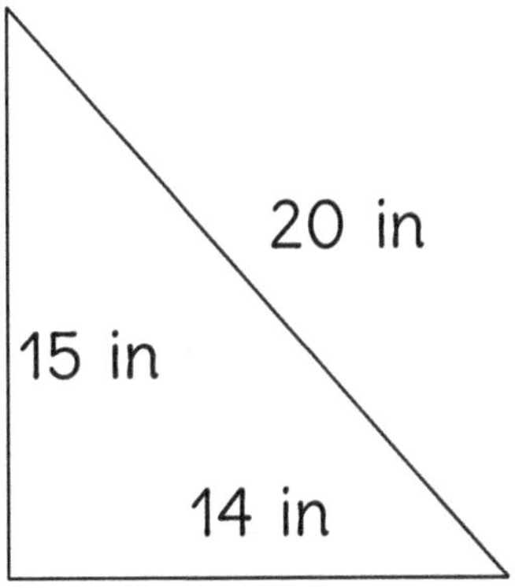
20 in
15 in
14 in

26)

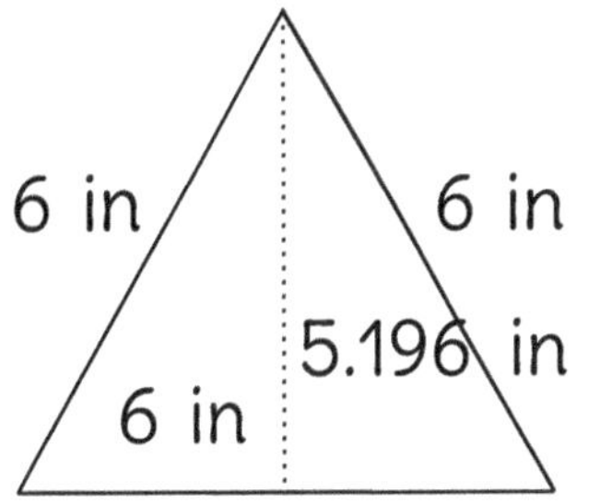
6 in
6 in
5.196 in
6 in

27)

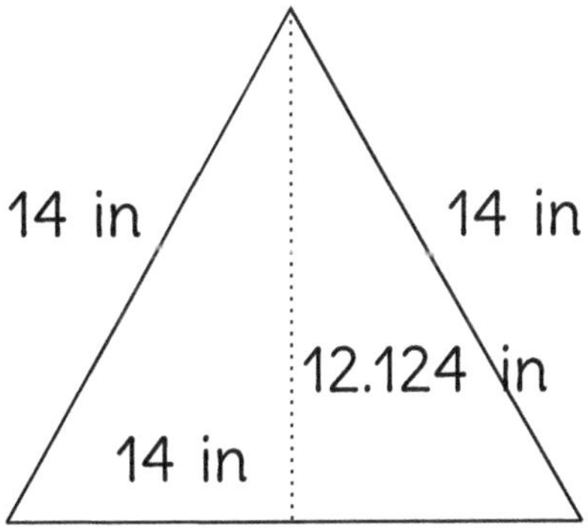
14 in
14 in
12.124 in
14 in

28)

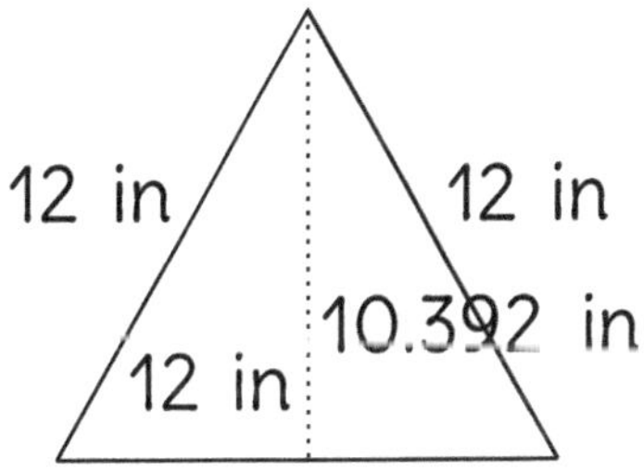
12 in
12 in
10.392 in
12 in

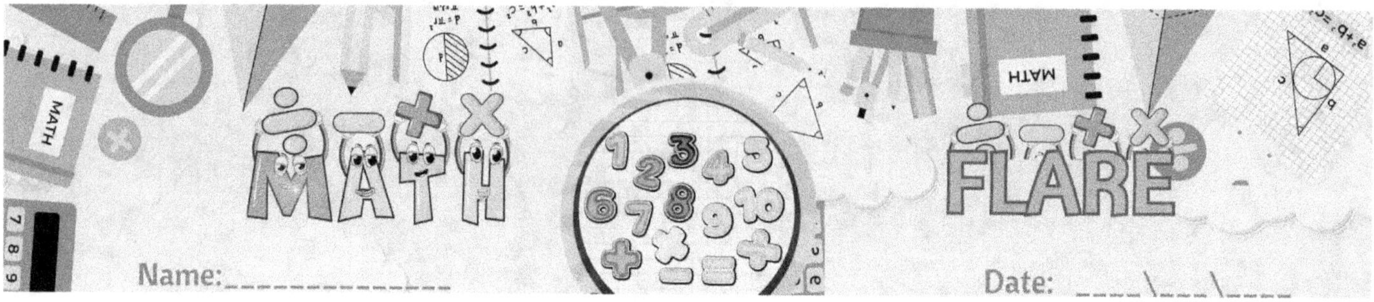
MATH
FLARE
Name:
Date:

29)

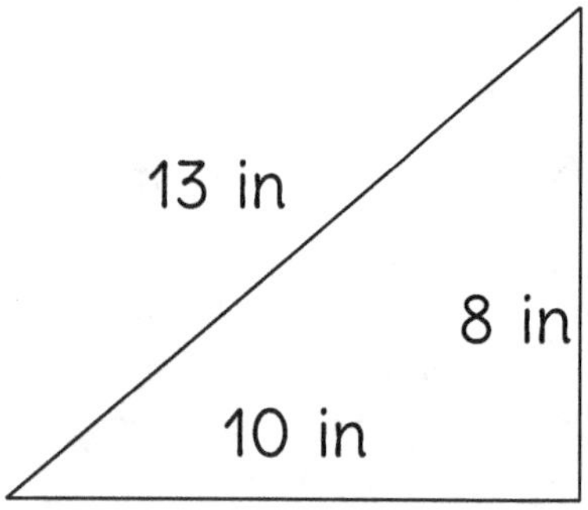
13 in
8 in
10 in

30)

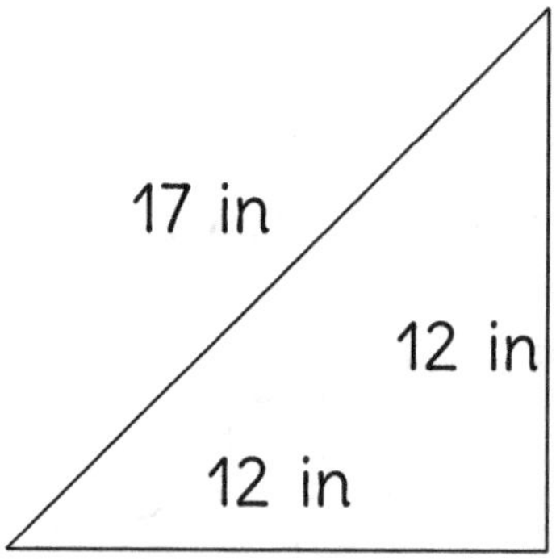
17 in
12 in
12 in

31)

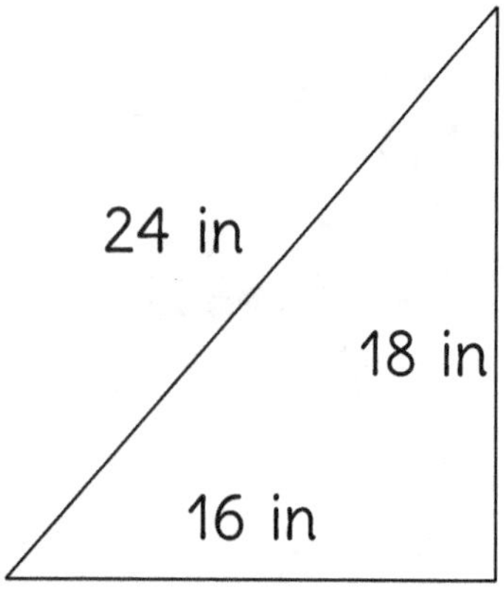
24 in
18 in
16 in

32)

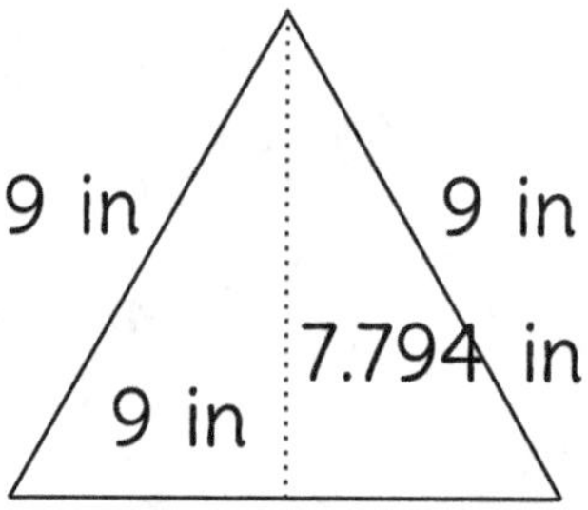
9 in
9 in
7.794 in
9 in

Name:_______________ Date: ___________

33)

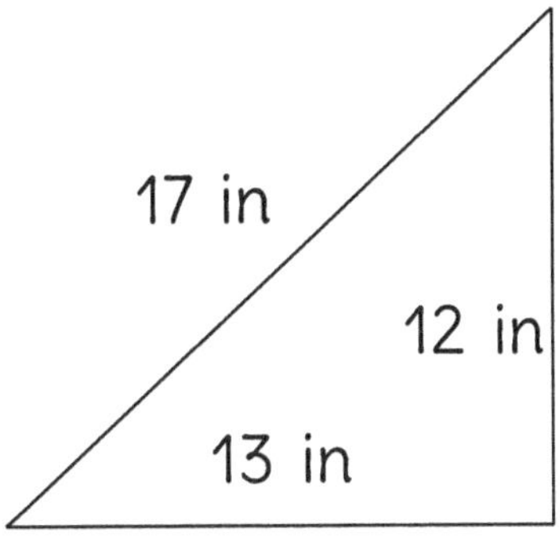

34)

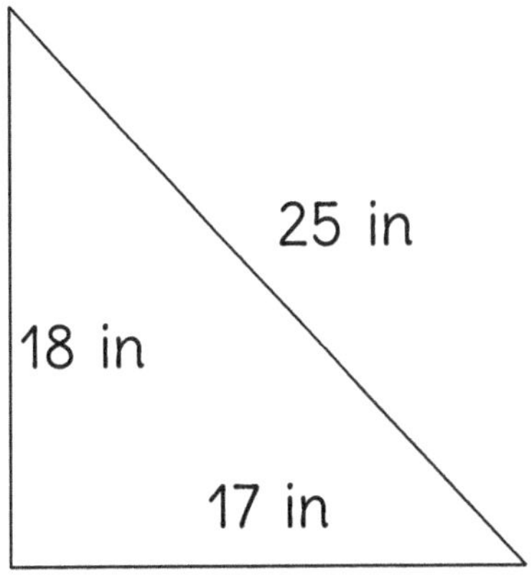

35)

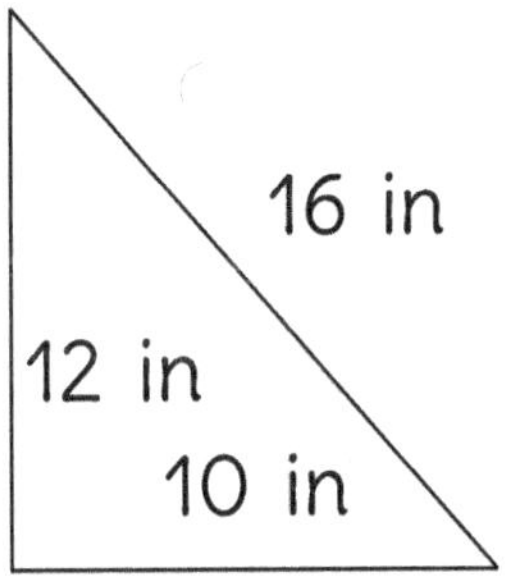

36)

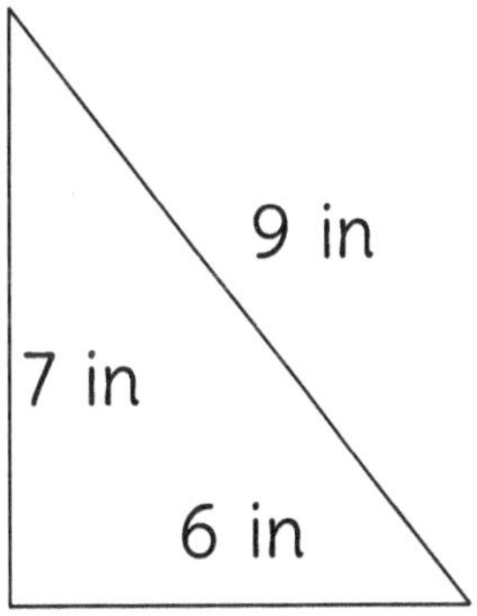

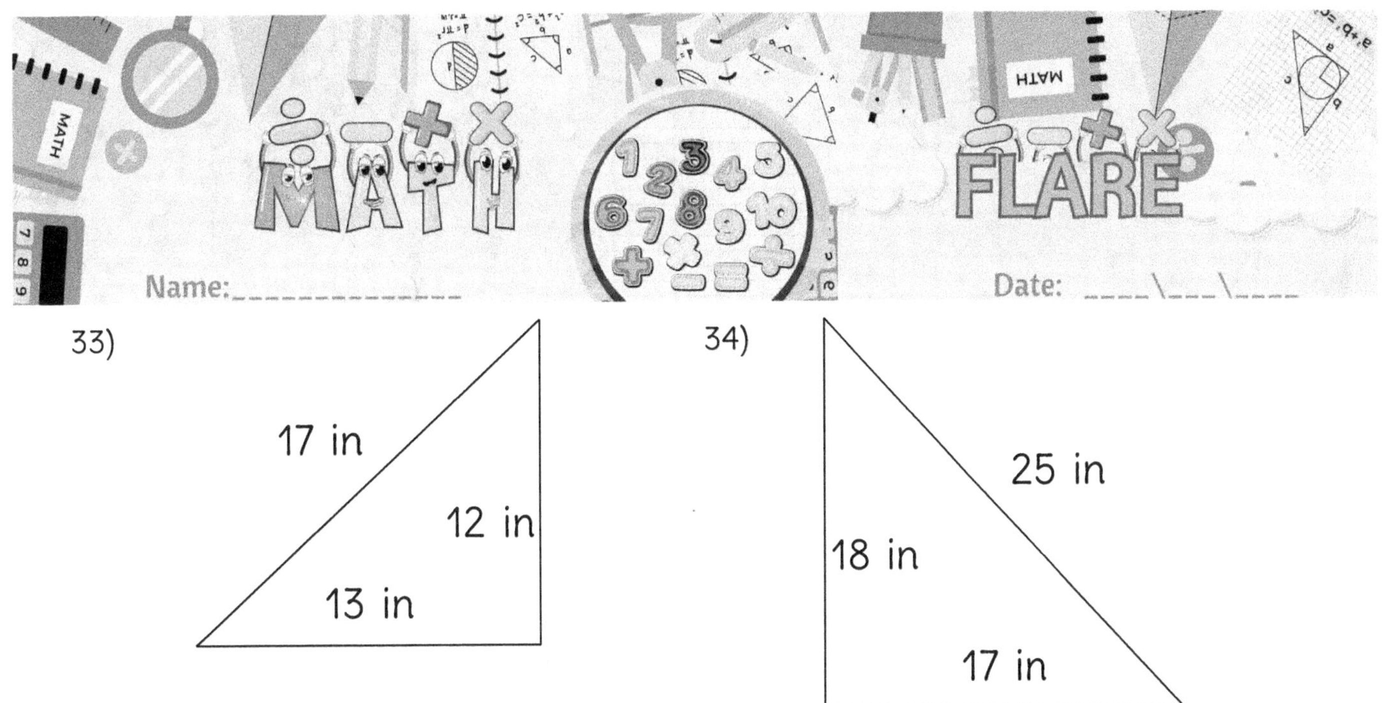

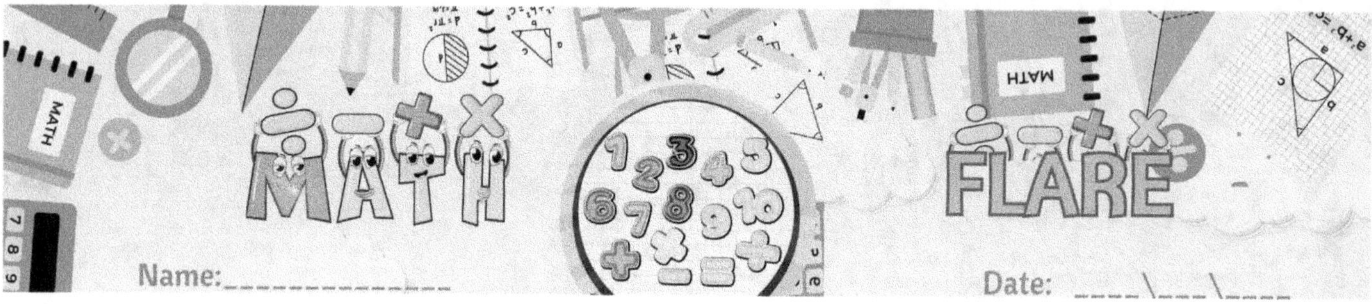
MATH
FLARE
Name:______________
Date: _________

37)

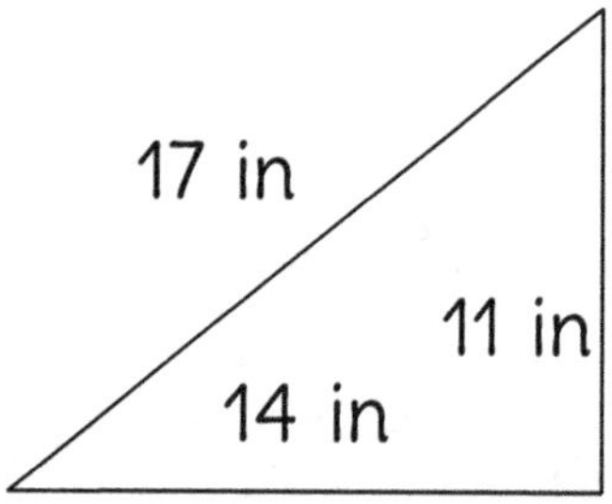
17 in
11 in
14 in

38)

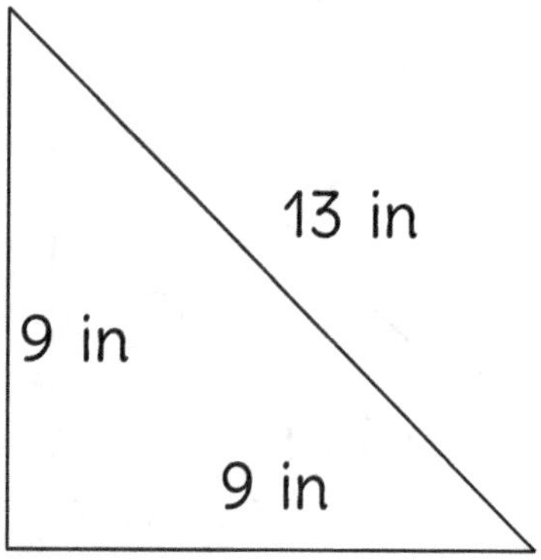
13 in
9 in
9 in

39)

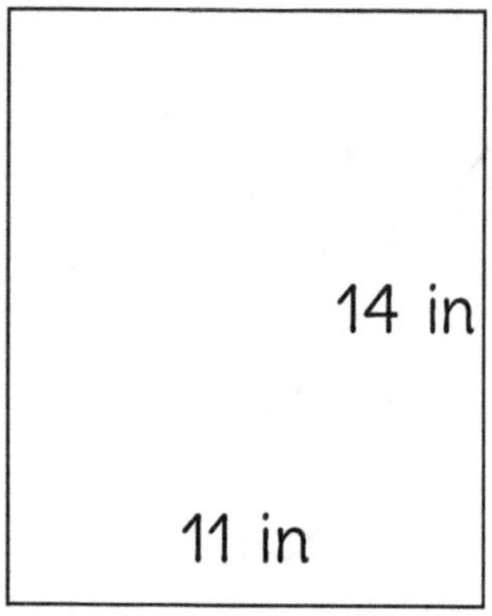
14 in
11 in

40)

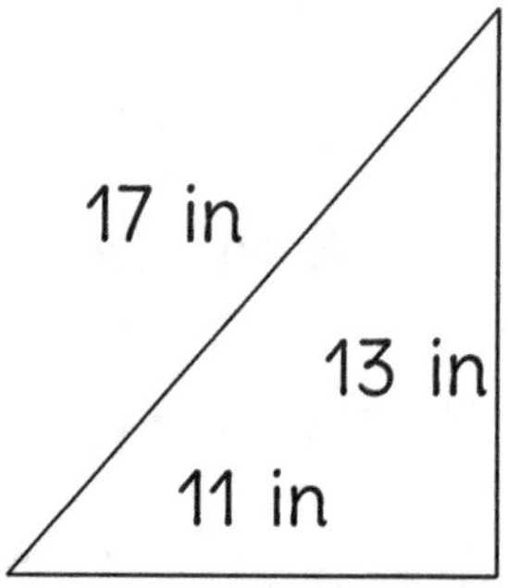
17 in
13 in
11 in

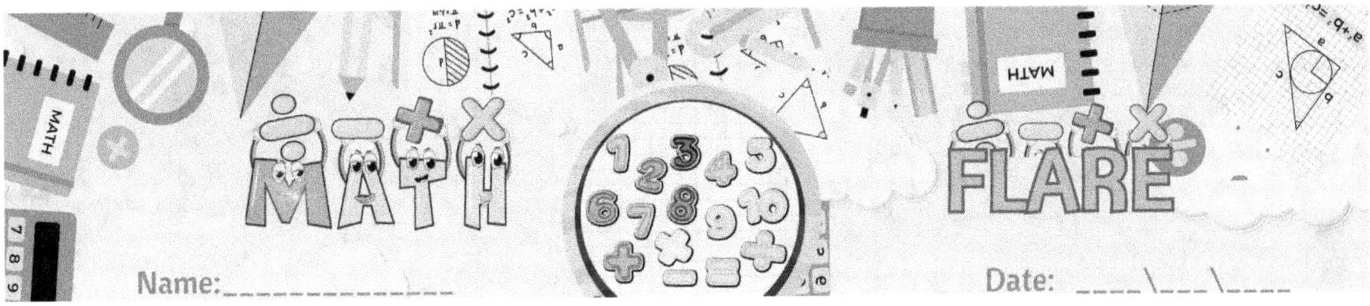
MATH
FLARE
Name:
Date:

41)

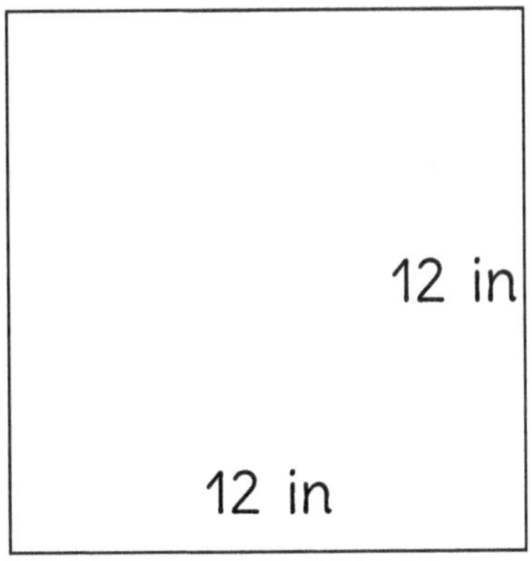
12 in
12 in

42)

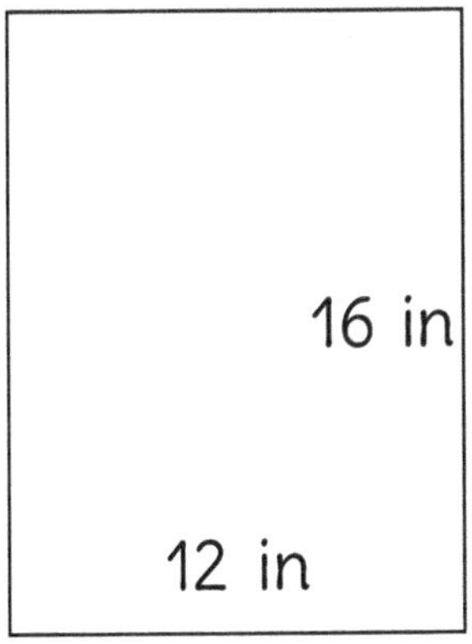
16 in
12 in

43)

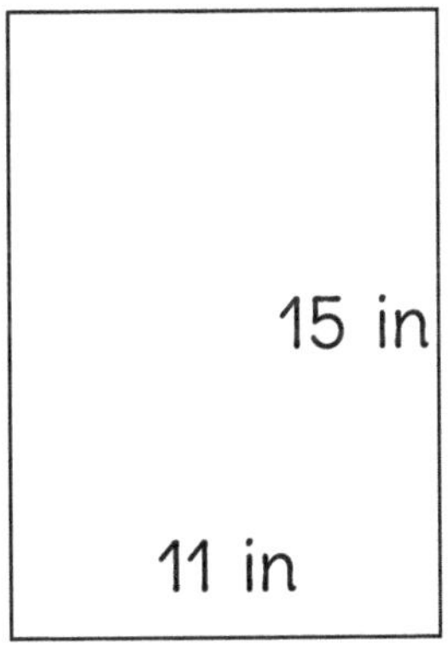
15 in
11 in

44)

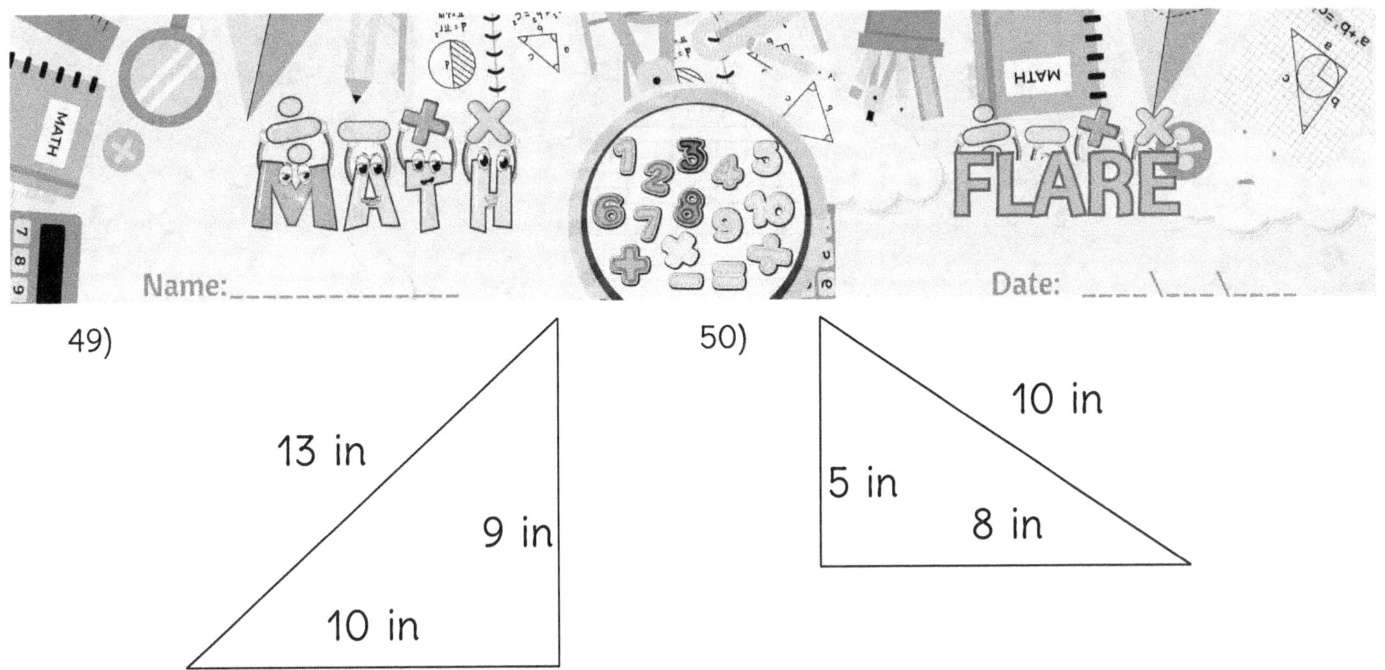

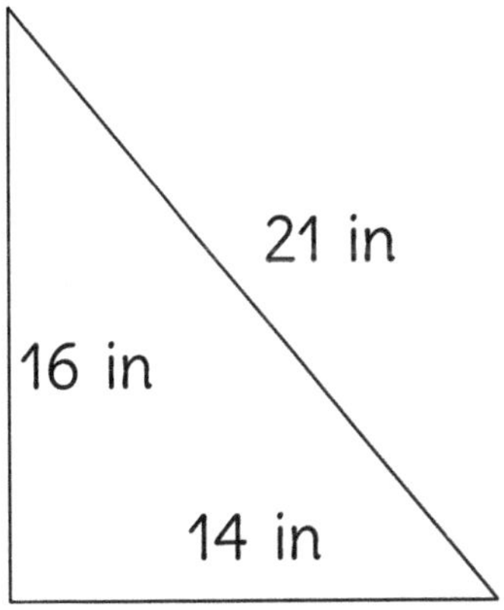
21 in
16 in
14 in

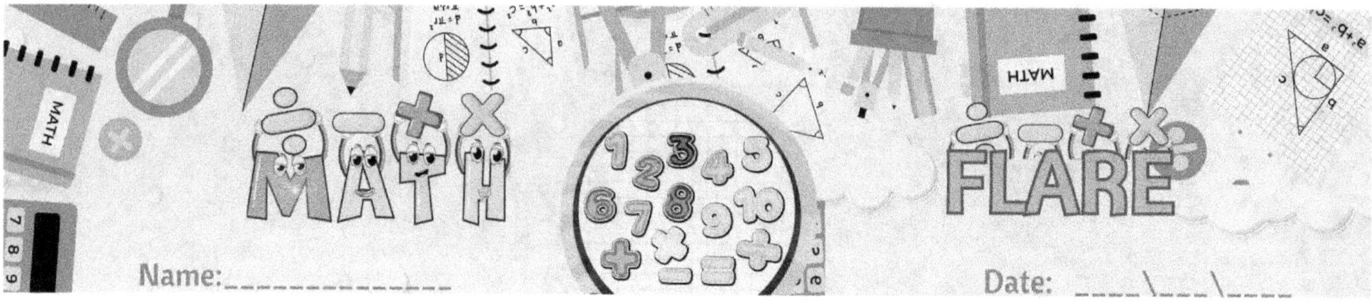

45)

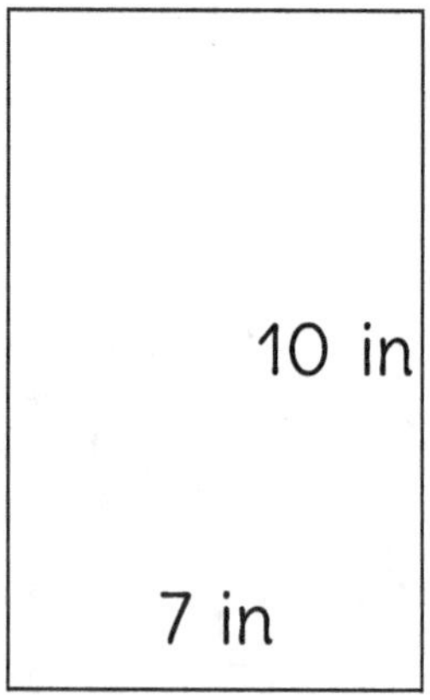

46)

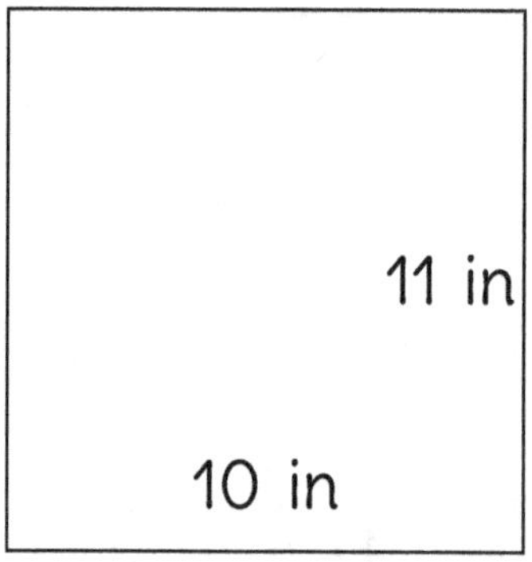

47)

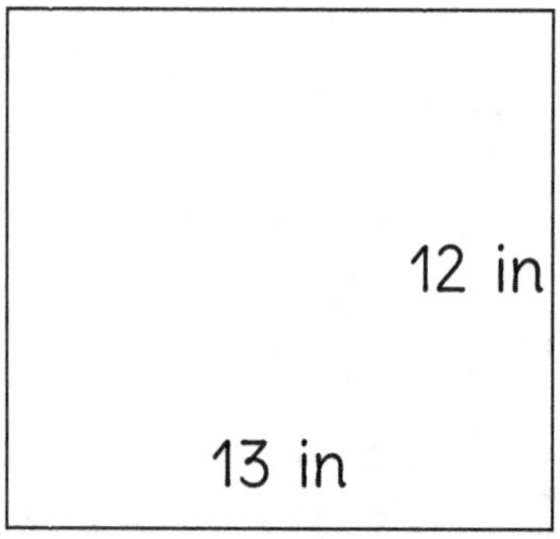

48)

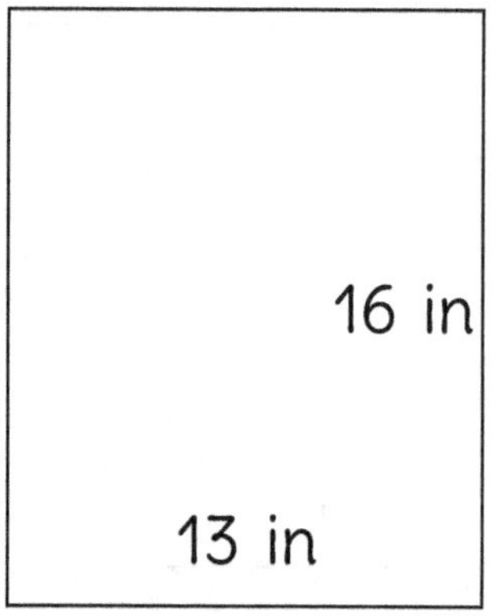

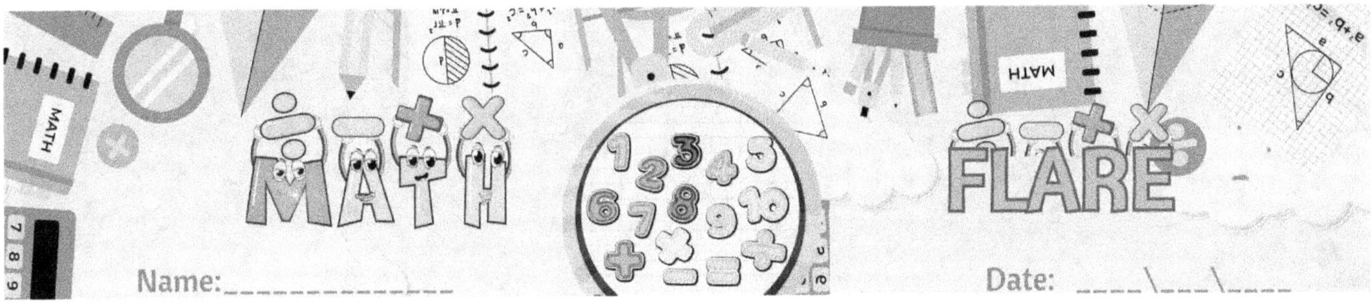
MATH
FLARE
Name:
Date: _________

49)

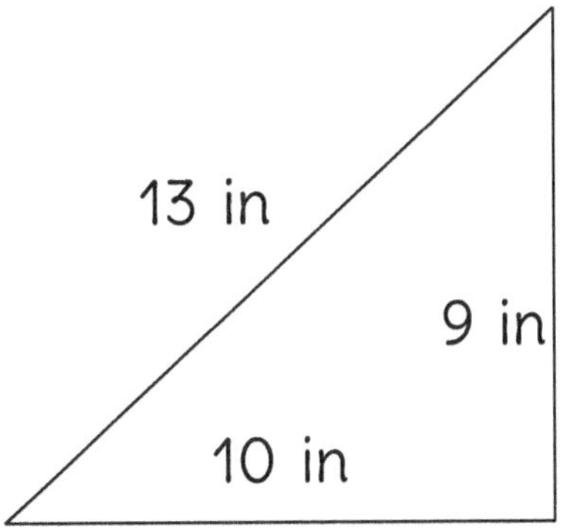
13 in
9 in
10 in

50)

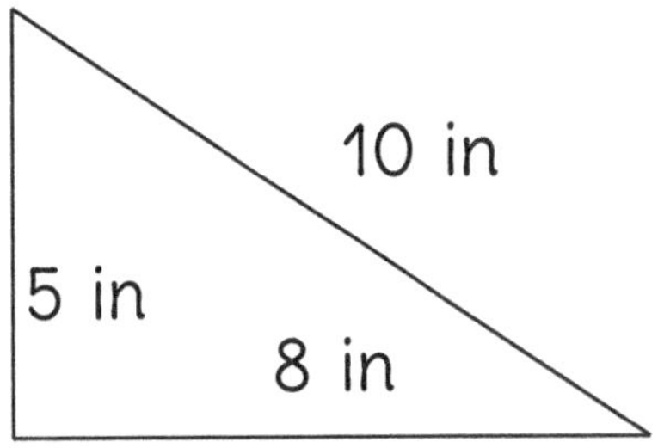
10 in
5 in
8 in

51)

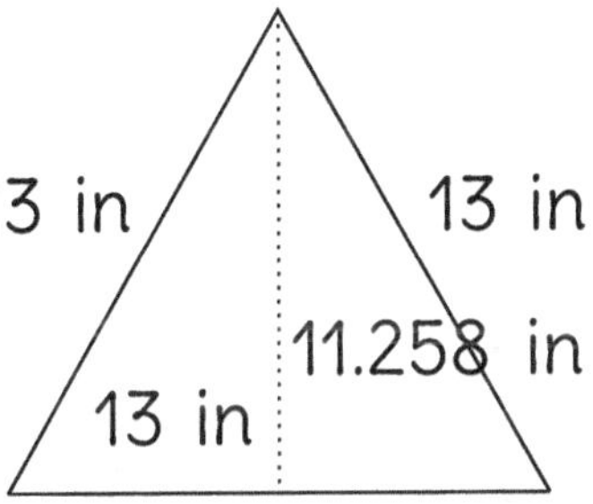
13 in
13 in
11.258 in
13 in

52)

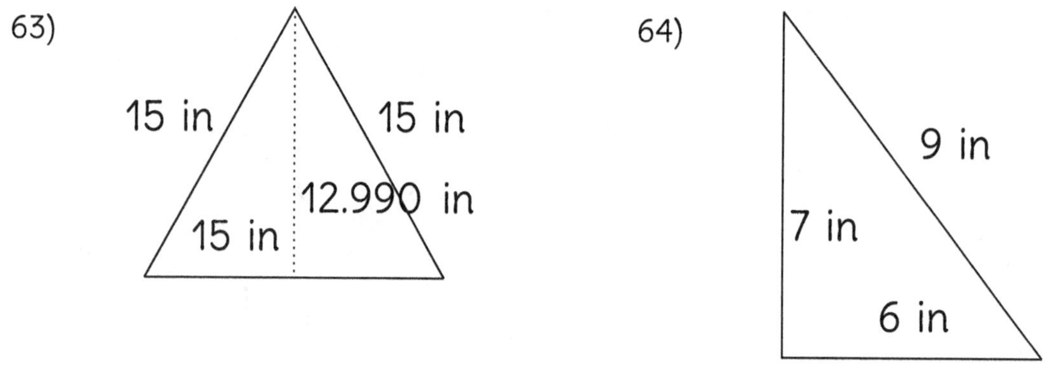

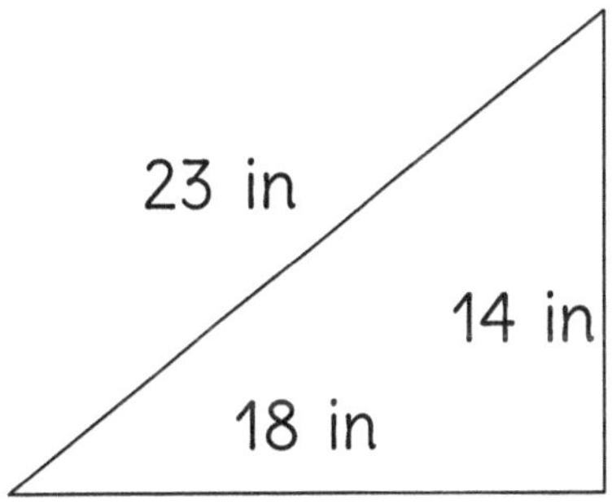
23 in
14 in
18 in

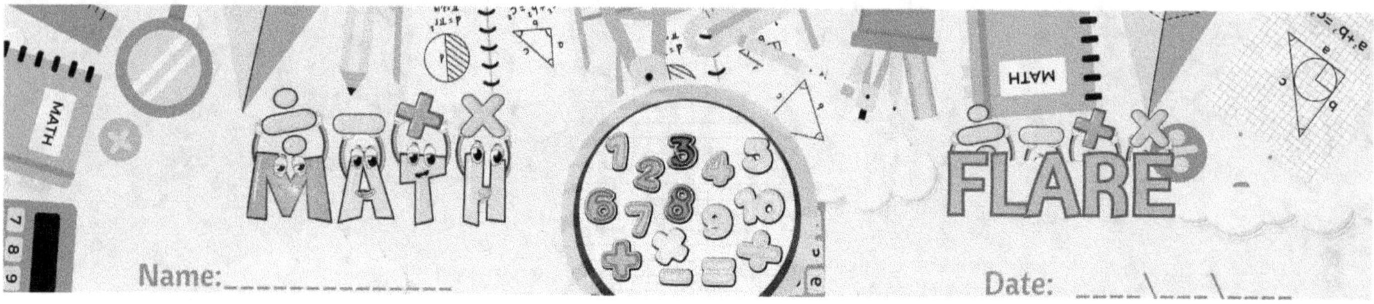
MATH
FLARE
Name:
Date:

53)

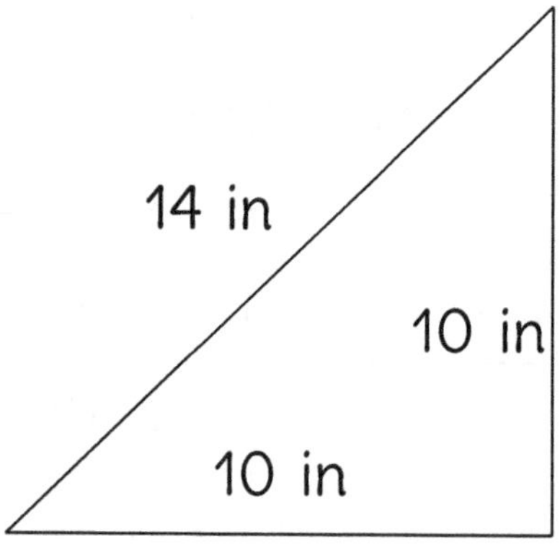
14 in
10 in
10 in

54)

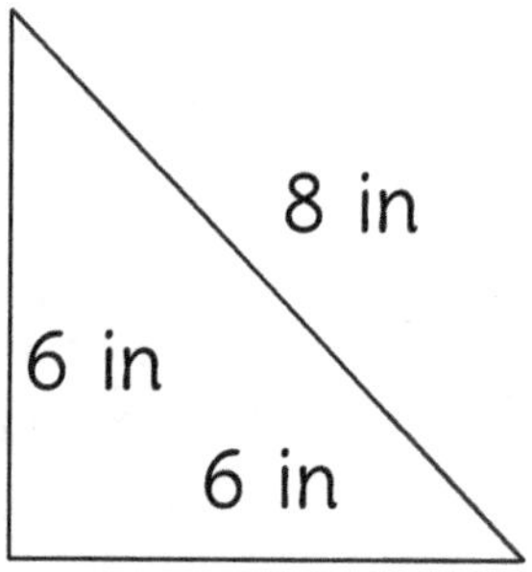
8 in
6 in
6 in

55)

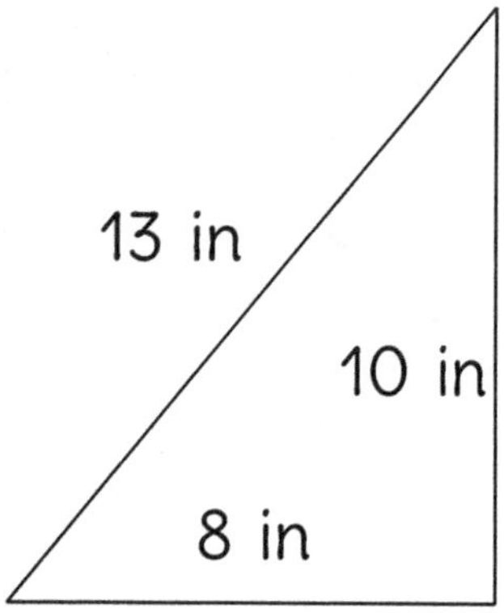
13 in
10 in
8 in

56)

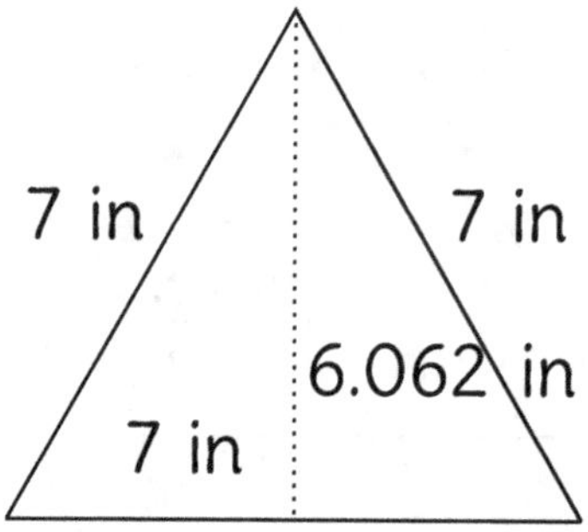
7 in
7 in
6.062 in
7 in

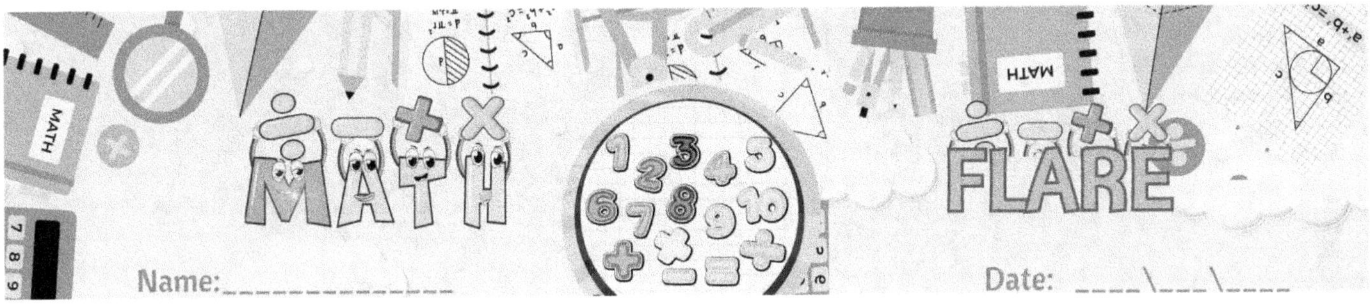
MATH
FLARE
Name:
Date:

57)

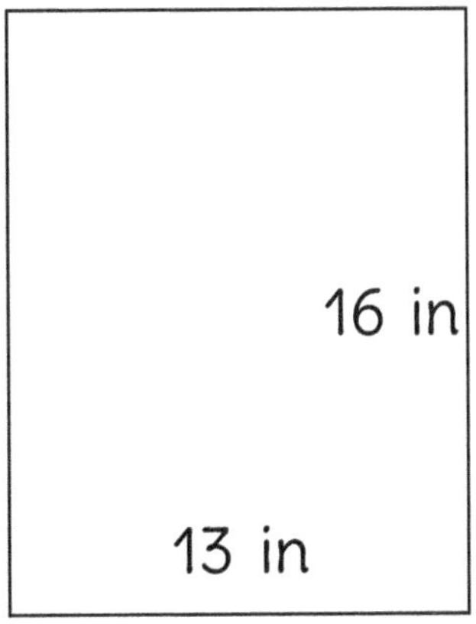
16 in
13 in

58)

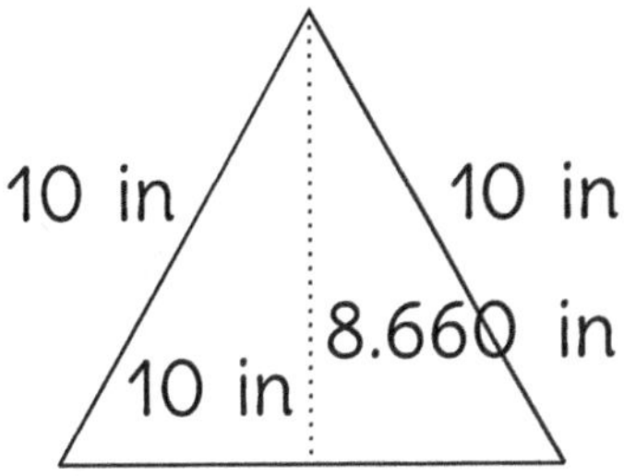
10 in
10 in
8.660 in
10 in

59)

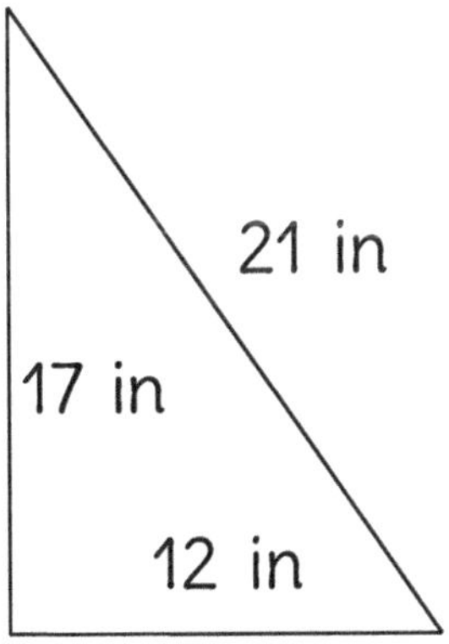
21 in
17 in
12 in

60)

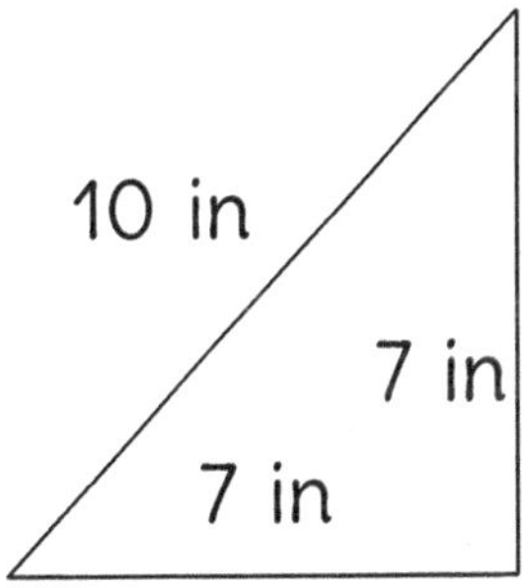
10 in
7 in
7 in

61)

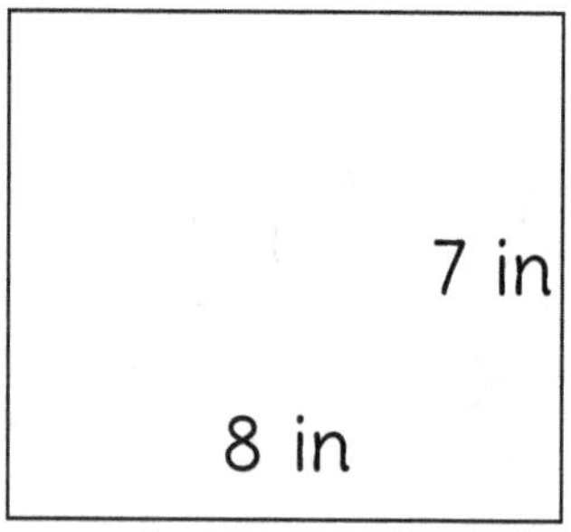

62)

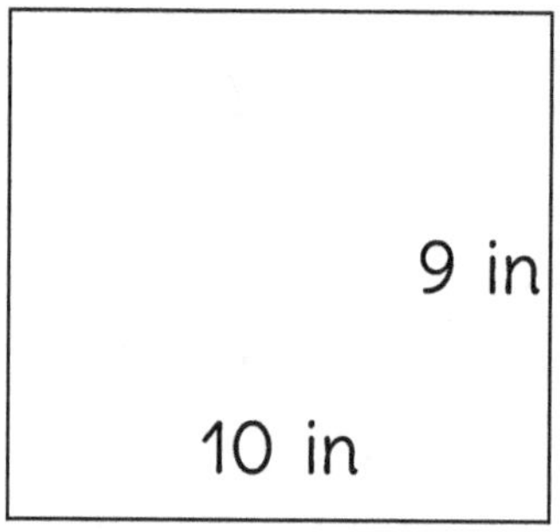

63)

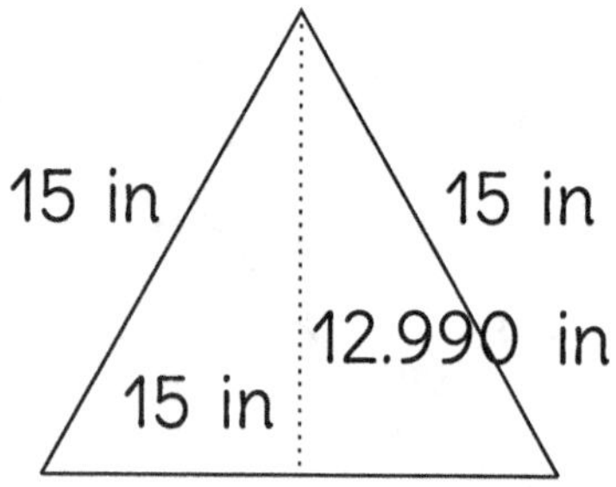

64)

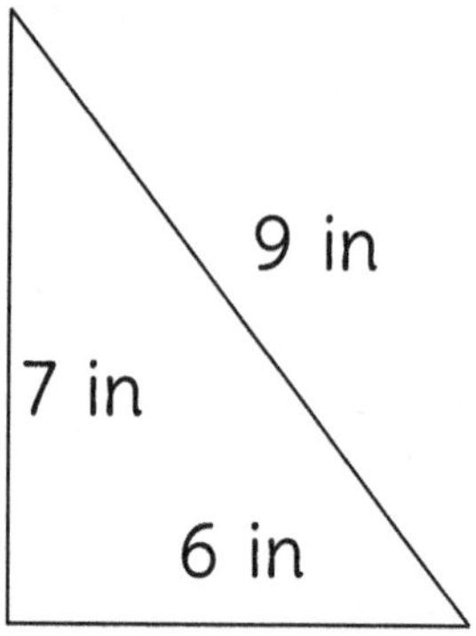

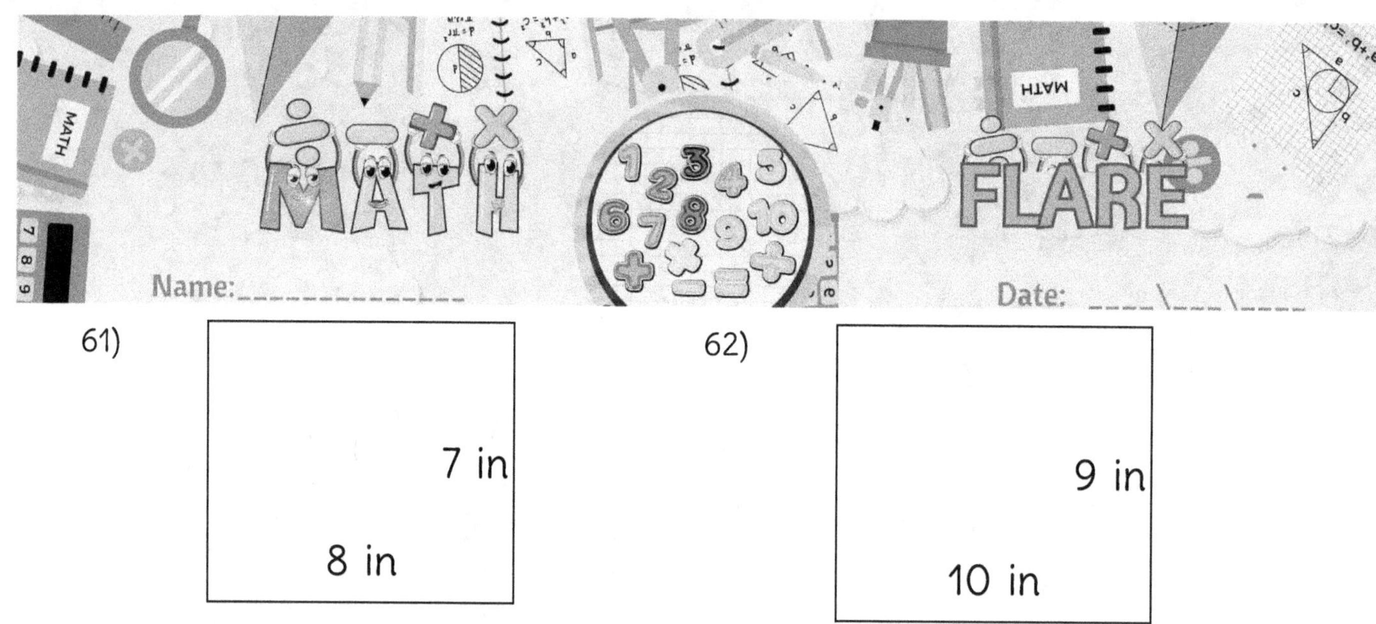

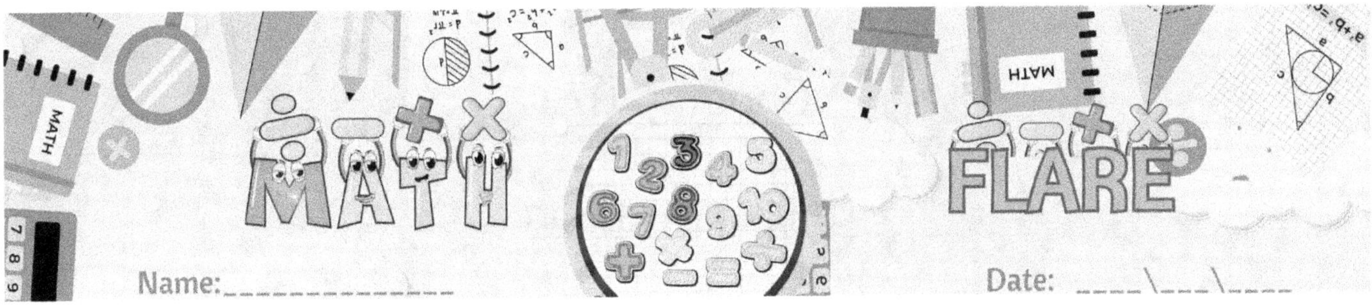
MATH
FLARE
Name:
Date:

65)

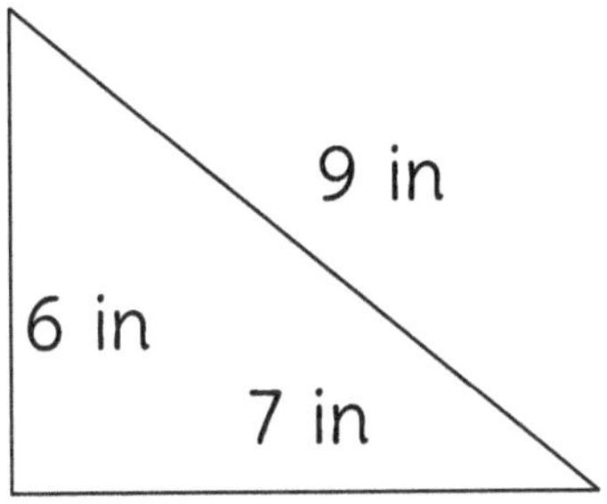
9 in
6 in
7 in

66)

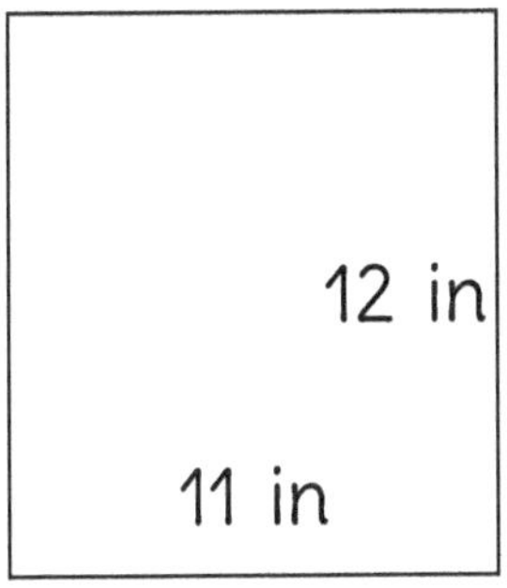
12 in
11 in

67)

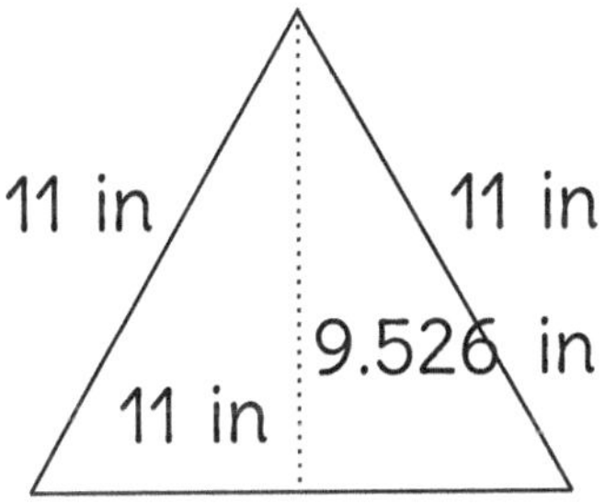
11 in
11 in
9.526 in
11 in

68)

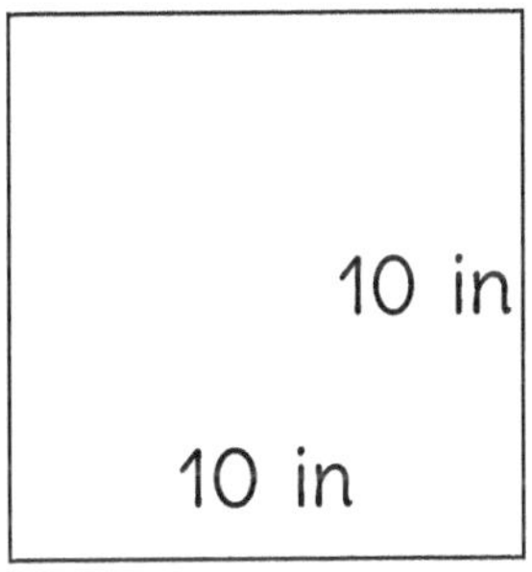
10 in
10 in

Chapter. 07

Unit Conversion

Metric Conversion
1 meter (m) = 100 centimeters (cm)
1 meter (m) = 1000 millimeters (mm)
1 kilometer (km) = 1000 meters (m)
1 hectare (ha) = 10000 square meters (m^2)
1 square meter (m^2) = 10000 square centimeters (cm^2)
1 cubic meter (m^3) = 1000 liters (L)

Weights and Measures
1 kilogram (kg) = 1000 grams (g)
1 liter (L) = 1000 milliliters (mL)
1 tonne (t) = 1000 kilograms (kg)
1 centimeter (cm) = 10 millimeters (mm)
1 gram (g) = 1000 milligrams (mg)
1 kilometer (km) = 100000 centimeters (cm)

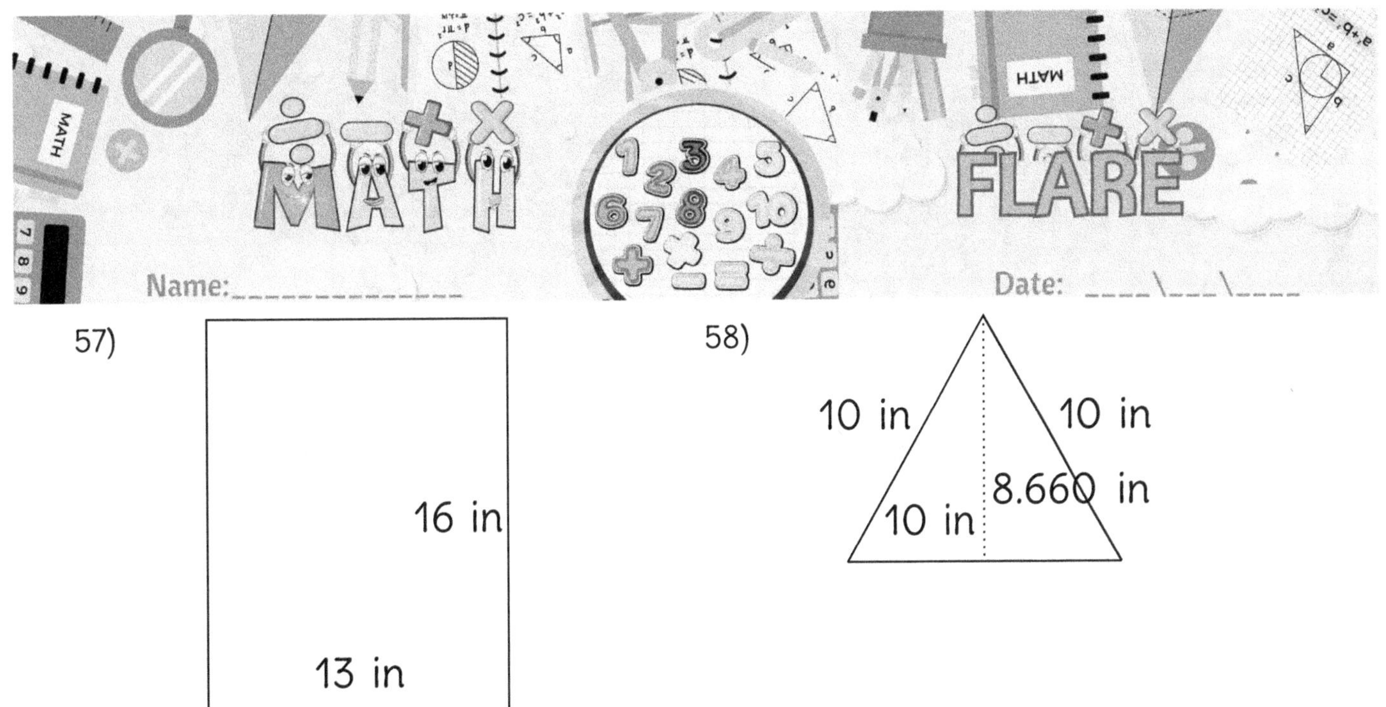

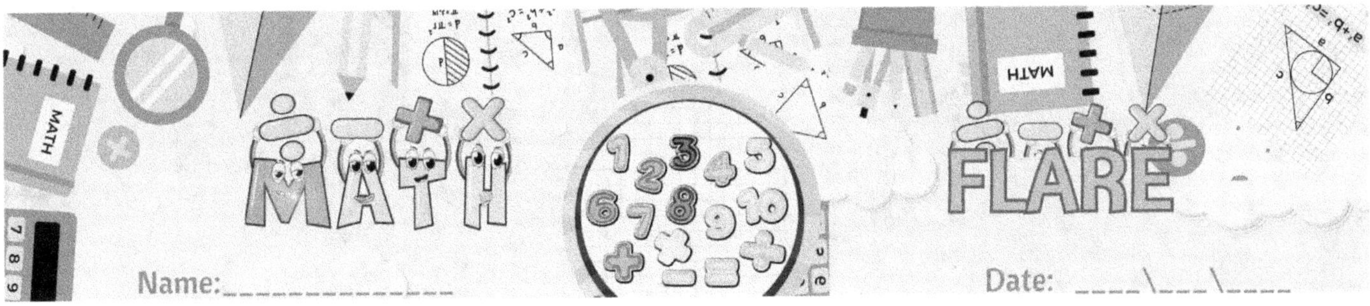

Metric Conversion

Convert the given measures.

1) 63 in = 1.600 m

2) 16 in = __________ m

3) 10 ft = __________ m

4) 97 ft = __________ m

5) 63 ft = __________ m

6) 55 ft = __________ m

7) 35 in = __________ m

8) 53 ft = __________ m

9) 96 ft = __________ m

10) 41 ft = __________ m

11) 33 in = __________ m

12) 24 in = __________ m

13) 62 in = __________ m

14) 66 in = __________ m

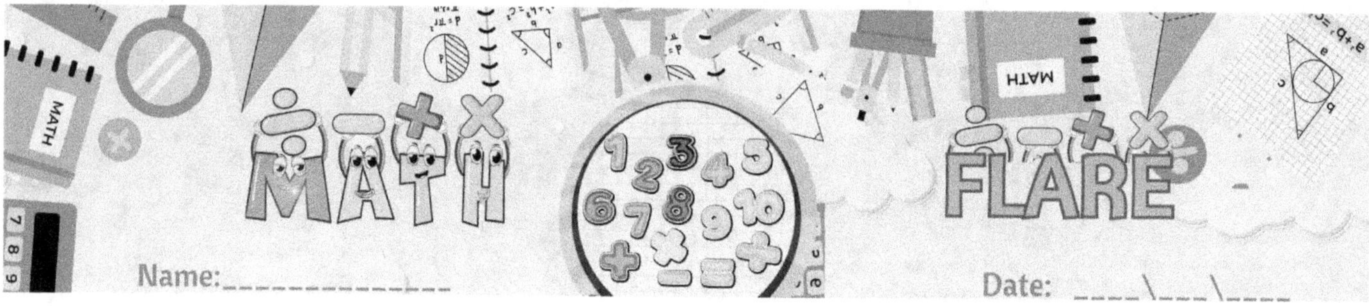

Name:______________ Date: __________

15) 41 in = ________________ m

16) 39 in = ________________ m

17) 60 in = ________________ m

18) 87 in = ________________ m

19) 42 in = ________________ m

20) 15 in = ________________ m

21) 63 in = ________________ m

22) 67 ft = ________________ m

23) 39 ft = ________________ m

24) 73 in = ________________ m

25) 23 ft = ________________ m

26) 55 ft = ________________ m

27) 50 in = ________________ m

28) 14 ft = ________________ m

29) 25 in = ________________ m

30) 68 ft = ________________ m

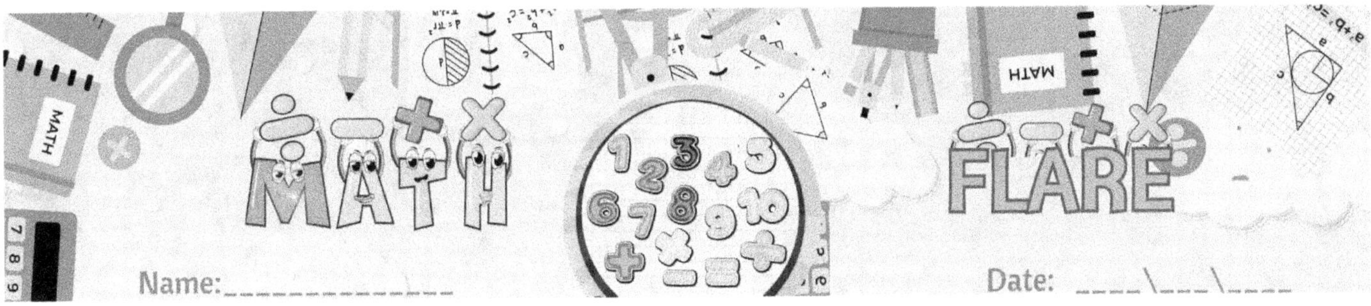

31) 15 ft = ______________ m

32) 24 ft = ______________ m

33) 22 in = ______________ m

34) 93 ft = ______________ m

35) 61 in = ______________ m

36) 55 ft = ______________ m

37) 39 ft = ______________ m

38) 97 in = ______________ m

39) 20 in = ______________ m

40) 13 ft = ______________ m

41) 28 in = ______________ m

42) 31 in = ______________ m

43) 80 ft = ______________ m

44) 71 in = ______________ m

45) 59 ft = ______________ m

46) 22 in = ______________ m

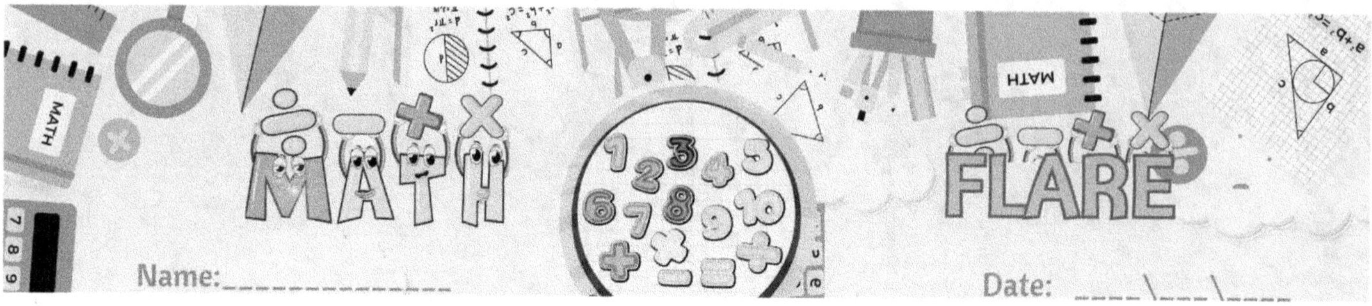

47) 11 in = ______________ m

48) 54 in = ______________ m

49) 76 ft = ______________ m

50) 61 ft = ______________ m

51) 91 ft = ______________ m

52) 58 ft = ______________ m

53) 69 in = ______________ m

54) 93 in = ______________ m

55) 67 in = ______________ m

56) 95 ft = ______________ m

57) 76 ft = ______________ m

58) 36 in = ______________ m

59) 83 ft = ______________ m

60) 18 ft = ______________ m

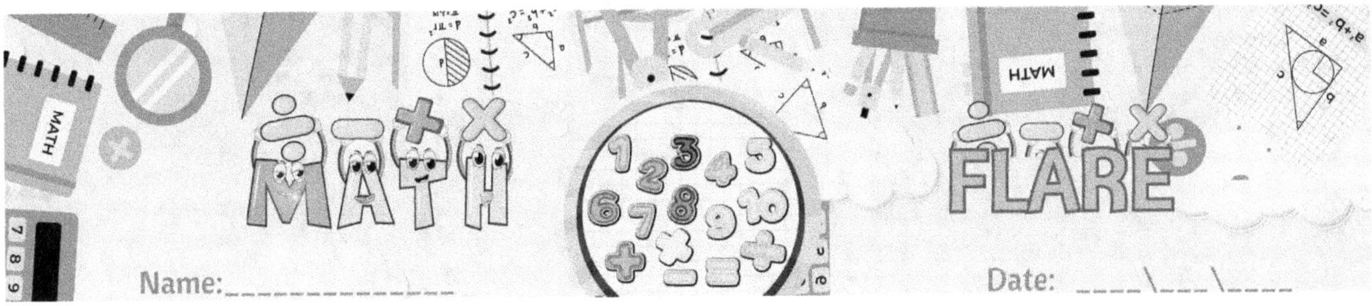

Metric Weights and Measures

Convert the given measures to new units.

1) 15 t = 15,000 kg

2) 31 t = ________ kg

3) 38 t = ________ kg

4) 38 cm = ________ km

5) 36 kg = ________ t

6) 19 g = ________ kg

7) 11 L = ________ mL

8) 67 cm = ________ m

9) 15 cm = ________ km

10) 85 t = ________ kg

11) 11 cm = ________ km

12) 62 m = ________ km

13) 77 km = ________ m

14) 40 cm = ________ km

Name:_______________ Date: __________

15) 86 kL = _______________ L

16) 43 t = _______________ kg

17) 86 km = _______________ m

18) 67 kL = _______________ mL

19) 24 km = _______________ cm

20) 11 kg = _______________ t

21) 53 m = _______________ km

22) 95 g = _______________ t

23) 37 t = _______________ kg

24) 63 mL = _______________ L

25) 76 kg = _______________ t

26) 56 cm = _______________ m

27) 54 km = _______________ cm

28) 29 mL = _______________ kL

29) 36 mL = _______________ L

30) 66 t = _______________ kg

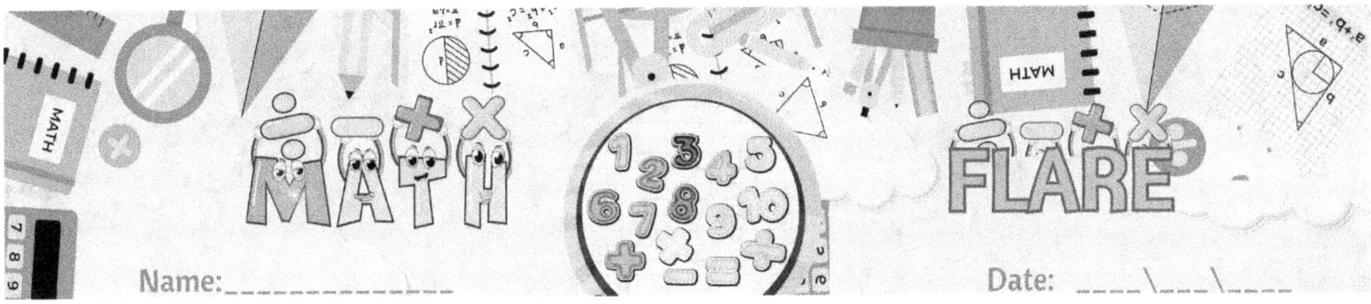

Name:______________ Date: ___________

31) 78 t = ______________ g

32) 12 km = ______________ cm

33) 23 mL = ______________ L

34) 12 cm = ______________ m

35) 97 t = ______________ g

36) 96 kg = ______________ t

37) 92 L = ______________ kL

38) 52 cm = ______________ km

39) 45 kL = ______________ L

40) 50 km = ______________ cm

41) 21 g = ______________ kg

42) 43 kg = ______________ t

43) 48 km = ______________ cm

44) 90 cm = ______________ m

45) 60 km = ______________ cm

46) 39 cm = ______________ m

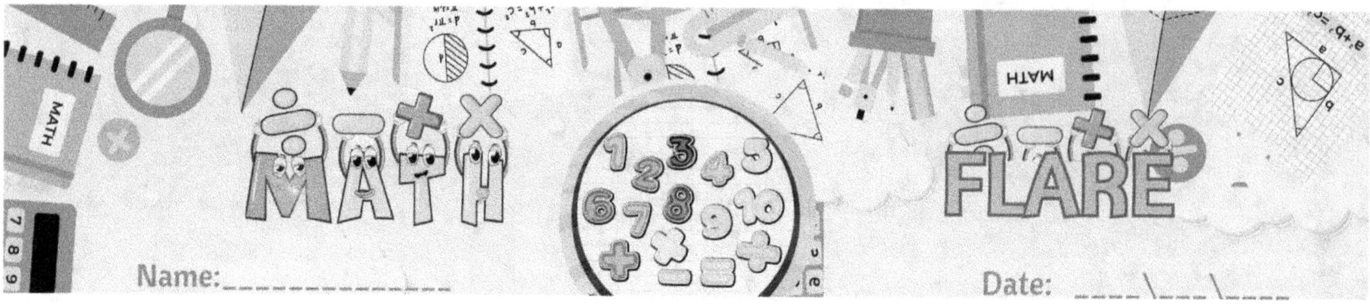

47) 80 kL = ____________ L

48) 40 km = ____________ m

49) 17 kL = ____________ L

50) 35 L = ____________ kL

51) 19 km = ____________ m

52) 19 L = ____________ mL

53) 22 km = ____________ m

54) 83 L = ____________ kL

55) 63 L = ____________ kL

56) 93 cm = ____________ m

57) 74 L = ____________ kL

58) 61 km = ____________ m

59) 78 t = ____________ kg

60) 64 g = ____________ kg

ANSWERS

Page 1: Addition with Regrouping

1. 16,111	2. 13,120	3. 14,642	4. 17,313	5. 13,310
6. 11,165	7. 13,330	8. 12,120	9. 14,124	10. 12,121
11. 12,386	12. 11,742	13. 12,142	14. 19,411	15. 11,340
16. 11,151	17. 12,172	18. 12,253	19. 12,122	20. 16,152
21. 12,410	22. 11,170	23. 12,140	24. 15,521	25. 12,421
26. 14,610	27. 11,310	28. 12,633	29. 13,113	30. 11,940
31. 18,120	32. 13,153	33. 12,224	34. 13,261	35. 12,262
36. 11,210	37. 11,311	38. 14,112	39. 19,110	40. 16,140
41. 17,333	42. 11,830	43. 14,110	44. 14,114	45. 11,110
46. 16,251	47. 11,140	48. 11,110	49. 11,522	50. 11,512
51. 11,642	52. 11,112	53. 13,310	54. 11,141	55. 11,320
56. 17,412	57. 15,130	58. 15,120	59. 14,340	60. 12,830
61. 11,450	62. 14,713	63. 11,121	64. 11,134	65. 16,111
66. 13,422	67. 11,311	68. 15,112	69. 11,244	70. 16,120
71. 16,120	72. 14,211	73. 11,565	74. 13,235	75. 11,270
76. 14,110	77. 14,785	78. 18,112	79. 15,111	80. 11,523
81. 14,691	82. 11,210	83. 11,114	84. 12,224	85. 13,218
86. 11,225	87. 18,712	88. 13,420	89. 11,131	90. 12,122
91. 14,820	92. 11,631	93. 12,220	94. 18,330	95. 13,233

96. 17,110	97. 15,753	98. 12,122	99. 13,310	100. 18,191

Page 6: Subtraction with Regrouping

1. 479	2. 852	3. 1,589	4. 378	5. 807	6. 4,885
7. 2,779	8. 682	9. 3,545	10. 879	11. 1,487	12. 2,887
13. 571	14. 2,856	15. 2,871	16. 887	17. 1,577	18. 385
19. 2,454	20. 665	21. 788	22. 4,889	23. 4,873	24. 784
25. 5,046	26. 2,862	27. 146	28. 4,482	29. 658	30. 884
31. 786	32. 88	33. 5,481	34. 2,884	35. 1,888	36. 2,881
37. 69	38. 5,883	39. 1,762	40. 4,875	41. 2,878	42. 1,889
43. 3,882	44. 586	45. 765	46. 1,887	47. 736	48. 5,825
49. 544	50. 663	51. 1,681	52. 2,886	53. 3,587	54. 581
55. 782	56. 2,889	57. 1,275	58. 655	59. 111	60. 617
61. 2,785	62. 1,761	63. 6,808	64. 388	65. 888	66. 1,876
67. 665	68. 5,789	69. 5,829	70. 3,365	71. 1,674	72. 1,467
73. 2,388	74. 2,781	75. 85	76. 3,881	77. 817	78. 1,576
79. 1,645	80. 1,581	81. 4,857	82. 486	83. 729	84. 1,633
85. 846	86. 5,123	87. 354	88. 5,883	89. 1,436	90. 1,388
91. 4,753	92. 2,854	93. 456	94. 2,387	95. 881	96. 3,331
97. 542	98. 1,672	99. 724	100. 1,888		

Page 11: Addition Word Problems

1. 92	2. 72	3. 40	4. 71	5. 56	6. 138	7. 114

8. 48	9. 158	10. 81	11. 162	12. 110	13. 106	14. 171
15. 112	16. 114	17. 185	18. 106	19. 158	20. 155	21. 120
22. 162	23. 89	24. 102	25. 84	26. 96	27. 132	28. 76
29. 92	30. 53					

Page 19: Subtraction Word Problems

1. 9	2. 8	3. 44	4. 18	5. 2	6. 60	7. 17	8. 26
9. 0	10. 43	11. 15	12. 7	13. 88	14. 0	15. 39	16. 4
17. 25	18. 19	19. 19	20. 5	21. 61	22. 10	23. 45	24. 23
25. 74	26. 2	27. 49	28. 33	29. 63	30. 1		

Page 27: Multiplication: 2 x 1

1. 30	2. 33	3. 40	4. 66	5. 46	6. 42	7. 64	8. 88
9. 69	10. 90	11. 50	12. 80	13. 88	14. 60	15. 86	16. 82
17. 84	18. 63	19. 44	20. 48	21. 20	22. 54	23. 99	24. 48
25. 80	26. 41	27. 93	28. 75	29. 96	30. 28	31. 57	32. 49
33. 61	34. 14	35. 40	36. 36	37. 84	38. 24	39. 22	40. 55

Page 29: Multiplication: 3 x 1

1. 808	2. 844	3. 309	4. 360	5. 882	6. 426	7. 806
8. 363	9. 711	10. 246	11. 550	12. 680	13. 682	14. 658
15. 480	16. 226	17. 843	18. 532	19. 500	20. 666	21. 595
22. 555	23. 639	24. 662	25. 448	26. 600	27. 630	28. 404
29. 633	30. 204	31. 484	32. 693	33. 505	34. 848	35. 888

36. 903 37. 824 38. 666 39. 963 40. 699

Page 31: Multiplication: 4 x 1

1. 4,808 2. 3,330 3. 4,888 4. 2,446 5. 4,440 6. 6,448
7. 4,044 8. 8,840 9. 2,266 10. 4,404 11. 6,333 12. 8,888
13. 4,444 14. 3,900 15. 3,096 16. 5,505 17. 8,000 18. 8,620
19. 4,260 20. 6,093 21. 8,264 22. 6,210 23. 6,693 24. 6,096
25. 6,206 26. 4,088 27. 6,339 28. 2,860 29. 9,939 30. 9,216
31. 4,640 32. 6,906 33. 2,013 34. 6,688 35. 4,048 36. 2,286
37. 4,402 38. 4,046 39. 9,390 40. 6,003

Page 33: Multiplication (double Digit)

1. 7,138 2. 1,239 3. 8,463 4. 1,323 5. 874 6. 378
7. 1,525 8. 2,464 9. 2,294 10. 2,352 11. 861 12. 3,825
13. 4,656 14. 2,255 15. 1,456 16. 1,209 17. 4,788 18. 1,449
19. 588 20. 2,607 21. 2,816 22. 768 23. 308 24. 540
25. 3,808 26. 3,481 27. 272 28. 1,296 29. 1,400 30. 1,860
31. 4,402 32. 2,170 33. 864 34. 4,268 35. 900 36. 6,966
37. 1,479 38. 6,004 39. 4,088 40. 1,755 41. 2,173 42. 6,106
43. 4,784 44. 6,072

Page 36: Multiplication (3 Digit)

1. 501,216 2. 51,625 3. 150,543 4. 195,908 5. 413,658
6. 746,630 7. 392,675 8. 310,660 9. 534,996 10. 157,746

11. 155,078	12. 123,087	13. 311,742	14. 160,402	15. 503,792
16. 651,406	17. 260,793	18. 366,800	19. 72,967	20. 120,910
21. 20,664	22. 264,546	23. 395,166	24. 729,118	25. 303,009
26. 31,496	27. 54,168	28. 100,345	29. 491,283	30. 631,734
31. 838,850	32. 744,513	33. 236,544	34. 697,300	35. 111,108
36. 141,940	37. 322,172	38. 256,959	39. 639,195	40. 52,947
41. 536,924	42. 245,690	43. 357,332	44. 160,881	

Page 39: Basic Division

1. 4	2. 5	3. 9	4. 2	5. 6	6. 2	7. 8	8. 2	9. 9
10. 5	11. 2	12. 10	13. 4	14. 4	15. 6	16. 5	17. 8	18. 2
19. 5	20. 4	21. 3	22. 3	23. 7	24. 1	25. 3	26. 9	27. 9
28. 9	29. 8	30. 3	31. 5	32. 7	33. 9	34. 7	35. 4	36. 10
37. 2	38. 8	39. 3	40. 4	41. 4	42. 5	43. 1	44. 6	45. 8
46. 2	47. 10	48. 1	49. 6	50. 5	51. 1	52. 6	53. 7	54. 3
55. 4	56. 2							

Page 42: Long Division (within 100)

1. 42	2. 52	3. 63	4. 47	5. 16	6. 96	7. 54	8. 99
9. 30	10. 96	11. 79	12. 41	13. 14	14. 13	15. 96	16. 92
17. 16	18. 62	19. 69	20. 11	21. 13	22. 32	23. 46	24. 21
25. 77	26. 40	27. 43	28. 22	29. 86	30. 44	31. 33	32. 35
33. 95	34. 41	35. 74	36. 24	37. 31	38. 74	39. 54	40. 51

41. 54 42. 69 43. 2 44. 88

Page 45: Long Division (within 1000)

1. 477	2. 160	3. 480	4. 37	5. 842	6. 263	7. 391
8. 133	9. 957	10. 394	11. 609	12. 990	13. 413	14. 634
15. 393	16. 515	17. 554	18. 176	19. 547	20. 675	21. 372
22. 769	23. 212	24. 601	25. 462	26. 883	27. 66	28. 652
29. 170	30. 769	31. 317	32. 848	33. 413	34. 210	35. 938
36. 139	37. 595	38. 438	39. 477	40. 746	41. 729	42. 285
43. 230	44. 874	45. 821				

Page 49: Multiplication Word Problems

1. 72	2. 38	3. 221	4. 176	5. 90	6. 44	7. 28
8. 108	9. 154	10. 20	11. 10	12. 168	13. 154	14. 70
15. 80	16. 55	17. 32	18. 112	19. 21	20. 196	21. 196
22. 289	23. 110	24. 80	25. 91	26. 96	27. 80	28. 18
29. 60	30. 190					

Page 57: Division Word Problems

1. 35	2. 20	3. 89	4. 20	5. 96	6. 23
7. 72	8. 32	9. 44	10. 4	11. 71	12. 33
13. 74	14. 92	15. 81	16. 88	17. 2	18. 46
19. 65	20. 30	21. 31	22. 2	23. 24	24. 20
25. 1,530	26. 34	27. 90	28. 86	29. 49	30. 38

Page 66: Adding Decimals

1. 1,225.89	2. 923.16	3. 1,578.65	4. 1,144.98	5. 1,732.44
6. 1,164.58	7. 317.90	8. 846.23	9. 1,305.89	10. 1,062.19
11. 1,545.66	12. 1,250.88	13. 897.19	14. 1,330.78	15. 922.41
16. 663.98	17. 1,128.16	18. 1,098.42	19. 945.94	20. 1,578.45
21. 1,481.31	22. 741.95	23. 880.54	24. 1,297.18	25. 1,455.63
26. 809.53	27. 1,632.00			

Page 68: Subtracting Decimals

1. 118.24	2. 154.37	3. 219.24	4. 428.12	5. 139.35
6. 371.51	7. 87.66	8. 123.83	9. 768.85	10. 614.62
11. 98.44	12. 46.35	13. 168.01	14. 178.35	15. 59.29
16. 254.93	17. 57.37	18. 465.20	19. 91.66	20. 146.15
21. 603.84	22. 282.65	23. 316.80	24. 367.76	25. 434.30
26. 460.02	27. 31.06			

Page 70: Place Value

1. 5 tenths	2. 7 hundreds
3. 1 hundred thousand	4. 8 ones
5. 8 ones	6. 9 tens
7. 3 thousands	8. 9 tens
9. 8 tenths	10. 0 tens
11. 0 hundredths	12. 6 thousands

13. 7 hundreds
14. 0 ones
15. 2 tens
16. 8 tens
17. 4 hundredths
18. 5 hundreds
19. 7 ones
20. 0 ones
21. 8 ten thousands
22. 6 ones
23. 1 hundred
24. 8 thousands
25. 4 thousands
26. 8 hundred thousands
27. 8 hundredths
28. 9 hundredths
29. 7 tenths
30. 5 thousandths
31. 0 tenths
32. 3 ten thousands
33. 2 tenths
34. 8 thousands
35. 3 hundreds
36. 2 ones
37. 5 hundreds
38. 5 thousands
39. 0 thousands
40. 4 ones
41. 0 hundreds
42. 4 ones
43. 4 hundredths
44. 7 ten thousands
45. 6 tenths
46. 8 thousands
47. 2 hundredths
48. 2 ten thousands
49. 1 ten thousand
50. 8 thousands
51. 8 hundredths
52. 0 tenths
53. 3 ones
54. 1 ten

55. 9 ones
56. 4 ones
57. 3 ones
58. 6 ones
59. 3 tenths
60. 7 tenths
61. 1 one
62. 2 thousandths

Page 78: Place Value: Expanded Notation

1. 891,479
2. 576.587
3. 375.801
4. 888.887
5. 977,292
6. 452.283
7. 992.784
8. 7,461.88
9. 1,230.90
10. 632,787
11. 757,872
12. 8,181.43
13. 293,130
14. 741,927
15. 125,968
16. 706.354
17. 4,822.71
18. 52,208.7
19. 723.889
20. 317.757
21. 95,678.1
22. 76,526.1
23. 48,292.8
24. 7,429.76
25. 8,673.13
26. 6,380.69
27. 1,186.98
28. 400.879
29. 20,070.9
30. 25,567.5
31. 70,736.1
32. 989,751
33. 7,814.20
34. 198.078
35. 397,763
36. 4,116.97
37. 9,019.55
38. 4,345.28
39. 690.876
40. 6,495.67
41. 91,639.7
42. 96,491.8
43. 3,043.79
44. 190,000
45. 78,142.3
46. 718,966
47. 950.065
48. 10,628.1
49. 9,232.31
50. 699.848
51. 59,770.2
52. 422.259
53. 31,021.4
54. 18,520.9
55. 9,312.83
56. 22,621.8
57. 19,365.9
58. 63,282.3
59. 1,215.75
60. 43,922.3
61. 43,358.5

Page 85: Place Value: Expanded Notation

1. 691,905	2. 645,479	3. 8,674.14	4. 925.424
5. 768,120	6. 13,672.3	7. 195.052	8. 4,441.64
9. 71,426.9	10. 804,397	11. 1,477.43	12. 83,121.0
13. 17,432.2	14. 401,359	15. 9,918.61	16. 56,088.2
17. 392,928	18. 9,615.53	19. 248.347	20. 68,800.3
21. 112,418	22. 47,764.7	23. 5,008.60	24. 657,972
25. 385.103	26. 77,953.7	27. 6,962.10	28. 26,679.4
29. 271,545	30. 31,803.8	31. 36,913.2	32. 41,295.4
33. 351,654	34. 31,598.2	35. 324,492	36. 41,944.0
37. 43,696.4	38. 26,457.4	39. 113,302	40. 6,822.43
41. 85,501.3	42. 662,116	43. 3,089.62	44. 8,954.50
45. 5,499.59	46. 591.048	47. 235.892	48. 783.850
49. 93,942.0	50. 665,334	51. 800,731	52. 671.269
53. 873.227	54. 751,218	55. 421.167	56. 3,142.58
57. 2,446.19	58. 30,944.2	59. 640,322	

Page 95: Place Value: Expanded Notation

1. 9 hundreds + 8 tens + 8 ones + 5 tenths + 8 hundredths + 2 thousandths
2. 4 hundreds + 4 tens + 5 tenths + 1 hundredth + 1 thousandth
3. 9 hundred thousands + 2 ten thousands + 8 thousands + 2 hundreds + 5 tens + 7 ones

4. 2 hundred thousands + 7 ten thousands + 2 thousands + 6 hundreds + 1 ten + 8 ones
5. 4 ten thousands + 9 thousands + 6 hundreds + 2 tens + 3 ones + 2 tenths
6. 5 hundred thousands + 3 ten thousands + 5 thousands + 2 hundreds + 6 tens + 5 ones
7. 7 hundreds + 3 tens + 4 ones + 7 tenths + 8 hundredths + 8 thousandths
8. 5 thousands + 7 hundreds + 9 tens + 5 ones + 5 tenths + 6 hundredths
9. 8 hundred thousands + 5 ten thousands + 8 thousands + 3 hundreds + 3 tens + 9 ones
10. 1 thousand + 7 hundreds + 6 tens + 8 ones + 6 tenths + 6 hundredths
11. 6 ten thousands + 7 thousands + 2 hundreds + 4 tens + 2 ones + 1 tenth
12. 2 hundreds + 2 tens + 3 ones + 9 tenths + 1 hundredth + 8 thousandths
13. 2 thousands + 2 hundreds + 8 tens + 3 ones + 5 tenths + 3 hundredths
14. 9 hundreds + 4 tens + 8 ones + 2 tenths + 5 hundredths + 1 thousandth
15. 5 thousands + 6 hundreds + 6 tens + 1 one + 2 hundredths
16. 8 hundred thousands + 3 ten thousands + 2 thousands + 9 hundreds + 8 tens + 9 ones
17. 4 hundred thousands + 5 ten thousands + 3 hundreds + 1 one
18. 2 hundred thousands + 6 ten thousands + 8 thousands + 6 hundreds + 8 tens + 5 ones
19. 6 hundreds + 5 ones + 4 tenths + 8 thousandths
20. 2 ten thousands + 8 hundreds + 1 one + 2 tenths
21. 7 hundreds + 9 tens + 4 ones + 5 hundredths + 4 thousandths

22. 6 ten thousands + 4 thousands + 3 hundreds + 6 tens + 4 ones + 5 tenths
23. 9 hundred thousands + 1 ten thousand + 2 thousands + 3 hundreds + 6 tens
24. 3 thousands + 2 hundreds + 7 tens + 3 ones + 7 tenths + 3 hundredths
25. 6 hundred thousands + 6 thousands + 2 hundreds + 1 ten
26. 5 ten thousands + 1 thousand + 7 hundreds + 3 tens + 6 tenths
27. 6 hundreds + 9 tens + 7 ones + 8 tenths + 6 hundredths + 2 thousandths
28. 5 hundreds + 3 tens + 9 ones + 7 tenths + 2 hundredths + 6 thousandths
29. 6 ten thousands + 4 tens + 3 ones + 5 tenths
30. 8 ten thousands + 9 thousands + 4 hundreds + 8 tens + 1 one + 4 tenths
31. 1 hundred + 1 ten + 2 tenths + 3 hundredths + 4 thousandths
32. 2 hundreds + 7 tens + 4 ones + 8 tenths + 2 hundredths + 1 thousandth
33. 2 ten thousands + 2 thousands + 7 hundreds + 5 tens + 2 ones + 1 tenth
34. 6 ten thousands + 2 thousands + 4 hundreds + 2 tens + 5 ones + 2 tenths
35. 1 hundred + 2 tens + 4 ones + 7 tenths + 1 hundredth + 9 thousandths
36. 3 hundreds + 4 tens + 1 one + 7 tenths + 3 hundredths + 2 thousandths
37. 9 thousands + 2 hundreds + 6 tens + 7 ones + 5 tenths + 5 hundredths
38. 4 thousands + 8 hundreds + 9 tens + 4 ones + 9 tenths + 8 hundredths
39. 8 hundreds + 1 ten + 2 ones + 7 tenths + 2 hundredths + 9 thousandths
40. 4 thousands + 6 hundreds + 1 one + 8 tenths + 5 hundredths
41. 8 thousands + 1 hundred + 5 tens + 1 one + 7 tenths + 1 hundredth

42. 1 hundred + 1 ten + 1 one + 4 tenths + 9 hundredths + 2 thousandths

43. 3 hundreds + 7 tens + 7 ones + 5 tenths + 5 hundredths + 2 thousandths

44. 7 hundred thousands + 6 thousands + 9 hundreds + 8 tens + 3 ones

45. 3 hundred thousands + 6 ten thousands + 6 thousands + 9 hundreds + 9 tens + 9 ones

46. 5 ten thousands + 4 thousands + 1 hundred + 4 tens + 1 one + 6 tenths

47. 6 ten thousands + 7 thousands + 2 hundreds + 3 tens + 7 ones + 7 tenths

48. 7 ten thousands + 2 thousands + 3 hundreds + 1 one + 8 tenths

49. 4 hundred thousands + 7 thousands + 1 hundred + 2 tens + 5 ones

50. 9 hundreds + 1 ten + 8 ones + 2 tenths + 2 hundredths + 8 thousandths

51. 9 hundreds + 7 tens + 8 tenths + 6 hundredths + 6 thousandths

52. 1 thousand + 4 hundreds + 5 tens + 5 ones + 7 tenths + 4 hundredths

53. 6 hundreds + 3 tens + 9 ones + 2 tenths + 1 hundredth

54. 2 hundred thousands + 1 thousand + 4 hundreds + 3 tens

55. 8 hundred thousands + 4 ten thousands + 6 thousands + 2 hundreds + 6 tens + 7 ones

56. 4 hundreds + 4 tens + 4 ones + 9 tenths + 3 hundredths + 7 thousandths

57. 5 ten thousands + 2 thousands + 8 hundreds + 1 ten + 5 ones + 1 tenth

58. 7 thousands + 8 ones + 8 tenths + 4 hundredths

59. 6 thousands + 6 hundreds + 6 tens + 4 ones + 7 hundredths

Page 105: Fraction Identification

1. 5/9 2. 3/5 3. 6/9 4. 1/8 5. 10/12 6. 5/6 7. 1/2

8. 4/5	9. 6/10	10. 2/3	11. 2/4	12. 5/7	13. 9/12	14. 1/3
15. 2/5	16. 1/9	17. 1/7	18. 4/8	19. 3/6	20. 7/10	21. 4/9
22. 7/8	23. 1/10	24. 5/12	25. 1/5	26. 4/10	27. 8/12	28. 3/4
29. 6/8	30. 2/7	31. 3/8	32. 2/9	33. 6/12	34. 4/7	35. 8/10
36. 1/4	37. 4/6	38. 8/9	39. 2/8			

Page 110: Compare the Fractions

1. >	2. >	3. >	4. <	5. <	6. <	7. >	8. =	9. >	10. >
11. <	12. <	13. <	14. >	15. <	16. >	17. <	18. >	19. <	20. >
21. <	22. >	23. <	24. >	25. <	26. >	27. <	28. <	29. <	30. >
31. >	32. <	33. >	34. <	35. >	36. <	37. >	38. >	39. >	40. =

Page 113: Convert Fractions to Decimals

1. 0.52	2. 0.5	3. 0.12	4. 0.94	5. 0.19	6. 0.52
7. 0.59	8. 0.62	9. 0.82	10. 0.94	11. 0.7	12. 0.17
13. 0.67	14. 0.87	15. 0.44	16. 0.25	17. 0.32	18. 0.81
19. 0.4	20. 0.45	21. 0.5	22. 0.48	23. 0.79	24. 0.93
25. 0.15	26. 0.2	27. 0.24	28. 0.29	29. 0.11	30. 0.30
31. 0.32	32. 0.04	33. 0.86	34. 0.84		

Page 115: Fractions Addition (Common Denominator)

1. 3/5	2. 3/4	3. 1/3	4. 11/12	5. 1/2	6. 2/5
7. 6/7	8. 8/9	9. 1/1	10. 7/8	11. 2/3	12. 3/11
13. 4/5	14. 3/4	15. 5/11	16. 3/7	17. 9/10	18. 5/6

19. 8/9	20. 1/2	21. 6/7	22. 9/11	23. 5/12	24. 4/5
25. 4/5	26. 5/8	27. 11/12	28. 2/3	29. 4/5	30. 7/11
31. 3/4	32. 3/10	33. 7/9	34. 2/3	35. 1/2	36. 7/10
37. 2/3	38. 4/11	39. 3/8	40. 6/7	41. 3/5	42. 4/5
43. 9/11	44. 8/9	45. 7/12	46. 3/4	47. 1/5	48. 1/4
49. 5/6	50. 2/3	51. 9/11	52. 5/6	53. 2/7	54. 6/7
55. 1/2	56. 10/11	57. 5/8	58. 4/9	59. 5/6	60. 9/10
61. 1/3	62. 5/9	63. 9/11	64. 5/7	65. 3/5	66. 6/11
67. 8/9	68. 1/2	69. 5/8	70. 2/3	71. 5/9	72. 3/8
73. 2/3	74. 5/7	75. 4/5	76. 10/11	77. 2/3	78. 3/10
79. 7/8	80. 7/12	81. 1/2	82. 4/5		

Page 121: Fractions Subtraction: (Common Denominator)

1. 5/11	2. 1/2	3. 2/5	4. 1/4	5. 1/3	6. 1/4	7. 7/10
8. 1/6	9. 2/7	10. 1/4	11. 3/5	12. 1/4	13. 1/7	14. 1/3
15. 1/5	16. 4/9	17. 2/3	18. 4/11	19. 2/11	20. 1/7	21. 1/6
22. 1/9	23. 1/4	24. 5/8	25. 1/5	26. 2/5	27. 1/8	28. 1/10
29. 1/8	30. 1/6	31. 1/7	32. 1/9	33. 7/12	34. 1/2	35. 3/11
36. 1/5	37. 2/9	38. 1/7	39. 1/3	40. 2/9	41. 3/7	42. 1/3
43. 1/8	44. 1/3	45. 1/10	46. 1/12	47. 1/9	48. 1/5	49. 1/11
50. 1/4	51. 1/8	52. 2/5	53. 3/7	54. 5/9	55. 6/11	56. 1/2
57. 1/5	58. 5/6	59. 1/3	60. 1/5	61. 5/11	62. 2/7	63. 1/12

64. 1/6	65. 2/5	66. 1/11	67. 1/8	68. 1/2	69. 4/9	70. 1/4
71. 1/11	72. 2/9	73. 3/10	74. 1/12	75. 1/6	76. 2/11	77. 3/7
78. 1/3	79. 5/11	80. 1/12	81. 1/2	82. 5/9		

Page 128: Area and Perimeter: Rectangles and Triangles

1. P=24 A=27.71	2. P=18 A=15.59	3. P=47 A=97.5
4. P=32 A=45	5. P=43 A=78	6. P=36 A=62.35
7. P=52 A=165	8. P=51 A=112.5	9. P=48 A=110.85
10. P=54 A=140.29	11. P=18 A=15.59	12. P=45 A=84
13. P=46 A=91	14. P=39 A=73.18	15. P=29 A=35
16. P=53 A=120	17. P=29 A=36	18. P=32 A=45
19. P=30 A=56	20. P=25 A=28	21. P=46 A=91
22. P=22 A=30	23. P=27 A=35.07	24. P=58 A=144.5
25. P=49 A=105	26. P=18 A=15.59	27. P=42 A=84.87
28. P=36 A=62.35	29. P=31 A=40	30. P=41 A=72
31. P=58 A=144	32. P=27 A=35.07	33. P=42 A=78
34. P=60 A=153	35. P=38 A=60	36. P=22 A=21
37. P=42 A=77	38. P=31 A=40.5	39. P=50 A=154
40. P=41 A=71.5	41. P=48 A=144	42. P=56 A=192
43. P=52 A=165	44. P=51 A=112	45. P=34 A=70
46. P=42 A=110	47. P=50 A=156	48. P=58 A=208
49. P=32 A=45	50. P=23 A=20	51. P=39 A=73.18

52. P=55 A=126	53. P=34 A=50	54. P=20 A=18
55. P=31 A=40	56. P=21 A=21.22	57. P=58 A=208
58. P=30 A=43.3	59. P=50 A=102	60. P=24 A=24.5
61. P=30 A=56	62. P=38 A=90	63. P=45 A=97.42
64. P=22 A=21	65. P=22 A=21	66. P=46 A=132
67. P=33 A=52.39	68. P=40 A=100	

Page 145: Metric Conversion

1. 1.600	2. 0.406	3. 3.048	4. 29.566	5. 19.202
6. 16.764	7. 0.889	8. 16.154	9. 29.261	10. 12.497
11. 0.838	12. 0.610	13. 1.575	14. 1.676	15. 1.041
16. 0.991	17. 1.524	18. 2.210	19. 1.067	20. 0.381
21. 1.600	22. 20.422	23. 11.887	24. 1.854	25. 7.010
26. 16.764	27. 1.270	28. 4.267	29. 0.635	30. 20.726
31. 4.572	32. 7.315	33. 0.559	34. 28.346	35. 1.549
36. 16.764	37. 11.887	38. 2.464	39. 0.508	40. 3.962
41. 0.711	42. 0.787	43. 24.384	44. 1.803	45. 17.983
46. 0.559	47. 0.279	48. 1.372	49. 23.165	50. 18.593
51. 27.737	52. 17.678	53. 1.753	54. 2.362	55. 1.702
56. 28.956	57. 23.165	58. 0.914	59. 25.298	60. 5.486

Page 149: Metric Weights and Measures

1. 15,000	2. 31,000	3. 38,000	4. 0.00038

5. 0.036	6. 0.019	7. 11,000	8. 0.67
9. 0.00015	10. 85,000	11. 0.00011	12. 0.062
13. 77,000	14. 0.00040	15. 86,000	16. 43,000
17. 86,000	18. 67,000,000	19. 2,400,000	20. 0.011
21. 0.053	22. 0.000095	23. 37,000	24. 0.063
25. 0.076	26. 0.56	27. 5,400,000	28. 0.000029
29. 0.036	30. 66,000	31. 78,000,000	32. 1,200,000
33. 0.023	34. 0.12	35. 97,000,000	36. 0.096
37. 0.092	38. 0.00052	39. 45,000	40. 5,000,000
41. 0.021	42. 0.043	43. 4,800,000	44. 0.90
45. 6,000,000	46. 0.39	47. 80,000	48. 40,000
49. 17,000	50. 0.035	51. 19,000	52. 19,000
53. 22,000	54. 0.083	55. 0.063	56. 0.93
57. 0.074	58. 61,000	59. 78,000	60. 0.064

www.ingramcontent.com/pod-product-compliance
Lightning Source LLC
Chambersburg PA
CBHW080937120726
48003CB00011B/3192
* 9 7 9 8 8 6 9 3 0 2 9 7 7 *